# Intellectual and Developmental Disabilities & the Criminal Justice System

*Voula Marinos, Samantha Stromski,
Lisa Whittingham & Dorothy Griffiths*

Copyright © 2020 NADD Press

12 Hurley Avenue
Kingston, New York 12401

All rights reserved.

No part of this book may be reproduced, stored in a retrieval system or transmitted in any form by means of electronic, mechanical, photocopy, recording or otherwise, without written permission of NADD, 12 Hurley Avenue, Kingston, New York 12401.

ISBN: 978-1-57256-122-9
LCCN: 2020903965

Printed in the United States of America

# Dedication

### *To Mark Pathak*

Mark first made his impression on Executives across Ontario when he presented his model on Witness Support, Preparation and Profiling at a workshop in 2011. Mark's intelligence, enthusiasm and dynamic speaking ability were evident. It became clear that Mark was compassionate, family focussed and driven to make a difference for those with intellectual and developmental disabilities who are justice-involved. Mark was tireless in his pursuit to bring equity and justice to those who needed it most. Mark has made a tangible difference in the lives of those he supported, worked with, and loved.

# Acknowledgements

This collection of chapters illustrates that each author is committed, through various forms and methods, to supporting this highly vulnerable population vis-à-vis the criminal justice system. We thank you for your hard work and patience in this process. We were saddened by the loss of our colleague and friend Mark Pathak. His work signified a paradigm shift that truly conceptualizes persons with intellectual disabilities as having credible voices in cases involving them when they are properly supported.

We would also like to thank everyone who supported us throughout the process of writing this book, including Edward Seliger at NADD and the anonymous reviewers. Thank you to Marc Goldman for his thoughtful foreword. As someone who has committed his career to work with offenders with intellectual and developmental disabilities, his reflections on the merits of this book are most appreciated and meaningful.

To Dorothy Griffiths: as your co-editors, we would like to thank you for dedicating your career as a tireless advocate on behalf of persons with intellectual and developmental disabilities and being the perfect mentor and colleague at Brock University. We thank you for spearheading this book project and for influencing us to collaborate together.

# Table Of Contents

**Foreword** *Marc Goldman* ................................................................................ ix

**Preface** *Voula Marinos, Samantha Stromski, Lisa Whittingham & Dorothy Griffiths* ..... xi

### PART I: Foundations in Understanding Persons with Intellectual and Developmental Disabilities and the Criminal Justice System

**Chapter 1** Complexities and Gaps in Understanding Persons with Intellectual and Developmental Disabilities and the Criminal Justice System. ......... 3
*Voula Marinos, Dorothy Griffiths, Samantha Stromski & Lisa Whittingham*

**Chapter 2** Classification and Identification of Accused Persons with Intellectual Disabilities in the Criminal Justice System. ............... 23
*Dorothy Griffiths, Voula Marinos, Jessica Jones, Amanda Jones, & Mary Gilmore*

### PART II: Persons with IDD in the Justice System

**Chapter 3** Accommodations and Supports to Participate in the Criminal Courts......................................................... 53
*Voula Marinos, Mihael Cole & Samantha Stromski*

**Chapter 4** Forensic Inpatient Involvement of Persons with Intellectual and Developmental Disabilities ........................................... 67
*Lisa Whittingham*

**Chapter 5** Bridging the Gap in the Criminal Justice System for Persons with Intellectual Disabilities: A Model Program................ 83
*Mark Pathak, John Clarke & Stephanie Ioannou*

### PART III: Supporting Individuals with IDD Who Have Offended in the Community

**Chapter 6** The Dignity of Risk and Culture of Care: Community Risk Assessment and Management for Offenders with Intellectual Disabilities................................................ 109
*Jessica Jones, Rebekah Ranger & Paul Fedoroff*

**Chapter 7** Challenges in Community Support for Offenders with Intellectual Disabilities Who Have Offended ...................................... 123
*Deborah Richards, Samantha Stromski & Dorothy M. Griffiths*

### PART IV: Special Topics/Populations

**Chapter 8** Offenders with Autism Spectrum Disorder: A Case of Diminished Responsibility ..................................................... 155
*Layla Hall & Jessica Jones*

**Chapter 9** Justice-Involved Individuals with Fetal Alcohol Spectrum Disorder: Risk, Interventions, and Protective Factors ............................................. 175
*Shelley Watson, Lisa Whittingham, Kelly Coons-Harding, & Elisa Richer*

**Chapter 10** *"I Met Another Man Who Was Wounded with Hatred"*: A Therapeutic Jurisprudence Analysis of How We Ignore the Sexual Needs and the Sexual Actions of Persons with Intellectual and Developmental Disabilities ......................................... 199
*Michael Perlin, Heather Ellis Cucolo & Alison J. Lynch*

**Authors** ................................................................................................................ 215

**Index** ................................................................................................................... 221

# Foreword

In the early 1990's, I was invited to develop a forensic unit at a State psychiatric facility for individuals with intellectual and developmental disabilities. The unit was created to treat individuals with intellectual and developmental disabilities who were mandated to the facility by the courts because they had been deemed either "Unfit to Stand Trial" or "Not Guilty by Reason of Insanity." At the time, these terms meant little to me. As a clinician who was working with persons with intellectual and developmental disabilities with behavioral disorders, I was familiar with proactive treatment approaches and treating aberrant behavior with a multimodal approach. I had, however, not a clue concerning the treatment of criminal behavior.

I began my research. A few trips to the library failed to increase my knowledge of those with developmental and intellectual disability who engaged in criminal behavior. Branching out in my library search to criminology literature, I was surprised to learn that many of the vulnerabilities related to engaging in crime were characteristics common to people with intellectual disabilities. Unfortunately, I was unable to find a comprehensive work at that time that considered the variety of issues surrounding this topic. I found little in general to assist with my task and learned that the field lacked literature on the topic. Upon reflection, I was in desperate need of this book.

I learned a considerable amount as I attempted to do what appeared to be required to support such individuals in a proactive and humane manner. To successfully support individuals who have engaged in offending behavior, regardless of whether or not the criminal justice system is or was involved, requires an understanding of the prevalence, nature, and development of offending by those with developmental and intellectual disabilities, the nature of the most effective treatment approaches as well as a solid understanding of the criminal justice system.

Treatment based on theory and evidence is central to good practice; alternative approaches simply take a chance on what might be effective based on guesses. Support, based on guesses, is more likely to result in more victims as opposed to those based on theory and evidence. Supports based on the individual's rights with disregard to community (including peer and support professional) safety not only increases the likelihood of victimization but increasingly punitive sanctions on the offender. The good news is that we now understand that with positive approaches we can change the direction of those with a history of offensive behavior. And we can prevent victimization.

At the onset, working with offenders requires education about the criminal justice system. Courts, with their unique rules, etiquette, and language might make us uneasy, and it makes the path of persons with intellectual and developmental disabilities even more complicated and stressful than for offenders without disabilities. It is essential that anyone working with or interested in those with IDD who engage in criminal behavior understand the structure and limitations of the criminal justice system.

This work considers many of the issues that need to be considered when working with this population in this challenging area of our practice. Many agencies and professionals are reluctant to accept into their system or caseload people with intellectual and developmental disabilities who have committed or are at risk of recommitting a criminal act. If accepted without knowledge of the appropriate way to provide support or treatment both in the criminal justice system and in the therapeutic environment, there is a likelihood that the risk might be minimized, thereby increasing the risk of committing crime in the future, or they may become unduly restrictive in their support or intervention which both is counterintuitive to good practice and often a rights violation. Either way it is likely that uninformed practice will lead to unfortunate results; the former increases the likelihood of another victim; the latter lacks any incentive for the individual to learn new behaviors and experience a meaningful life. Community support must also address inequalities that persons with IDD most often face, including increased risks of poverty, unemployment, victimization, and discrimination. It is for this reason that I was pleased to have the opportunity to review and comment on this book. This book reviews a very impressive variety of topics that will assist anyone working with individuals with intellectual disabilities who are at risk of criminal behavior. A strong team is required to successfully support such individuals. The information within this volume should be considered part of the team.

I believe that if this book had been on my reference shelf in the 90's, I would have been much more effective.

Marc Goldman, MS
Licensed Psychological Associate

# Preface

*Voula Marinos, Samantha Stromski, Lisa Whittingham & Dorothy Griffiths*

There continues to be a high representation of individuals with intellectual and developmental disabilities (IDD) in the criminal justice system. Yet there continue to be challenges and complexities in the court system as legal matters are still primarily carried out in a traditional fashion that is designed for more "able bodied" individuals. This book not only provides a foundational approach to supporting justice-involved individuals with IDD but also examines practical difficulties and dilemmas for them when involved in the justice system. This book will assist professionals supporting those with IDD to gain a deeper understanding of the challenges when interacting with the criminal justice system and varying accommodations that are available in various jurisdictions nationally and internationally, while also introducing students to the complexities of supporting persons with IDD in the criminal justice system. The following chapters are meant to open a dialog and emphasize the need to reframe our approach to persons with IDD in the criminal justice system – one that is multidisciplinary, person-centered, and builds on a biopsychosocial approach that can result in more substantive and equitable experiences for those with IDD when interacting with the justice system.

This book is divided into four parts. We begin with Part 1 entitled *Foundations in Understanding Persons with IDD & the Criminal Justice System*, which offers our multi-dimensional approach to understanding important issues, dilemmas, and gaps for persons with IDD in the criminal justice system and professionals and the systems that respond to them. The book then goes on in Parts 2, 3, and 4 to offer and reflect on dilemmas in a substantive way that plague a justice system and the community-based services that are meant to assist them. Issues of identification, risk assessments, court supports, and accommodations inside and outside of the justice system are addressed. Some chapters are more focused, recognizing unique issues and dilemmas to consider for persons with ASD and FASD, as well as those charged with sexual offenses.

Chapter 1 provides the reader with a historical, social, psychological, and legal context for the dilemmas and complex issues which persons with IDD face in the justice system, as well as how systems – including family, criminal justice, and community agencies – respond to justice-involved individuals. Chapter 2 specifically explores a critical foundation of one's interactions within the justice system and how systems respond: classification and identification. This topic challenges the myth that persons with IDD are easily identified and classified, paving the way to discussions in Section II of the book – supports in the criminal justice system.

Part 2 is focused on *Persons with IDD and the Criminal Justice System*. Chapter 3 reviews accommodations and supports in Canada, including key gaps that should be addressed for access to justice. Chapter 4 reviews and addresses some of the challenges associated with transferring people with IDD to a forensic inpatient unit if they are found unfit to stand trial or not criminally responsible for their offenses. Chapter 5 describes, highlights, and analyzes an innovative program that reframes participation and justice for persons with IDD.

Part 3 shifts our attention away from the criminal justice system to the community: *Supporting Individuals with IDD Who Have Offended in the Community*. This section extends the substantive and applied issues in Part II and addresses ways to support individuals beyond the courtroom. Chapters 6 and 7 specify critical issues of support, including risk assessments in the community and programs within the community.

Part 4 is dedicated to *Special Topics/Populations*. Chapters 8, 9 and 10 of the book represents chapters, overall, that are focused on special populations with unique needs – such as those with ASD and FASD – or particular topics that present challenges for the courts relating to persons with IDD – namely sexual offenses. The final chapter offers a thought-provoking perspective that a paradigm shift towards therapeutic jurisprudence can produce the conditions to respect the sexual rights of persons with IDD.

# Part I:

## Foundations in Understanding Persons with Intellectual and Developmental Disabilities and the Criminal Justice System

*Chapter 1*

# Complexities and Gaps in Understanding Persons with Intellectual and Developmental Disabilities and the Criminal Justice System

*Voula Marinos, Dorothy Griffiths, Samantha Stromski & Lisa Whittingham*

## Intellectual Disabilities and Developmental Disabilities

Universally accepted definitions of intellectual and developmental disabilities have not been developed. This is in large part due to the diversity observed in persons labelled as having an intellectual or developmental disability, but also due to the various spheres in which definitions are needed (e.g., clinical, research, legal, etc.) (Harris & Greenspan, 2016; Owen & McFarland, 2002). Regardless of the sphere of practice, most definitions are aligned with the American Association on Intellectual and Developmental Disabilities (AAIDD) definition and describe intellectual disability as having an onset before 18-years-old and characterized by "significant limitations in both intellectual functioning and adaptive functioning, which covers many every day social and practical skills" (AAIDD, 2018). Limitations in intellectual functioning may include deficits in problem-solving, reasoning, and/or verbal language skills; whereas, limitation in adaptive functioning may include areas such as social skills, home management, and/or ability to obey rules/laws (AAIDD, 2018). In comparison, a developmental disability "is an umbrella term that includes intellectual disability but also includes [other] disabilities that are apparent during childhood" (AAIDD, 2018). These disabilities have an onset before the age of 18 and may be primarily characterized by physical disabilities (e.g., cerebral palsy), cognitive disabilities (e.g., autism spectrum disorder), or both (e.g., Down syndrome) (AAIDD, 2018).

Many people use the terms *intellectual disability* and *developmental disability* interchangeably; however, it is important to ensure that there is discrimination between these two terms since not all persons diagnosed with a developmental disability will have an intellectual disability. For example, fetal alcohol spectrum disorder (FASD) is a developmental disability, characterized by an onset before the age of 22, the presence of physical disabilities (e.g., skeletal anomalies or heart defects), and challenges in executive functioning and cognitive ability (e.g., impairments in judgement, attention, and memory) (Streissguth, 1997). However, not all persons with FASD meet the criteria for intellectual disability. Several authors have identified that IQ scores for persons with FASD ranges between 20 to 120, with approximately 10% of persons meeting the criteria for an intellectual disability (i.e., have an IQ of 70 or less) (Mattson, Crocker, & Nyguen, 2011; Streissguth, 1997). The impact of this difference between intellectual disability and developmental disabilities means that many individuals with FASD will experience the challenges associated with having a developmental disability and require accommodations but will not qualify for the services designated for persons with an intellectual disability (Mattson et al., 2011; Streissguth, 1997). This book is concerned with both intellectual and developmental disability. In some cases, the authors have focused on a particular developmental disability alone, such as FASD, while other authors have chosen to focus on intellectual disability and the challenges these individuals face when navigating the court system.

We argue that it is important to have a multidimensional and multidisciplinary conceptualization of persons with intellectual and developmental disabilities (IDD) as they interact with the criminal justice system. Before addressing this theoretical framework, it is important to consider briefly the history of persons with IDD and their interactions with the criminal law, and their current prevalence and challenges when faced with a criminal justice system that is rooted in ableism.

## *A Brief History of Intellectual and Developmental Disabilities and Interactions with the Law*

Many attempts in the past few centuries have been made to demonstrate the relationship between intelligence and criminal behavior. For example, Charles Goring reported in 1913 that individuals who were likely to commit criminal offenses had lower intelligence and were of shorter stature. He based these conclusions on talking to 3000 incarcerated individuals and deciding for himself whether they were intelligent (White & Haines, 2002). While the flaws in Goring's research design are obvious, there have been more organized efforts to demonstrate the relationship between individuals with IDD and offending behavior.

In the late 19$^{th}$ and early 20$^{th}$ centuries the social hygiene movement involved a group of professionals and well-intending citizens who were committed to keeping citizens both safe and healthy using the science of Darwin (i.e., evolution) and Galton (i.e., intelligence testing) (Griffiths et al., 2016; White & Haines, 2002). Under the guise of creating a more caring and supportive society, efforts were made to use the scientific method to control individuals suggested to be responsible for the moral decline of society and to reduce the influence and continuation of vice and crime through eugenics and segregation. One of the groups of individuals caught up in the net of this movement was persons with IDD. In 1910, Henry Goddard proposed that a nomenclature could be used to evaluate and classify persons using the intelligence quotient (IQ) (Griffiths et al., 2016; Wehmeyer, 2013). That is, citizens could be measured using the intelligence test and categorized according to mental defectiveness (or "feeble-mindedness") ranging from "idiot" to "moron." He suggested that anyone labeled as a moron (i.e., with the mental age between eight to twelve) was unfit for society and should be controlled through institutionalization, sterilization, or both (Griffiths et al., 2016; Wehmeyer, 2013). This idea that individuals could be classified and sorted according to feeble-mindedness (and subsequently risk) led to widespread sterilization and segregation of individuals with IDD in institutions in many countries (i.e., Canada, the United States, and England) for nearly a century.

The last half of the 20th century saw changes in how persons with IDD were conceptualized. Rather than exclude persons with IDD from society and prevent their development as a population, there was a shift in recognition to how society could play a role in their success. We have witnessed how changes in the available supports for persons with IDD have shifted from institutionalization to include more opportunities for residency and participation in the community (Griffiths et al., 2016; Owen & McFarland, 2002). Unfortunately, one of the possible outcomes of this shift in support has been more individuals with IDD becoming involved in the criminal justice system (Jones, 2007). This has left criminal justice professionals responsible for not only determining whether an individual has an IDD, but also whether the presence of an IDD played a role in the decision-making to commit the offense and/or whether it will influence the person's ability to participate in the proceedings. These new challenges make it important for professionals from both the criminal justice and the forensic systems to ensure they are adequately educated about IDD and/or have the support from other sectors (i.e., developmental services).

One of the critical reasons to improve the knowledge and support of persons with IDD is to guard against the use of stereotypes and/or inaccurate or outdated information in decision-making and criminal proceedings. Prior research has suggested that in the absence of accurate knowledge or support, court professionals have relied on the use of stereotypes to inform their arguments regarding persons with IDD. This may include the use of fictional characters or "cherry-picking" facts to support their case regarding persons with IDD. For example, Harris and Greenspan (2016) identified that the fictional character, Lennie from John Steinbeck's novel *Of Mice and Men*, was cited in the Briseno doctrine (which addresses how Atkins v. Virginia (2003) should be implemented) as an example of "the kind of severely and obviously impaired person for whom judicial relief should be limited" (p. 34). Furthermore, they suggested that lawyers and forensic professionals who are not familiar with the assessment of IDD are at risk of misinterpreting acts not typically associated with persons with IDD (e.g., driving a car) as proof of "normal functioning" and query the validity or reliability of the diagnosis of intellectual disability. That is, based on their own knowledge or beliefs about person with IDD and what they are capable of, they believed that participation in these activities was evidence enough that an intellectual disability was not present, even if a deeper examination indicated that their participation was not successful (e.g., inability to maintain car insurance or frequent accidents) (Harris & Greenspan, 2016). Better knowledge regarding persons with IDD and/or the increased use of interdisciplinary teams to support persons with IDD in the criminal justice system may help to increase the awareness that intellectual disability is not determined solely by an IQ score; rather, it is a continuum of skills that are both quantifiably and qualitatively different (Griffiths, Taillon-Wasmund, & Smith, 2002).

## *Prevalence and Demographics*

According to a recent meta-analysis, persons with intellectual and developmental disabilities (IDD) in the community comprise just over 1% of the population (Maulik, Mascarenhas, Mathers, Dua, & Saxena, 2011). With regards to the criminal justice system, studies have estimated a considerable range regarding prevalence of intellectual and developmental disabilities (i.e., between 2 to 40%) (Holland, 2004; Lindsay, Law, & Macleod, 2002; Noble & Conley,1992). In a singular study that examined aggregate prison data from six countries, the prevalence rate ranged from 0% to 2.8% (Fazel, Xenitidis, & Powell, 2008). Other researchers have also noted a significant range in prevalence and have suggested that this range may be due to the variance in the inclusionary criteria for the participants being involved in the study, how intellectual and developmental disability have been operationally defined, and the methods employed to gather the data (Jones, 2007; Lindsay, Hastings, Griffiths, & Hayes, 2007). While many researchers have indicated that offenders with IDD are overrepresented amongst the offender population (i.e., Loucks, 2007), Lindsay, Hastings, and Beech (2011) suggested that it is difficult to conclude that persons with IDD are overrepresented given the vast differences in research methods.

As suggested by Lindsay and colleagues (2011), when discussing prevalence rates of offending committed by persons with IDD, there are four overarching cautions that need to be addressed. First, the prevalence research for this population is characterized by poor research designs including inconsistent definitions (e.g., intellectual v. developmental disability) (Bradley, 2009), identification protocols (e.g., the measurements selected) (McBrien, Hodgetts, & Gregory, 2003), and a lack of control groups (Lindsay, 2002). Second, greater clarity is needed when reporting prevalence rates regarding challenging behaviors that are deviant and may require interpretation to be considered criminal (e.g., administrative offenses) compared to behaviors that are clearly criminal (e.g., sexual assault) (Holland, Clare & Mukhopadhyay, 2002). Third, persons with intellectual and developmental disabilities may be more likely to become entangled with the legal system and fare more poorly in the criminal justice system than neurotypical persons (Jones, 2007). Researchers have suggested that some of the risks contributing to the overrepresentation of persons with IDD in the criminal justice system include their willingness to confess or to disclose information that is not in their best interest and they are more likely to receive longer sentences (Jones, 2007).

Finally, it is important to recognize how research is being conceptualized. There is a vast difference between statements made that people with IDD are more likely to commit crimes than other populations compared to people with IDD are disproportionately represented within the criminal justice system (Griffiths, Hingsburger, Hoath & Ioannou, 2018). It is important to recognize the nuanced difference between these two sentences. From our perspective, the first statement suggests that persons with IDD are more likely to commit crimes because they have more criminogenic or risk factors than others. While it is clearly important to understand statistics about the frequency of crime, such statements are meaningless without a careful understanding of the underlying circumstances that lead to crime. One cannot have a meaningful discussion about criminal offending without asking critical questions about the criminal justice system itself and how crime is responded to. The second statement should lead us to ask more critical questions: is it possible that persons with IDD are overrepresented in the criminal justice system because they are more likely to engage in particular behavior that brings them to the attention of the police and criminal justice system? Are persons with IDD more vulnerable to criminal charges and do they experience greater challenges navigating the system than others because the system lacks accessibility, such as legal aid/public defenders, support in attending court dates, communicating with their lawyer, understanding court conditions and expectations?

Early research indicated that arson, theft, and sexually related offenses were the most common offenses committed by persons with intellectual disability (Day, 1993; Denkowski & Denkowski, 1986; Klimecki, Jenkinson, & Wilson, 1994; Walker & McCabe, 1973), however more recent research has refuted these statements. More recent research has suggested that the most common offenses committed by persons with IDD are acts involving aggression (McBrien et al., 2003; O'Brien et al., 2010; Wheeler, Clare, & Holland, 2013). For example, O'Brien and colleagues reported the following statistics on the most prevalent offenses: physical aggression (50%) and verbal aggression (33%), followed by property destruction (19%), inappropriate sexualized contact (15%), and sexualized behavior (14%). More specifically, Lindsay and colleagues (2010) identified that the latter statistics regarding sexualized behaviors differ depending on the type of settings from which the data were gathered. In addition, Simpson and Hogg (2001a, b) noted that individuals with borderline intellectual disability may engage in higher incidences of sexual offending, criminal damage, and burglary but may engage in lower incidence of murder or armed robbery.

Furthermore, there is an emerging body of literature that indicates that persons with IDD appear to represent two types of person who become entangled with the law (Holland et al., 2002; Lindsay et al., 2010; Wheeler et al., 2009). The first group of individuals is characterized by young males with a higher IQ but greater social disadvantage, including high rates of mental illness and substance use (Wheeler et al., 2009), and a history of childhood behavioral problems (Holland et al., 2002); whereas, the second group of individuals is characterized by lower IQ and is more likely to be receiving community-based support services prior to the offense (Wheeler et al., 2009). Furthermore, their offenses were also often described as being part of an escalation continuum, that included non-criminal actions, such as verbal and physical aggression. This is not surprising given that aggression has been reported to be the most frequent challenging behavior amongst persons with IDD (Emerson, 2001).

In Canadian, U.S., and U.K. criminal law, a crime is said to have occurred when an individual engages in an act that is both in violation of the law (*actus reus*), and the individual has intent to commit a criminal act (*mens rea*). It is the role of court actors to demonstrate that the act took place but also that there was intention to commit the act if conviction is to take place. Clare and Murphy (1998) suggested that "the criteria for a crime and of being involved meaningfully in criminal justice procedures is much greater for people with mild intellectual disabilities and it is this sub-group of people with problem behavior who are the most likely to come into contact with the criminal justice system" (p.155). Researchers and scholars often interpret these results as focusing on individuals with a mental disorder (i.e., psychiatric illness); however, for persons with IDD, it may mean that the nature of the person's disability needs to be examined for the role it plays in the commission of the crime. For example, what role does Prader Willi syndrome (a genetic disorder characterized by an insatiable appetite for food) play in the case involving an individual who stole some donuts? Or what role does Williams syndrome (a genetic disorder characterized by hyper-sociability) play in the case of the individual who has been encouraged to be a lookout for his 'apparent friends' while they go into a store and rob it?

Persons with IDD who have offended are similar to neurotypical offenders: young, male, unemployed, socio-economically disadvantaged (Emerson & Halpin, 2013). However, offenders with IDD are also more likely to have experienced institutional life or out-of-home placement, and less likely to have been provided appropriate education that could lead to employment (Ali, Ghosh, Strydom, & Hassiotis, 2016). And while intellectual disability has been shown to be a vulnerability for offending (Farrington & Welsch, 2006), the elevated rates do not indicate that diminished intelligence is the cause of the offending behavior. Persons with intellectual and developmental disabilities experience a range of psychosocial crises in their developing years as a result of both the nature of their disability and their resultant challenges faced in society (Gilson & Levitas, 1987). This may include social exclusion and isolation and histories of abuse and neglect. It should be noted that offenders with IDD that have been abused and/or neglected are disproportionately overrepresented when compared to offenders without IDD (Marinos et al., 2009).

Considerable literature has emerged on the characteristics of offending in the general and intellectual and developmental disability (IDD) populations. Most offenders with IDD have a mild intellectual or borderline IQ (i.e., IQ score ranging 55-85), though research has shown that individuals with a borderline IQ (i.e., IQ score of 70-85) are more likely to offend than individuals with a mild IQ (i.e., IQ score of 55 – 70) (Baldry, Clarence, Dowse, & Trollor, 2013; Hayes, Schackell, Mottram, & Lancaster, 2007; Lindsay et al., 2010; McLachlan, 2016). Additionally, there appears to be very low prevalence of persons with a severe or profound IQ in the criminal justice system. Holland (2004) suggested that it is likely that individuals with more severe disabilities are typically diverted away from the criminal justice system since police and other court officials assume they do not possess the *mens rea* to be convicted of a crime.

Challenges associated with intellectual and developmental disabilities often include language and social skills deficits; cognitive deficits including difficulties with learning, reasoning, and problem solving; inability to complete activities of daily living without assistance; and social skills (Schalock et al., 2010). With regards to criminal offending behavior, problems with communication, social skills, judgment, impulse control, gullibility, and delays in moral development may put persons with IDD at greater risk of engaging in offending behavior (Clare & Gudjonsson, 1993; Lindsay, Sturmey, & Taylor, 2004). Additionally, once involved with the criminal justice system, persons with IDD may experience greater disadvantage since they may not understand or know their rights, may acquiesce to suggestions, may lack appropriate legal support, may want to please the officer, or may plead guilty to a crime they did not commit (Marinos et al., 2009).

Finally, persons with IDD may be at greater risk of engaging in crime due to increased challenges associated with poor health and mental health. Research has demonstrated that persons with IDD have higher rates of comorbid psychiatric challenges; specifically, the rates amongst offenders with IDD ranged 32%-46% with a gradual increase in risk as an individual's age increases (Dekker, Koot, Ende, & Verhulst, 2002; Einfeld et al., 2006; Einfeld & Tonge, 1996). This is comparable to persons with IDD (not accused of an offense) regarding specific psychiatric diagnoses. For example, Cooper and van der Speck (2009) indicated that compared to the general population, adults with IDD experience depression, schizophrenia, and bipolar disorder at twice the rate. The increased risk for a psychiatric diagnosis may be the direct result of biological or neurological differences or may be the result of challenges in coping, communication, problem-solving and judgment, and poor environmental fit (Deb et al., 2001). For example, these comorbid psychiatric conditions may interfere with the individual's access to community inclusion, support, placement, and employment (Bruininks, Hill & Morreau, 1988; Parmenter, Einfeld, Tonge, & Dempster, 1998). It is also possible that the elevated risk of mental illness might also be related to the historical life experience of persons with intellectual disabilities (Deb et al., 2001). For example, Hughes and colleagues (2012) examined the prevalence of abuse in persons with disabilities and found that estimates ranged between 26% and 90% for women with disabilities, whereas, the range was 28.7% to 86.7% for men with disabilities.

## Challenges in the Criminal Justice System

Navigating the criminal justice system as an accused person can be extremely challenging and complex. Individuals with IDD commonly have inadequate understanding of the criminal justice system and the rights they have within the legal system (Barron, Hassiotis, & Barnes, 2002). According to Marinos et al. (2009), individuals with intellectual disabilities are less likely to understand their legal rights, such as the right to remain silent or to have a lawyer present. As a result, individuals with an intellectual disability may be more apt to incriminate themselves by unintentionally providing false confessions (Barron et al., 2002), saying what they believe to be expected by police, being easily led by the interviewer, or not fully understand the implications to their statements (Jones, 2007; Marinos et al., 2009). Moreover, research by Clare and Gudjonsson (1995) found that the participants who had an intellectual disability were more likely to think that a false confession would not have serious consequences or believed that a suspect's innocence would be evident to police officers, even if a false confession was provided when compared to those with average intelligence. This can pose a significant vulnerability for those with intellectual disability as they often lack the abstract understanding of the complex system and the consequences of this in relation to providing a false confession or pleading guilty to a crime they did not commit.

The justice process also involves complex language, court processes, and procedures that can pose a significant challenge for those with intellectual disabilities. There are responsibilities placed on the accused person to navigate the processes and follow up with all necessary expectations of the court in a timely manner. For instance, the accused person is responsible for applying for legal aid in provinces and territories throughout Canada and in the U.S., coordinating with a lawyer to represent them, instructing their lawyer, and remembering their upcoming court dates. In addition, they must be aware of the formal rules of the courtroom as well as unwritten rules that can vary depending on what jurisdiction they are in, such as being aware of where to stand and what to do when their name is called in court. The court process is abstract and hard to understand for anyone trying to navigate but can be even more challenging for individuals with IDD who understand and learn differently. For example, research by Howard, Phipps, Clarbour and Rayner (2015) explored the court experiences of individuals with intellectual disabilities. They found that persons with IDD had a lack of understanding in terms of their role in the court system and how to navigate it. Persons with IDD reported feeling as though they were filtered through the system with limited understanding and support. This can result in this population being more susceptible to making decisions about their court case that could result in negative consequences such as being denied bail or pleading guilty for a crime they did not commit.

Finally, while research has identified different characteristics and challenges faced by persons with IDD in the criminal justice system, it is important to remember that individuals with intellectual disability are not a homogenous group, and there are a number of cognitive and genetic disorders with varying characteristics that can manifest in different struggles for individuals when they are interacting in the justice system. The following chart (see Table 1), although not exhaustive, outlines varying disabilities, challenges, and recommended accommodations to assist individuals when interacting with the justice system.

## Table 1: Challenges in the criminal justice system and suggested accommodations for a variety of disabilities

| Disability | Challenges while in the CJS | Accommodations |
| --- | --- | --- |
| Fetal Alcohol Spectrum Disorder | - Suggestibility<br>- Impulse control<br>- Understanding the concept of consequences<br>(Fast & Conry, 2009; Streissguth, Barr, Kogan and Bookstein, 1996). | - Screening tools to identify FASD while in the courts (i.e., ALARM Screening tool) (Fast & Conry, 2009, p. 252)<br>- Use clear and plain language<br>- Slow down the court process<br>- Simplify bail and probation orders to include concrete language (Jeffery, 2010) |
| Autism | - Lack of empathy<br>- Difficulty understanding social cues<br>- Obsessive behaviors (King & Murphy, 2014) | - Provide justice professionals specific information about individual and ways to support them<br>- Ask individuals specific questions<br>- Avoid sarcasm (Allen et al. 2008) |
| Williams Syndrome | - Exhibit high rates of fear and anxiety<br>- Vulnerable to manipulation by others due to friendly nature<br>(Dykens, Hodapp, Finucane, 2000, p.97-135) | - Minimize distractions<br>- Have a support person present in court process to alleviate anxieties |
| Fragile X Syndrome | - Trouble focusing<br>- Socialization skills<br>- Short Term Memory<br>(Dykens et al, 2000, p. 137-167) | - Provide training to the individual in advance to allow time to understand expectations of the court process<br>- Support person present to assist with focusing and keeping the individual on track<br>- Copies of bail and probation orders with upcoming dates provided to individual |
| Prader-Willi Syndrome | - Compulsive and obsessive behaviors (often with food)<br>- Stubborn behaviors<br>- Impulse control<br>- Negative self-evaluation<br>(Dykens et al., 2000 p. 169-205) | - Provide training and education prior to court date to ensure individual knows what to expect from the court process |

## Shifting the Paradigm for Understanding IDD and Offending Behavior

While it is important for criminal justice professionals to be familiar with intellectual and developmental disabilities, it is impractical to expect them to be solely responsible for meeting the needs of persons with IDD in the criminal justice system. The system itself needs to be structured to allow for access to justice. A conceptual framework is key to developing an accessible structure that lends itself to justice professionals and other key actors making decisions and providing services that are lawful and equitable. It is important to have a framework that is "flexible, creative, and seamless, virtually eliminating jurisdictional and professional barriers to appropriate service" (Dart, Gapen, & Morris, 2002, p. 293).

Developing this framework is challenging given a person with IDD may be seen in multiple sectors as having different needs and labels. Take for example, the *common client*, an individual seen by professionals in multiple sectors (e.g., mental health, developmental services, health services, and the criminal justice system) (Griffiths et al., 2002, p. 407). As the individual moves through these various sectors, different assessments will be conducted, different labels will be attached, and different recommendations for intervention will be made. One individual may be labelled as having autism spectrum disorder and referred for behavior consultation in developmental services; when seen in the mental health sector, they may be labeled as having an intellectual disability and a mood disorder and prescribed medication; and finally, they may be labeled as a high-risk offender and managed for risk by the criminal justice sector. In this scenario, the individual has not changed; however, they have been given several different labels and recommendations for treatment based on the title of the professional assessing them and the mandate of each sector (Griffiths et al., 2002).

Given that multiple sectors may be involved in supporting persons with IDD in the criminal justice system, it is important that any framework used is person-centered, uses a multidimensional, multimodal approach for understanding behavior, and focuses on maintaining individual human rights.

### *A Person-Centered Approach*

While the obvious feature of a person-centered approach is the idea that the individual is included and at the heart of the planning, it goes beyond this idea to include several other principles, including modification to the processes to promote genuine inclusion of the individual, incorporating caregivers and other supports when it is appropriate, and ensuring that the individual with IDD expresses satisfaction with the process as well as the outcome (Holburn, Jacoson, Vietze, Schwartz, & Sersen, 2000).

The Law Commission of Ontario (2012) developed a framework for understanding and promoting the inclusion of persons with disabilities in law proceedings. They also identified the importance of using a person-centred approach to ensure that persons with disabilities are the primary focus of legal proceedings involving them. They suggested that it was important for all court actors to focus on principles such as respecting dignity and worth, fostering autonomy and independence, and promoting social inclusion and participation when involved in a case with a person with a disability or when developing and implementing laws that may affect persons with IDD.

## A Multidimensional Approach and Multidisciplinary Team

Given that researchers and professionals have moved away from a medical model that focuses on disability as an impairment or deficit within the individual alone to a holistic social model, which focuses on a multitude of variables within the environment that can interact with an impairment to create the experience of disability, any framework developed needs to account for the many possible variables that may contribute to the offending behavior of the individual with IDD. Griffiths and Gardner (2002) proposed the *biopsychosocial model* as a multidimensional model that can be used to understand challenging behaviors in persons with IDD and dual diagnosis (i.e., developmental disability and mental health diagnosis). Specifically, they identified that challenging behavior, including offending behavior, is often the result of intertwined influences of biological, psychological, and social factors.

**Table 2: Examples of biological, psychological, and social factors that may influence offending behavior in persons with IDD**

| Biological Factors | Psychological Factors | Social Factors |
|---|---|---|
| • Genetic syndromes (e.g., Down Syndrome)<br>• Psychiatric disorders (e.g., schizophrenia)<br>• Traumatic brain injury<br>• Medical illness (e.g., diabetes)<br>• Alcohol/drug use<br>• Medication side effects<br>• Physical discomfort and pain | • Boredom<br>• Misunderstanding of social cues<br>• Poor personal boundaries<br>• Communication deficits (receptive/expressive)<br>• Impulsivity and poor self-management<br>• History of trauma<br>• Cognitive distortions<br>• Poor judgement abilities | • Crowded, noisy environments<br>• The presence of specific people (e.g., children)<br>• Lack of resources and support available<br>• Specific events (e.g., birthdays)<br>• Access to pornography<br>• Undesirable location (e.g., school) |

The biopsychosocial model provides a framework that promotes a person-centered approach and enables a multidisciplinary team to address the multiple risk factors contributing to offending behavior and subsequent involvement in the criminal justice system. A multidisciplinary team is highly beneficial in addressing challenging or offending behavior in persons with IDD. For example, a youth with fetal alcohol spectrum disorder (FASD) charged with drug possession may require the support of a lawyer, psychiatrist, addictions counsellor, occupational therapist, case manager/coordinator, and a behavior therapist to understand the causes associated with the offenses, the underlying circumstances, and to develop an intervention(s) to reduce recidivism. It is unlikely that a reduction in the risk of reoffending will come from one of these professionals, but instead will result from the cumulative effort of each team member supporting the individual with IDD within their scope of practice and according to the unique professional and disciplinary skills they bring to working within the context of the criminal justice system.

## Attention to Human Rights and Quality of Life

Finally, a multidimensional and multidisciplinary framework points to the importance of human rights that considers, among many principles, formal and substantive rights. Article 13 in the UN Convention on the Rights of Persons with Disabilities recognizes the rights of persons with intellectual disabilities to justice (United Nations, 2006). This includes both "procedural and age-appropriate accommodations, in order to facilitate their effective role as direct and indirect participants, including as witnesses, in all legal proceedings, including investigative and other preliminary stages" (United Nations, 2006, p. 9). Hamelin, Marinos, Robinson, & Griffiths (2012) identified that professionals working with persons with IDD must be familiar with both the individual and the nature of the disability to effectively ensure that the rights of persons with IDD are recognized and respected in practice. They go on to suggest that regular partnership between developmental services and the judicial system will help to ensure that the rights of persons with IDD are respected, ultimately leading to substantive equality.

Similarly, this partnership also needs to extend into ensuring that persons with IDD have the funding and community resources to reduce the likelihood of recidivism. In the absence of these services, prisons have become the social safety net for persons not receiving adequate supports to ensure quality of life in the community (Baldry et al., 2013; Lerner-Wren, 2002).

## Limitations in Knowledge: What Do We Know About the Gaps in Understanding Persons with IDD in the Criminal Justice System?

### *Structural Gaps and Persons with IDD*

On the whole, the gaps in the literature regarding persons with IDD and the criminal justice system alert us to a system that could benefit from enhanced structural changes to make it more inclusive for everyone. Foundationally, there have been important developments in the criminal justice system to facilitate service delivery to persons identified with IDD. For example, in Ontario, the Ministry of the Attorney General's *Diversity, Inclusion, and Accessibility Office* has hired diversity officers, which is part of the broader objective to provide accessible justice in Ontario and to meet the mandate of the *Accessibility for Ontario with Disabilities Act* (AODA) (2005). The AODA requires the province, in its public institutions and services, to be accessible and accommodating by 2025. Similarly, the British Columbia Public Service intends on being fully accessible by 2024 (British Columbia, 2018). Specific to the criminal justice system in Ontario is the addition of the Dual Diagnosis Justice Case Management (DDJCM) workers who are supported by the Ontario Ministry of Community and Social Services. At this time, there are over 23 DDJCM workers in Ontario. They assist persons with IDD or dual diagnosis (i.e., mental health and/or behavioral issues) who currently are involved in the criminal justice system. They help with obtaining a lawyer, legal aid, acting as a liaison with the court, working collaboratively with community partners that are part of the mental health diversion, and post-custody planning and supports (Community Networks of Specialized Care, 2019). In the United States, some progress has been made, depending upon the state, to support persons with intellectual and developmental disabilities. In New Jersey, for example, the Criminal Justice Advocacy Program (CJAP) assists persons with intellectual and developmental disability by providing alternatives to prison and serving as a conduit between the various systems in which they interact (Camden ResourceNet, 2019).

In addition, while Canada as a nation, ratified the United Nations Convention on the Rights of Persons with Disabilities (UNCRPD) in 2010, Canada recently tabled the Optional Protocol to the UNCRPD. Support of this optional protocol allows Canadian citizens with disabilities to file complaints with the UN Committee about possible rights violations in Canada (Almeida, 2017). This development alerts us to Canada's continued commitment to substantive changes for persons with intellectual and developmental disabilities. Clearly rights are less meaningful if violations cannot be addressed through official means and remedies cannot be provided. But all of this requires identification at the outset, and this is one of the most critical elements of the discussion. These developments reflect a commitment and collaboration between the justice and developmental sectors regarding effective support for persons with IDD in the criminal justice system; however, there is a lack of research on the impact of the training, the effectiveness of services delivered to persons with IDD, and outcomes. It is also unclear whether and to what extent training has translated within and across the justice sector – policing, bail, courts, and corrections.

## *Diversion and Persons with IDD*

Like other persons suspected of committing criminal offenses, the first point of contact with the criminal justice system is the police. As the gatekeepers of the system, they have an immensely challenging job of having to interact with a variety of individuals, including persons with IDD, who might find themselves being charged with a criminal offense. Police need to be prepared to respond to all individuals, regardless of their range of backgrounds – that is, differences in age, race/ethnicity, class, gender, sexuality, abilities, in addition to different personalities, experiences, expectations, and momentary emotional states. One of the biggest challenges facing police when interacting with persons with IDD is determining whether the individual has an intellectual or developmental disability (Henshaw & Thomas, 2012). We all tend to approach individuals in our day-to-day interactions as though they clearly understand our language and the nuances of our communications. The police are no exception to this rule. Henshaw and Thomas (2012) found that finding effective communication strategies for police with persons with IDD needs to be further examined and developed. In addition, the police also 'open the gate' to persons with IDD into the formal court process. Despite the breadth and depth of the justice system and its multiple specialized courts in Canada, the U.S., and the U.K. (i.e., mental health court, drug court, Aboriginal court), there has been relatively little consistent research on the involvement of persons with IDD in this literature.

Moreover, while most literature has focused on incarceration and persons with IDD (e.g., Hayes, 2004; Jones, 2007), some additional literature points to the importance of understanding how and why persons with intellectual and developmental disabilities enter the criminal justice system. Few studies have looked at the interactions between persons with IDD and police officers. In one of the few studies examining police interactions with persons with IDD, a comparison of the individual pathways before and after police interactions indicated that individuals with IDD who had a history of involvement with a community-based forensic team were more likely to be charged for a criminal offense, regardless of the nature of the offense, than being sent to the emergency department or dealt with informally by police (Raina, Arenovich, Jones, & Lunsky, 2013). They also noted that when offenses involved physical aggression, the individual with IDD was more likely to being charged. Future research should focus on the ways in which police divert persons with IDD away from the formal criminal justice system.

Another key area of research that would be informative is with the use of specialized courts for persons with IDD. Using the framework of therapeutic jurisprudence (TJ), 'problem-solving' courts have been developed with the underlying assumption that the law and legal actors who implement the law act as "...social forces that may produce therapeutic or antitherapeutic consequences" (Wexler 1997 at p. 233). Mental health courts typically act as diversionary judicial proceedings outside of the traditional adversarial court. They include collaborative interactions between legal actors and community mental health representatives with the goal of addressing the underlying mental health factors influencing the individual's behavior while at the same time making the person accountable for their actions. A variety of mental health and/or behavioral challenges could qualify an individual to be diverted to a mental health court.

Finally, the term 'mental disorder' is found in the Canadian Criminal Code (C.C.C.) (section 2) and criminal law in most other countries (i.e., United States, United Kingdom, Australia) to describe individuals who may have engaged in actions that are considered criminal but lack the *mens rea* to appreciate these actions. These expectations allow for the court to make exceptions for individuals who might be suffering from a mental disorder (i.e., psychiatric illness, acquired brain injury) provided it is severe enough that the person is unable to appreciate the nature and consequences of their actions. In this case, the individual may be found unfit to stand trial and/or not criminally responsible on account of mental disorder (section 16 C.C.C.). In many states, an insanity defense is possible with the burden of proof being on the defendant (FindLaw, 2019). While persons with IDD may qualify to be diverted under these sections of the Criminal Code, it is important that persons with a mild IDD is identified to be considered. At this time, there is little research on the experiences of persons with IDD within the criminal courts regarding diversion.

A multidimensional and multidisciplinary framework is required for understanding and working with persons with IDD within the justice system. A biopsychosocial, human- and rights-centered approach that is geared towards recognizing the social factors influencing crime can increase access to justice. At the same time, persons with IDD are interacting with a justice system that is, by its very structure, ableist. While there is clear evidence of a shifting paradigm towards equity and accessibility within the justice system, much more work needs to be done. It is essential to support professionals within the criminal justice system to collaborate with other professionals within the developmental, mental health, social welfare, and other sectors to assist them in their interactions with persons with IDD as accused, victims, and witnesses.

# References

Ali, A., Ghosh, S., Strydom, A., & Hassiotis, A. (2016). Prisoners with intellectual disabilities and detention status. Findings from a UK cross sectional study of prisons. *Research in Developmental Disabilities, 53*, 189-197.

Allen, D., Evans, C., Hider, A., Hawkins, S., Peckett, H., & Morgan, H. (2007). Offending behaviour in adults with Asperger syndrome. *Journal of Autism Developmental Disorders, 38*, 748-758.

Almeida, J. (2017, November 30). *The Government of Canada tables the Optional Protocol to the United Nations Convention on the Rights of Persons with Disabilities.* Retrieved from: https://www.canada.ca/en/employment-social-development/news/2017/11/the_government_ofcanadatablestheoptionalprotocoltotheunitednatio.html

American Association on Intellectual and Developmental Disabilities (AAIDD). (2018). Frequently Asked Questions on Intellectual Disability. Retrieved from: https://aaidd.org/intellectual-disability/definition/faqs-on-intellectual-disability#.WvUattMvwcg

Baldry, E., Clarence, M., Dowse, L., & Trollor, J. (2013). Reducing vulnerability to harm in adults with cognitive disabilities in the Australian criminal justice system. *Journal of Policy and Practice in Intellectual Disabilities, 10*(3), 222-229.

Barron, P., Hassiotis, A., & Banes, J. (2002). Offenders with intellectual disability: The size of the problem and therapeutic outcomes. *Journal of Intellectual Disability Research, 46*(6), 454-463.

Bradley, K. (2009, April). *The Bradley Report: Lord Bradley's review of people with mental health problems and learning disabilities in the criminal justice system.* London: Department of Health. Retrieved from: https://webarchive.nationalarchives.gov.uk/20130123195930/http://www.dh.gov.uk/en/Publicationsandstatistics/Publications/PublicationsPolicyAndGuidance/DH_098694

British Columbia. (2018). *Building a Better B.C. for People with Disabilities.* Retrieved from: https://www2.gov.bc.ca/gov/content/governments/about-the-bc-government/accessibility

Bruininks, R. H., Hill, B. K., & Morreau, L. E. (1988). Prevalence and implications of maladaptive behaviors and dual diagnosis in residential and other service programs. In J. A. Stark, F. J. Menolascino, M. H. Albarelli, &V. C. Gray (Eds.), *Mental retardation and mental health: Classification, diagnosis, treatment, & services* (pp. 3-29). New York, NY: Springer Press.

Camden ResourceNet. (2019). *The Arc of New Jersey Criminal Justice Advocacy Program (CJAP).* Retrieved from https://www.camdenresourcenet.org/search/the-arc-of-new-jersey-criminal-justice-advocacy-program/

Clare, I., & Gudjonsson, G. (1993). Interrogative suggestibility, confabulation, and acquiescence in people with mild learning-disabilities (mental handicap) - Implications for Reliability during Police Interrogations. *British Journal of Clinical Psychology, 32*, 295-301.

Clare, I.C.H., & Gudjonsson, G. H. (1995). The vulnerability of suspects with intellectual disabilities during police interviews: A review and experimental study of decision-making. *Department of Psychiatry, 8*(2), 110-128.

Clare, I. C. H., & Murphy, G. H. (1998). Working with offenders or alleged offenders with intellectual disabilities. In E. Emerson, C. Hatton, J. Bromley & A. Cane (Eds.), *Clinical psychology and people with intellectual disabilities* (pp. 154-176). Chichester, UK: Wiley.

Community Networks of Specialized Care (2019). *Dual Diagnosis Justice Case Managers.* Retrieved from http://www.community-networks.ca/collaboration/dual-diagnosis-justice-case-managers/

Cooper, S. A., & van der Speck, R. (2009). Epidemiology of mental ill health in adults with intellectual disabilities. *Current Opinion in Psychiatry, 22*(5), 431-436.

Dart, L., Gapen, W., & Morris, S. (2002). Building responsive service systems. In D. M. Griffiths, C. Stavrakaki, & J. Summers (Eds.), *Dual diagnosis: An introduction to the mental health needs of persons with developmental disabilities* (pp. 387 – 418). Sudbury, ON: Habilitative Mental Health Resource Network.

Day, K. (1994). Male mentally handicapped sex offenders. *British Journal of Psychiatry, 165*, 630-639.

Deb, S., Matthews, T., Holt, G., & Bouras, N. (2001). *Practice guidelines for the assessment and diagnosis of mental health problems in adults with intellectual disability.* Pavilion, Brighton: The European Association for Mental Health in Mental Retardation.

Dekker, M. C., Koot, H. M., Ende, J. V. D., & Verhulst, F. C (2002). Emotional and behavioral problems in children and adolescents with and without intellectual disability. *Journal of Child Psychology and Psychiatry, 43*(8), 1087-1098.

Denkowski, G.C., & Denkowski, K.M. (1986). Characteristics of the mentally retarded adolescent offender and their implications for residential treatment design. *Behavioral Interventions, 1*(1), 73-90.

Dykens, E. M., Hodapp, R. M., & Finucane, B. M. (2000). *Genetics and mental retardation syndromes: A new look at behavior and interventions.* Baltimore: Paul. H. Brookes Publishing Co.

Einfeld, S. L., Piccinin, A. M., Mackinnon, A., Hofer, S. M., Taffe, J., Gray, K. M., ... & Tonge, B. J. (2006). Psychopathology in young people with intellectual disability. *Journal of the American Medical Association, 296*(16), 1981-1989.

Einfeld, S. L., & Tonge, B. J. (1996). Population prevalence of psychopathology in children and adolescents with intellectual disability II: Epidemiological findings. *Journal of Intellectual Disability Research, 40*(2), 99-109.

Emerson, E. (2001). *Challenging behaviour: Analysis and intervention in people with severe intellectual disabilities.* Cambridge, UK: Cambridge University Press.

Emerson, E., & Halpin, S. (2013). Anti-social behaviour and police contact among 13 to 15-year-old English adolescents with and without mild/moderate intellectual disability. *Journal of Applied Research in Intellectual Disabilities, 26*(5), 362-369.

Farrington, D. P., & Welsh, B. C. (2006). Individual factors. In D. P. Farrington & B. C. Welsh (Eds.), *Saving children from a life of crime: Early risk factors and effective interventions* (pp. 37-54). Oxford, UK: Oxford University Press.

Fast, D. K., & Conry, J. (2009). Fetal alcohol spectrum disorders and the criminal justice system. *Developmental Disabilities Research Reviews, 15*, 250-257.

Fazel, S., Xenitidis, K., & Powell, J. (2008). The prevalence of intellectual disabilities among 12,000 prisoners: A systematic review. *International Journal of Law and Psychiatry, 21*, 369–373.

FindLaw. (2019). *The Insanity Defense Among States.* Retrieved from https://criminal.findlaw.com/criminal-procedure/the-insanity-defense-among-the-states.html

Gilson, S. F., & Levitas, A. S. (1987). Psychosocial crises in the lives of mentally retarded people. *Psychiatric Aspects of Mental Retardation Reviews, 6*(6), 27-31.

Griffiths, D. M., & Gardner, W. I. (2002). The integrated biopsychosocial approach to challenging behaviours. In D. M. Griffiths, C. Stavrakaki, & J. Summers (Eds.), *Dual diagnosis: An introduction to the mental health needs of persons with developmental disabilities* (pp. 387 – 418). Sudbury, ON: Habilitative Mental Health Resource Network.

Griffiths, D., Hingsburger, D., Ioannou, S., & Hoath, J. (2018). Ethical considerations in working with people with intellectual disabilities who have offended. In W.R. Lindsay & J.L. Taylor (Eds.), *The Wiley handbook on offenders with intellectual and developmental disabilities: Research, training and practice* (pp. 105-122). Chichester, UK: Wiley.

Griffiths, D., Owen, F., Hamelin, J., Feldman, M., Condillac, & Frijters, J. (2016). History of institutionalization: General background. In D. M. Griffiths, F. Owen, & R. A. Condillac (Eds.), *A difficult dream: Ending institutionalization for persons with intellectual disabilities with complex needs* (pp. 7 – 16). Kingston, NY: NADD Press.

Griffiths, D., Taillon-Wasmund, P., & Smith, D. (2002). Offenders who have a developmental disability. In D. M. Griffiths, C. Stavrakaki, & J. Summers (Eds.), *Dual diagnosis: An introduction to the mental health needs of persons with developmental disabilities* (pp. 387 – 418). Sudbury, ON: Habilitative Mental Health Resource Network.

Hamelin, J., Marinos, V., Robinson, J., & Giffiths, D. (2011). Rights and the justice system. InD. Griffiths, F. Owen, S. Watson (Eds.), *The rights agenda: An action plan to advance the rights of persons with intellectual disabilities* (pp. 223-254). Welland, ON: 3Rs Community University Research Alliance.

Harris, J. C., & Greenspan, S. (2016). Definition and nature of intellectual disability. In *Handbook of evidence-based practices in intellectual and developmental disabilities* (pp. 11-39). New York, NY: Springer Publishing Company.

Hayes, S. (2004). Pathways for offenders with intellectual disabilities. In W. R. Lindsay, J.L. Taylor, & P. Sturmey (Eds.), *Offenders with developmental disabilities* (pp. 68-89). Chichester, England: John Wiley & Sons Ltd.

Hayes, S., Shackell, P., Mottram, P., & Lancaster, R. (2007). The prevalence of intellectual disability in a major UK prison. *British Journal of Learning Disabilities, 35*, 162-167.

Henshaw, M., & Thomas, S. (2012). Police encounters with people with intellectual disability: prevalence, characteristics and challenges. *Journal of Intellectual Disability Research, 56*(6), 620-631.

Holburn, S., Jacobson, J. W., Vietze, P. M., Schwartz, A. A., & Sersen, E. (2000). Quantifying the process and outcomes of person-centred planning. *American Journal of Mental Retardation, 105*, 402 – 416.

Holland, A. J. (2004). Criminal behaviour and developmental disability: An epidemiological perspective. In W. R. Lindsay, J. L. Taylor, & P. Sturmey (Eds.), *Offenders with developmental disabilities* (pp. 23-34). Chichester UK: John Wiley & Sons.

Holland, T., Clare I., & Mukhopadhyay, T. (2002). Prevalence of 'criminal offending' by men and women with intellectual disability and the characteristics of 'offenders': Implications for research and service development. *Journal of Intellectual Disability Research 46*(1), 6-20.

Howard, R., Phipps, E., Clarbour, J., & Rayner, K. (2015). "I'd trust them if they understood learning disabilities" support needs of people with learning disabilities in the criminal justice system. *Journal of Intellectual Disabilities and Offending Behavior, 6*(1), 4-14.

Hughes, K., Bellis, M., Jones, L., Wood, S., Bates, G., Eckley, L., McCoy, E., Mikton, C; Shakespeare, T., Officer, A. (2012). Prevalence and risk of violence against adults with disabilities: A systematic review and meta-analysis of observational studies. *The Lancet, 379*(9826), 1621-1629.

Jeffery, H. M. I. (2010). An Arctic judges' journey with FASD. *Journal of Psychiatry & Law, 38,* 585-617.

Jones, J. (2007). Persons with intellectual disabilities in the criminal justice system: Review of the issues. *International Journal of Offender Therapy and Comparative Criminology, 51*(6), 723 – 733.

King, C., & Murphy, G. H. (2014). A systemic review of people with autism spectrum disorder and the criminal justice system. *Journal of autism and Developmental Disorders, 44*(11), 2717-2733.

Klimecki, M.R., Jenkinson, J., & Wilson, L. (1994). A study of recidivism among offenders with an intellectual disability. *Journal of Intellectual and Developmental Disability, 19*(3), 209-219. doi:10.1080/07263869400035241.

Law Commission of Ontario. (2012, September). *A framework for the law as it affects persons with disabilities: Advancing substantive equality for persons with disabilities through law, policy and practice.* Retrieved from: https://www.lco-cdo.org/wp-content/uploads/2012/12/disabilities-framework.pdf

Lerner-Wren, G. (2002). An innovative approach to the mentally disabled in the criminal justice system. In G. Landsberg, M. Rock, & L. Berg (Eds.), *Serving mentally ill offenders: Challenges & opportunities for mental health professionals* (pp. 128 – 132). New York, NY: Springer Publishing Company.

Lindsay, W.R. (2002). Research on sex offenders with intellectual and developmental disabilities. *Journal of Intellectual Disability Research, 46*(1), 74-85.

Lindsay, W. R., Hastings, R. P., & Beech, A.R. (2011). Forensic research in offenders with intellectual and developmental disabilities, 1: Prevalence and risk assessment. *Psychology, Crime and Law, 17*(1), 3-7.

Lindsay, W. R., Hastings, R. P., Griffiths, D. M., & Hayes, S. C. (2007). Trends and challenges in forensic research on offenders with intellectual disability. *Journal of Intellectual and Developmental Disability, 32,* 55–61.

Lindsay, W. R., Law, J. & MacLeod, F. (2002). Intellectual disabilities and crime: Issues in assessment, intervention and management. In A. Needs & G. Towl (Eds.), *Applying psychology to forensic practice* (pp. 97-114). Oxford: British Society Books/Blackwell.

Lindsay, W. R., O'Brien, G., Carson, D., Holland, A. J., Taylor, J. L., Wheeler, J. R., ... & Johnston, S. (2010). Pathways into services for offenders with intellectual disabilities: Childhood experiences, diagnostic information, and offense variables. *Criminal Justice and Behavior, 37*(6), 678-694.

Lindsay, W. R., Sturmey, P., & Taylor, J. L. (2004). Natural history and theories of offending in people with developmental disabilities. In W. R. Lindsay, J. L. Taylor, & P. Sturmey (Eds.), *Offenders with developmental disabilities* (pp. 3-22). West Sussex: John Wiley and Sons.

Loucks, N. (2007). *No one knows: The prevalence and associated needs of offenders with learning difficulties and learning disabilities.* Retrieved from www.prisonreformtrust.org.uk/uploads/documents/NOKML.pdf.

Marinos, V., Griffiths, D., Gosse, L., Robinson, J., Olley, G., & Lindsay, W. (2009). Legal rights and persons with intellectual disabilities. In F. Owen, & D. Griffiths. (Eds.). *Challenges to the human rights of people with intellectual disabilities.* Kingston, NY: NADD Press.

Mattson, S. N., Crocker, N., & Nguyen, T. T. (2011). Fetal alcohol spectrum disorders: Neuropsychological and behavioral features. *Neuropsychology Review, 21*(2), 81-101.

Maulik, P. K., Mascarenhas, M. N., Mathers, C. D., Dua, T., & Saxena, S. (2011). Prevalence of intellectual disability: A meta-analysis of population-based studies. *Research in Developmental Disabilities, 32*(2), 419-436.

McBrien, J. (2003). The intellectually disabled offender: Methodological problems in identification. *Journal of Applied Research in Intellectual Disabilities, 16*(2), 95-105.

McBrien, J., Hodgetts, A., & Gregory, J. (2003). Offending and risky behaviour in community services for people with intellectual disabilities in one local authority. *Journal of Forensic Psychiatry & Psychology, 14*(2), 280-297.

McLachlan, K. (2016). Intellectual disability among offenders in correctional forensic settings. In R. Roesch & A. N. Cook (Eds.), *Handbook of Forensic Mental Health Services* (p. 344). New York: Taylor & Francis.

Noble, J. & Conley, R. (1992). Toward an epidemiology of relevant attributes. In R. W. Conley, R. Luckasson, & G.N. Bouthelet (Eds.), *The criminal justice system and mental retardation* (pp. 17-53). Baltimore: Paul H. Brookes.

O'Brien, G., Taylor, J., Lindsay, W., Dundee, U., Anthony, J., Holland, A., ... Steptoe, L. (2010). A multi-centre study of adults with learning disabilities referred to services for antisocial or offending behaviour: Demographic, individual, offending and service characteristics. *Journal of Learning Disabilities and Offending Behaviour, 1*(2), 5-15.

Owen, F. & McFarland, J. (2002). The nature of developmental disabilities. In D. M. Griffiths, C. Stavrakaki, & J. Summers (Eds.), *Dual diagnosis: An introduction to the mental health needs of persons with developmental disabilities* (pp. 387 – 418). Sudbury, ON: Habilitative Mental Health Resource Network.

Parmenter, T., Einfeld, S., Tonge, B., & Dempster, J. (1998). Behavioural and emotional problems in the classroom of children and adolescents with intellectual disability. *Journal of Intellectual & Developmental Disability, 23*(1), 71-77.

Raina, P., Arenovich, T., Jones, J., & Lunsky, Y. (2013). Pathways into the criminal justice system for individuals with intellectual disability. *Journal of Applied Research in Intellectual Disabilities, 26*(5), 404-409.

Schalock, R. L., Borthwick-Duffy, S. A., Bradley, V. J., Buntinx, W. H., Coulter, D. L., Craig, E. M., ... & Shogren, K. A. (2010). *Intellectual disability: Definition, classification, and systems of supports.* Washington, DC: American Association on Intellectual and Developmental Disabilities.

Simpson, M.K., & Hogg, J. (2001a). Patterns of offending among people with intellectual disability: A systematic review. Part 1: Methodology and prevalence data. *Journal of Intellectual Disability Research, 45*(5), 384-396.

Simpson, M.K. , & Hogg, J. (2001b). Patters of offending among people with intellectual disability: A systemic review. Part II: Predisposing factors. *Journal of Intellectual Disability Research, 45*(5), 397-406.

Streissguth, A. P. (1997). *Fetal alcohol syndrome: A guide for families and communities.* Baltimore, MD: Brookes Publishing.

Streissguth, A. P., Barr, H. M., Kogan, J., & Bookstein, F. L. (1996, September 29). *Understanding the occurrence of secondary disabilities in clients with fetal alcohol syndrome*

*(FAS) and fetal alcohol effects (FAE)*. Retrieved from: http://lib.adai.uw.edu/pubs/bk2698.pdf

United Nations (2006). Convention on the rights of persons with disabilities. Retrieved https://www.un.org/development/desa/disabilities/convention-on-the-rights-of-persons-with-disabilities.html

Walker, N., & McCabe, S. (1973). *Crime and insanity in England* (vol. 2). Edinburgh: University Press.

Wehmeyer, M.J. (2013). Disability, disorder and identity. *Journal of Intellectual and Developmental Disabilities, 51*(2), 122-126.

Wexler, D. B. (1997). Therapeutic jurisprudence in a comparative law context. *Behavioral Sciences & the Law, 15*(3), 233-246.

Wheeler, J. R. Clare, I. C. H., & Holland, A. J. (2013). Offending by people with intellectual disabilities in community settings: A preliminary examination of contextual factors. *Special Issue: Pathways, Assessment and Treatment of Offenders with Intellectual Disability, 26*(5), 370-438.

Wheeler, J. R., Holland, A. J., Bambrick, M., Lindsay, W.R., Carson, D., Steptoe, L., Johnston, S., Taylor, J.L., Middleton, C., Price, K., & O'Brien, G. (2009). Community services and people with intellectual disabilities who engage in anti-social or offending behaviour: referral rates, characteristics, and care pathways. *Journal of Forensic Psychiatry & Psychology 20*(5), 717-740.

White, R. D., & Haines, F. (2002). *Crime and criminology: An introduction*. Toronto, ON: Oxford University Press.

*Chapter 2*

# Classification and Identification of Accused Persons with Intellectual and Developmental Disabilities in the Criminal Justice System[1]

*Dorothy Griffiths, Voula Marinos,
Jessica Jones, Amanda Jones, & Mary Gilmore*

## Introduction

The literature regarding accused persons with intellectual or developmental disabilities typically emphasizes the importance of identification and accommodation in the criminal justice system (CJS) to ensure equity and justice (i.e., Baldry, Clarence, Dowse & Trotter, 2013; Petersilia, 2000). However, emerging research has shown that there are real or perceived risks that can be associated with identification and classification of a person with an intellectual or developmental disability (Jones, 2014). In the chapter that follows, the prevalence rates of people with an intellectual or developmental disability as the accused within the justice system is discussed, followed by a review of the definitions of intellectual or developmental disability, the issues of identification, and the potential benefits and challenges that might result from that identification. We argue that classification and identification of persons with intellectual or developmental disability within the criminal justice system are not simple and obvious decisions; they need to be considered within the context of the interests and needs of the accused person with a disability and the stage of the justice process. The chapter will end with a discussion of screening and assessment strategies and best practice protocols for identification of an accused person with an intellectual disability or developmental disability.

---

[1]Portions of this chapter are excerpted from the theses of:
Fraser, M. (2017). *Individuals with intellectual disabilities and their experiences within the criminal justice system* (Unpublished Honours Thesis). Brock University: St. Catharines, Canada.
Jones, A. (2014). *Bridging the conceptualization of youth with intellectual disabilities to sentencing under the YCJA* (Unpublished Master's thesis). Brock University, St. Catharines, Canada.

## Prevalence Rates of Offenders with Intellectual Disabilities in the Criminal Justice System

Defining what is an intellectual or developmental disability, now combined under the umbrella term intellectual developmental disorder (IDD), the confusion between these diagnoses with mental illness (MI), and the disregard for dual diagnosis (co-morbid IDD and MI), create challenges when trying to determine the exact number of persons with intellectual developmental disabilities who are within the criminal justice system. Persons with developmental disorder represent 1-3% of the general population (ARC, 2017), yet between 4% and 14% of individuals in the U.S. under custody are diagnosed as individuals with an IDD (Petersilia, 2000). Stewart, Wilton and Sapers (2016) demonstrated that 25% of offenders incarcerated in federal custody in the Pacific region of Canada had some level of cognitive deficit. Out of 157 men tested in prison, 33 responded positively to having experienced some form of 'reading problem' or 'intellectual difficulties,' or had stated their attendance to a 'special school' (Murphy, Harnett, & Holland, 1995). More recent research reported that 12% of the prison population had an intelligence quotient below 70 (the upper cut off for an intellectual disability) and 30% scored in the borderline range disability (80 to 90) (Baldry et al., 2013).

As seen by the data presented above, prevalence studies report diverse percentages based on how data are collected, ranging anywhere from 2-40% (Cockram, Jackson, & Underwood, 1992; Cockram, Jackson, & Underwood, 1998; Hayes, 2007; Holland, 1991; Jones, 2007; Lindsay et al., 2010; Mallet, 2009). There are differences and challenges when studying the prevalence of offenders with intellectual or developmental disorders that relate to the definition of IDD, poorly constructed research methods, as well as the geographical area that the study is taking place in (Simpson & Hogg, 2001).

Loucks (2007) noted there are three main ways that incidence data are collected. The first is through assessing the prevalence of IDD within the offender population, the second is by surveying the social services that support persons with IDD, and the third is through self-report from offenders. Day (1994) has cautioned that incidence data, based on prison populations, does not fully account for the number of offenders with IDD because many are not charged or are diverted to facilities for persons with IDD. McBrien and Murphy (2006) have further identified that social service agencies may be reluctant to report an offense committed by a person with an IDD due to fear of reprisal or because of policy direction or lack thereof in their agency. Additionally, some individuals with an IDD may not be served within social service systems (Loucks, 2007).

Lastly, Loucks (2007) suggested self-reporting in persons with IDD has the inherent flaws of memory and failure to disclose either their offense or their disability. Many people with IDD tend to hide their disability for fear of stigmatization; the term cloak of competence was coined in 1967 by Edgerton to describe the phenomenon where a person with a disability may attempt to conceal their disability.

Griffiths, Watson, Lewis, and Stoner (2004) cautioned that research data regarding persons with IDD in the criminal justice system have often been based on prison populations or arrest/conviction rates. This type of data, showing higher prevalence rates, is typically interpreted to suggest that this population is at a higher risk to offend. Alternatively, these data may support a rival hypothesis of higher rates of apprehensions, arrests, confessions, and convictions (Murphy, Coleman & Haynes, 1983; Santamour & West, 1977). Griffiths and Fedoroff (2008) noted that the apparent overrepresentation of persons with disabilities within the offender population may not indicate a greater incidence of offending but an increased vulnerability to engage in offending due to social pressure or because of disadvantages experienced within the criminal justice system. Lindsay (2009) highlighted the overrepresentation within the offender population is related to inappropriate identification of persons with borderline or low average intellectual ability.

Statistics Canada (2015a) reported that administration of justice offences (e.g., failure to comply with a court order or failure to appear in court) typically represented a large majority of completed criminal cases, approximately 23% from 2013-2014. These charges are described as the strongest predictor of pre-trial detention for both adults and youth in Canada (Statistics Canada 2011; Statistics Canada, 2016). Custodial sentences are the most commonly imposed sentence in adult cases involving administration of justice charges (Statistics Canada, 2015b). Persons with an IDD may have a more difficult time adhering to traditional court orders. One mental health worker in Jones (2014) stated,

> If you had a young person who had a learning disability or a developmental delay and you gave them a piece of paper that says that is where you need to report to, this is what you need to do, number one they will likely lose the paper, number two they will likely not be able to read it, and number three they maybe can't even understand it. (p. 94)

Another lawyer described how one offender was required to write an apology as part of a diversion program. This particular offender had completed the community service portions of their diversion program but was unable to read and write and did not finish this letter and thus was not successful in completing the diversion program (Jones, 2014). Although it is not clear how large a role this offender's disability played in their ability or inability to successfully complete a diversion program, it is evident that these challenges and barriers may make it harder for persons with an intellectual disability to comply with traditional court orders. This may contribute to higher prevalence rates among this population within the justice system.

Further, Cockram (2005) noted differences in sentencing trends for persons with disabilities within Australia. While more likely to receive discharge, dismissal, or a withdrawal of charges at the front end of the system, individuals with an IDD, who were processed through the system were more likely to receive custodial sentences or more restrictive diversion conditions when compared to other offenders. Jones (2014) reported that for less serious crimes persons with an IDD were eligible for diversion, withdrawal, or dismissal; but for more serious crimes the presence of the disability was viewed as a risk factor which may lead to more restrictive sentencing. Thus, high prevalence rates within custodial facilities may in part, reflect sentencing disparities rather than differences in the propensity to offend.

## Definitions and Classifications of Intellectual Disability

Before discussing the benefits of identification of a disability, it is important to elaborate on the definitions and classifications used in identification. Jones (2014) found that many professionals in the criminal justice field had misconceptions about what constitutes an IDD, including associated risk/need factors. Carulla et al. (2011) suggested the use of the term intellectual is broadly accepted as an umbrella term that refers not only to cognitive functioning, but,

> Adaptive behaviour and learning that is age appropriate and meets the standards of culture appropriate demands of daily life. Even though "cognitive" may be seen as a more precise term that more closely reflects underlying phenomena of IDD, it also has a broader meaning in psychology. The use of the term "cognitive" in connection with dementia and schizophrenia may also cause confusion. (p.175)

The term developmental is often used in reference to the presence of this disability in the developing years to emphasize that the disability is dynamic (Carulla et al., 2011). However, among lawyers, Jones (2014) found that intellectual and developmental disabilities were described as a stable or unchanging cognitive deficit, with limited insight into cognitive and adaptive differences across individuals or the impact of social factors on overall health and wellness. These descriptions further blurred intellectual disabilities with mental health disorders and learning disabilities more generally. This understanding of what an intellectual disability entails makes it challenging for professionals in the justice system to see rehabilitation as a worthwhile sentencing goal.

Intellectual disability (formerly mental retardation), and now more broadly termed intellectual developmental disability (IDD) is the term used to describe a variety of syndromes characterized by low intelligence and significant limitations in adaptive functioning that occurs during the developmental period. Reynolds, Zupanick, and Dombeck (2013a, 2013b, 2013c, 2013d) wrote four incisive papers describing the current definitions used to diagnose and support persons with IDDs. They noted that there are two definitions for intellectual developmental disabilities routinely used in the field. The medical field largely relies on the definition created by the American Psychiatric Association (APA) and published in Diagnostic and Statistical Manual of Mental Disorders (DSM-5; APA 2013). The APA diagnostic criterion is typically used to diagnose IDD. In social services, the definition employed is often based on a similar definition from the American Association on Intellectual and Developmental Disabilities (AAIDD formerly AAMR, 2017). The AAIDD definition is typically employed as a tool for service planning. Although they are both relatively similar, there are differences in language and severity ratings.

The APA definition (APA, 2013) has three criteria: (i) deficiency in intellectual functioning (70 or below) as measured using a standardized IQ test and representing deficiency in reasoning, problem solving, planning, abstract thinking, judgement, academic learning, and experiential learning, (ii) deficits in adaptive functioning such as communication, social skills, personal independence, school or work functioning based upon clinical impressions, and (iii) the deficits must be apparent during childhood or adolescence.

Reynolds et al. (2013d) described the rating levels of disability: mild, moderate, severe, or profound. They noted that 85% of individuals with disability have a mild level of intellectual disability, meaning they typically can complete elementary academic levels, can be relatively self-sufficient, and require low levels of support. Ten percent of individuals with intellectual disabilities are labelled moderate and demonstrate basic communication skills, can perform most self-care activities and be employed in jobs that require limited social or conceptual skills. However, they noted that these individuals may require support in areas of social judgement and will typically live in settings such as group homes for support. Severe and profound levels of disability are found in 3-4 and 1-2 percent, respectively, of the population of persons with intellectual disabilities. Persons labelled as severely intellectually disabled have basic communication skills and supervision and supportive assistance in areas such as self-care. According to Reynolds et al. (2013d), these individuals will typically be living in a residential setting. Profound intellectual disability is typified as requiring 24-hour care and support; many will also experience comorbid physical and sensory disabilities.

Reynolds et al. (2013d) noted that the use of categories to classify intellectual disability implies that the various levels are distinct. However, they suggested instead that intellectual disability represents a continuum, rather than a distinct categorical label. They further questioned whether a unidimensional factor of severity provides information that can translate into practice suggesting that the meaning of a severity label tells little about the real needs of the individual. Additionally, they cautioned that within a category of severity that the support needs may vary significantly between individuals with the same label.

The AAIDD (2017) also employed the same three main criteria: (i) limitations in intellectual functioning (i.e., 70-75 or below as measured using a standardized IQ score), (ii) limitations in adaptive behaviour including conceptual skills, social skills and practical skills that are one standard deviation below the average on a standardized tool, and (iii) onset before the age of 18. However, the focus of their definition was on identification of limitations to enable the development of individualized support planning and the level of intensity of supports needed. The AAIDD rating of severity has been based on the Supports Intensity Scale (AAIDD, 2017); this scale explores both limitations and strengths as a basis for determining the levels of support needed. There are four levels: intermittent, limited, extensive, and pervasive. Intermittent support is identified for individuals who require only additional supports at times of change or stress. Limited supports are provided for individuals who may require additional training and support to manage daily living. Extensive support is provided for individuals who require daily support. Pervasive support is identified for individuals who require daily supervision to manage daily living. The four levels correspond to the APA severity levels.

Griffiths and Marinos (2005) cautioned against the use of the concept of Mental Age (MA) when describing intellectual functioning; this term is misunderstood and misused when identifying an individual within the criminal justice system. Often the professional expert making the designation is more experienced in mental health assessments for the courts, rather than assessments of persons with an intellectual disability, and as such there is a tendency to rely on the concept of MA as a description of the person's functioning. In practice, the MA refers to the level of questions the individual was able to respond correctly to on the test as compared to a normative standard based on age; it does not imply that the person functions overall at the level indicated by a mental age. Thus, although an adult with an intellectual disability may receive a mental age equivalent to a child, it does not in any way account for the person's experiences, general learning, or physical maturation as an adult. In addition, as Aiken (1994) warned, many of the IQ tests have less acceptable levels of predictive validity and as such must be used with great prudence as predictors of behavior.

## Distinguishing Intellectual Disability from Mental Disorder

The criminal justice system has generally paid greater attention to the identification and accommodations for persons with mental health needs. Intellectual disability is often subjugated under the title of mental disorders, thereby blurring the differentiation between mental health needs and challenges associated with intellectual disability. With a mental disorder caused by a mental health problem the premise is that with diversion to a psychiatric facility for treatment, and if treatment is forthcoming and effective, then the person can then proceed within the criminal justice system. However, persons with intellectual disabilities cannot be treated with medication or therapy to eliminate the intellectual disability that may prohibit them from effectively participating in the criminal justice system. Additionally, the accommodations needed for each group are significantly different.

Canadian courts have a number of resources available that can be utilized to help guide the justice process for offenders with mental health disorders. Pre-sentence reports (PSRs), psychological assessments, fitness trials, not-criminally responsive (NCR) defenses, mental health diversion programs, and specialized mental health courts are used to both identify the unique needs/risks of offenders and to tailor an appropriate judicial response. Being subjugated under the umbrella title of mental disorders, offenders with an intellectual disability are able to access and be referred to these resources and services. However, resources such as PSR's and psychological assessments are used with discretion by defense counsel because they have the potential to highlight not only mitigating factors but more importantly, aggravating factors which may negatively impact sentencing (Jones, 2014). Mental health diversion programs and mental health courts offer a court response that is tailored to the unique needs of offenders. Unfortunately, these services are not available in all jurisdictions nor available to all offenders due to the offense type, issues with identification, and differences in referral patterns due to prosecutorial discretion across courts (Jones, 2014).

In the courts, if a person is found incompetent or unfit to stand trial because they do not understand the criminal justice system procedures, then training can be provided to allow some individuals to learn what is needed to meet the criteria: understanding the nature or object of the proceedings; understanding the possible consequences of the proceedings; or communicating with their lawyer (section 2 of the *Canadian Criminal Code*). In some cases, this may be effective in rendering the person able to participate in the criminal justice process, but not always (Wall & Christopher, 2012). However, the training does not eliminate the disability. Wall and Christopher (2012) caution that while their study suggested that some accused with an intellectual disability were able to attain the ability to acquire and use the information in training, it was with reduced efficiency; other individuals, regardless of training were unable to attain trial competence standards. Thus, if the disability is extensive then no amount of training will produce the type of change that would enable the person to effectively participate in the criminal justice proceedings.

Given that these resources are limited and may highlight aggravating factors or place accused in treatment facilities for an indeterminate amount of time, they are typically reserved for more serious cases. "The extent to which any competency attainment efforts will succeed depends on a variety of factors, including the severity and type of a defendant's disability, the seriousness of the criminal charges, and any co-morbid psychiatric disorders that may affect trial competence" (Wall & Christopher, 2012, p. 371). The use of these training procedures may be justified if the disability or mental health condition of the offender is significant, the charge is of a serious nature, or the accused is a repeat offender with additional needs (Jones, 2014). With the exception of mental health diversion and mental health court, these resources, which could be used to gather detailed information about the accused, are not usually employed for a large majority of offenders (Jones, 2014). Instead, the use of reports previously obtained outside of the court system, such as individual education plans or input from support workers or community services, are preferred methods for obtaining information about an accused with intellectual disabilities or mental health disorders (Jones, 2014). Unfortunately, not all offenders have these reports or supports available.

Pertersila (2000) noted that the distinction between persons with an intellectual disability and a person with mental illness has been non-existent in some justice agencies. She further notes that the lack of distinction creates a serious problem. The accommodations within the courts that would be needed for persons with an intellectual disability might be significantly different from the needs of a person with a mental health or psychiatric problem. Persons with an intellectual disability pose unique cognitive, emotional, and psychological barriers that can interfere with their active participation in the criminal justice system from arrest to trial.

## Comorbid Mental Health Needs

Comorbid mental health factors present frequently as a second but interwoven diagnostic variable when identifying offenders within the criminal justice system. Research has demonstrated that 20-35% of persons with an intellectual disability will experience a comorbid mental health challenge (Nezu, Nezu, & Gill-Weiss, 1992); within the population of offenders with intellectual disabilities this percentage range from 30-47% (Steiner, 1984; White & Wood, 1988). Einfeld et al. (2006) noted that persons with dual diagnoses (intellectual disability and mental health problems) have difficulty accessing services; psychiatric services for the neurotypical population are now not always trained to identify mental health problems in persons with intellectual disabilities or to provide adapted services. Moreover, Baldry et al. (2013) noted that offenders with dual diagnoses have even less opportunity to receive appropriate assessment or treatment.

Persons with intellectual disability, when combined with a dual diagnosis or other social disadvantage, are vulnerable within the Criminal Justice System (Baldry et al., 2013). Thus, the identification of the needs of offenders with intellectual disabilities can often present a complexity in both assessment and intervention for the criminal justice system.

## Identification of an Intellectual Disability

McAfee and Gural (1988) reported that seventy-five percent of offenders with intellectual disability are identified at arrest; however 10% are not identified until they are in prison. Marinos et al. (2017) similarly found that mental health professionals reported that some individuals are not identified until sentencing has occurred and the individual is in custody facilities.

Under-identification has been reported to occur because of inadequate screening protocols, lack of training for criminal justice personnel, lack of experience with persons with intellectual disabilities by the psychologists or psychiatrists who typically assess cases involving mental health to judge competence of persons based on intellectual ability, and because of the reluctance on the part of the accused to self-identify (Bonnie, 1992; McAfee & Gural, 1988; Schilit, 1989; Smith & Broughton, 1994). Additionally, many offenders with intellectual disabilities do not show physical features that would be readily identifiable to the general population. There are many causes for an intellectual disability, and not all individuals with an intellectual disability will present with the same needs and challenges. Although most of the general population may be able to identify a person with Down syndrome, many of the other genetic and nongenetic causes of intellectual disability do not present with features that would allow the untrained profession to identify the person visually. Additionally, their presenting challenges and needs for support can be vastly different depending on the etiology. For example, a person with fetal alcohol spectrum disorder (FASD) will show a vastly different profile than a person with Down syndrome. The heterogeneity of the population is a large factor in under-identification. In the Jones (2014) study, a mental health provider remarked:

> I think FASD is a really challenging one to work with because young people, you know like if you think about other developmental disabilities like Downs syndrome, it is visible, a really visible disability, FASD, it's considered a brain disorder, like a brain injury, but like you look at those people and there is no visible disability, so we expect them to be able to react, and behave and perform. (p.56)

This under-identification raises the question as to whether there are benefits or risks to identifying persons with intellectual disabilities as they enter the criminal justice system as accused. Would identification lead to fewer persons with intellectual disabilities being unjustly charged, convicted, and imprisoned? Or does the identification set up conditions where we are seeking a different standard of responsibility for persons with intellectual disabilities that may lead to either an inequitable system of justice or further stigmatization of the person with a disability?

On one hand, we do not wish to excuse the criminal behaviors of offenders who are cognitively impaired. In a world where such persons are finally moving back into local communities and striving to be treated with equality, it would make no sense to demand a double standard in criminal justice matters. In a normalized world, one has to live within society's rules, and accept the consequence of one's actions.

> On the other hand, many offenders with cognitive disabilities may not be so much "lawbreakers" as they are low functioning citizens who lack education

on how to function responsibly in a complex society. Some research suggests that they are frequently used by other criminals to assist in law-breaking activities without understanding their involvement in a crime or its consequences. (Pertersila, 2000, p.5)

The ethical dilemma posed by Pertersila sheds light on one of the elements to take into consideration when persons with intellectual disabilities (cognitive disabilities) are accused of a crime within the criminal justice system. Identification of the person with an intellectual disability should not be seen as a way to overlook a crime committed by a person with intellectual disability but as a means of understanding the conditions that may have led to the crime, the *mens rea* associated with the crime, and what accommodations the person might need to ensure equity within the justice system. However, there also may be some risks in identification of a person's intellectual disability. If a person is suspected of not being deemed competent or fit to stand trial, then they may be diverted to a mental health facility where they will spend up to 60 days in being assessed, and potentially, could spend time in a facility until found fit or otherwise given a stay of proceedings if permanently unfit (*R. v. Demers, 2004*). If fit, the individual might also be viewed as permanently having cognitive impairments that could, on the face of it, be argued as being unable to benefit from rehabilitation.

## Benefits of Identification

Baldry and her colleagues (2013) noted that "[e]arly intervention for this group is crucial to preventing the escalation in vulnerability as individuals with complex cognitive impairment move into and through the CJS" and suggested that "there would be clear benefits of disability recognition and support at these early points in individuals' trajectories" (p.228).

However, Crocker, Cote, Toupin and St-Onge (2007) noted defendants with an intellectual disability in a pre-trial holding center in Quebec were found to be largely indistinguishable based on their physical or criminal profile cues from their neurotypical counterparts, and as such the probability of early screening and subsequent supports for these individuals was unlikely. One of the reasons primarily argued for identification is so that individuals would have the opportunity for accommodations. When someone is identified as requiring support for medical, personal, physical or communication reasons, then the law allows for accommodations such as the use of a hearing or sound amplification device, the use of an interpreter, Bliss symbols or sign language. In Ontario, victims and witnesses are eligible to testify using closed circuit television or behind a screen (section 486.2 Canadian Criminal Code). They can also benefit from the support and resources of the Victim Witness Assistance Program (Marinos, Griffiths, Fergus, Stromski, & Rondeau, 2014).

There is an abundance of research that demonstrates that individuals with intellectual disabilities are highly vulnerable in the criminal justice system. Fraser (2017) noted that there is evidence to show that individuals with intellectual disabilities experience challenges at each stage of the justice process: commission of crime, arrest, bail, trial, sentencing, conviction, corrections and release. Within each stage, she examined relevant research to discover different challenges and themes that arose.

*Prior to an arrest,* some persons with intellectual disabilities may have an increased vulnerability to commit a crime. According to Greenspan (2006), the three key vulnerabilities relate to cognitive ability (e.g., deficits in controlling temper, emotions, and decision processing/making), practical adaptive skills (e.g., self-care, lifestyle, home life, work, and community involvement), and social skills (leading to social isolation and increased risk for gullibility and seeking approval of others). Hingsburger (2013) coined the phrase *counterfeit criminality* to refer to those individuals who have criminally offended because of a lack of social belonging, self-advocacy skills, or the inability to discriminate situations that are risky.

*At the stage of arrest,* persons with intellectual disabilities may be at higher risk of mistreatment because of some common characteristics associated with the disability. For example, Perske (2004) developed a list of propensities of individuals with an ID. The list outlines vulnerabilities and factors that may contribute to false confession, therefore leading to wrongful conviction. Perske (2004) noted that persons with intellectual disability are more likely to rely on others to find solutions and seek to please authority figures and as such watch for clues from the interviewer as to the appropriate response, often bluffing an answer if none is forthcoming. In addition, they are more likely to respond affirmatively to the last question or change their answer if the question is repeated, under the assumption that the first response was incorrect. He also noted the desire to please persons in authority, a quickness to take blame, and lack of plea-bargaining.

O'Connell, Garmoe and Goldstein (2005) found that persons with intellectual disabilities were more likely to change their answer if they received friendly feedback. Essentially, it is then implied that regardless of accuracy, defendants may display confidence in their answers when repeatedly asked a question about a specific event (O'Connell, et al., 2005). Additionally, because they are more suggestible in the interrogative situation they are more easily coerced into providing false information (Everington & Fulero, 1999), are quick to take blame, and when exhausted will "surrender all defences" (Perske, 2004, p. 486). As a result, they are more likely to confess, provide evidence that is incriminating, or fail to plea-bargain (Edwards & Reynolds, 1997; Gudjonsson, 1990; Leo & Ofshe, 1998; Perske, 2004).

Persons with intellectual disabilities also have a greater challenge understanding legal rights and cautions (Leo & Ofshe, 1998). Ericson and Perlman (2001) compared the knowledge of terms related to the law and the courts of participants with and without ID; only 8 out of the 34 terms on the questionnaire were understood fully by the majority (75% or more) of the group with ID. In comparison, the majority (85% or more) of the group without an ID demonstrated a full understanding of all but 6 of the 34 terms. This has implications for their interactions throughout the remaining stages of the criminal justice system.

In a thematic analysis of the literature of the experiences of offenders with ID within the criminal justice system, three common themes and one overarching theme emerged; Hyun, Hahn and McConnell (2014) found that during arrest participants were a) not understanding what was happening, b) feeling lonely and unsupported, and c) uncertain about what to say or do. The overarching theme was social isolation, both prior to and within the criminal justice system. They have also been noted to seek approval from the police by giving what they think the officer may want to hear (Ellis & Luckasson, 1985).

Of significance during the period of arrest, researchers have noted that police officers often have little experience with persons with intellectual disability and may hold negative attitudes. For example, police in three police districts in the southeastern United States completed a questionnaire on their perceptions concerning persons with ID; Eadens, Cranston-Gingras, Dupoux and Eadens (2016) reported that 84.1% of the officers stated they had little or no training on ID, 62.9% had no contact with persons with ID, and 78.2% expressed negative attitudes towards the population.

*Following arrest,* offenders with intellectual disabilities were more likely to be remanded or denied bail compared to their counterparts who were released pre-trial (Ali, Ghosh, Strydom & Hassiotis, 2016; Cockram, 2000), to be held in pretrial custody (Cockram, 2000), to be jailed pretrial because of a failure to meet bail or personal recognizance (Toberg, 1992), and to be declared unfit to stand trial (Valenti-Hein & Schwartz, 1993), often resulting in institutionalization that lasted longer than if tried and convicted (Fedoroff, Griffiths, Marini, & Richards, 2000). People who are held pre-trial have been found to be more likely to be convicted (Toberg, 1992). If tried and convicted, they often serve longer terms than offenders without intellectual disabilities (Laski, 1992).

Cockram (2000) compared persons with and without ID through the criminal justice system and found that over one quarter of offenders with ID were held in pre-trial custody compared to only 17% of the comparison group, and nearly half of the group with ID were denied bail compared to only 44% of the comparison group. The findings suggest that offenders with ID are denied bail and placed in remand custody more than the general population (Cockram, 2000).

In a study conducted by White, Batchelor, Pulman and Howard (2015), 35 professionals from New South Wales, Australia participated in a semi structured interview regarding their overall understanding of those who are questionably fit/unfit to stand trial, and the process involved. The two themes that emerged were a) participants having a quite poor understanding and b) having limited experience working with these populations. These themes imply a need for professionals that specialize in this population and understand them effectively.

One of the major themes found in Hyun, Han and McConnell's (2014) thematic analysis of literature on offender's experiences within the criminal justice system was that of feeling unsupported. Although services exist for offenders with ID, the question is whether these services are available and accessible. The complexity of the trial process requires these supports to be not only available for individuals with ID, but also offered without any hesitation.

*Sentencing:* Cockram (2005) reported that persons with an intellectual disability were more likely to be sentenced to custody, that suspension of custodial sentences were not granted to persons with intellectual disability, and that fewer were provided with community-based orders. Steadman, Redlich, Callahan, Robbins, and Vesselinov (2011) however found that when cases were adjudicated in mental health courts, more favorable terms of sentencing, specifically for custodial sentences, were granted.

Cockram (2005) compared sentences of offenders with an ID to those without an ID in Western Australia. A total of 843 adults were tracked throughout the criminal system over a span of 11 years. Cockram found that for first time offenders of both groups, 11.3% of offenders with an ID were sentenced to custody compared to 8.9% of the comparison group. No custodial sentences were suspended for an offender with an ID compared to the comparison group in which 13 offenders from the general population were provided with a suspended sentence. Finally, fewer people in the comparison group were provided with community-based orders, but were instead ordered to pay a fine (Cockram, 2005).

Haskins and Friel (1973) conducted a study over 2 months that included 500 participants, 35 with an ID. All participants were offenders admitted to the Texas Department of Corrections. In-depth interviews were conducted to reveal experiential information prior to corrections, and during. Statistics from the study demonstrated that 34% of the group with an ID received probation, compared to 45% of the comparison group. Haskins and Friel (1973) suggested that prevalent negative attitudes from justice professionals resulted in the disproportionality of probations given.

Diversion options and the use of alternative measures for offenders with ID should be considered (Hayes, 2007). Diversionary options should consider the individual using a bio-psycho-social lens to develop a successful, rehabilitative option. However, it is a complicated matter for a judge to consider when diversion is the better option for the individual and his/her human rights (Hayes, 2007). In Canada, diversion is not typically considered if the crime is violent in nature. However, it may be offered for class 1 offenses such as theft, or fraud, as well as for class 2 offences such as break and enter and public mischief (Hartford, Carey, & Mendola, 2004).

*While in custody,* individuals with intellectual disabilities have been found to be slow to adjust to the institutional expectations and as a result are cited for more violations (Santamour & West, 1977; Smith, Algozzine, & Schmid, 1990). Talbot (2008) interviewed 154 offenders with an ID and 19 offenders without an ID at 14 different prisons across England, Wales, and Scotland. Through the interviews, Talbot (2008) found that 52% of prisoners with an ID were suffering from depression, and 70% were likely suffering from anxiety. In comparison, 19% of offenders without an ID were likely suffering from depression and 25% from anxiety. Participants with an ID used mainly negative terms to describe their experiences. Themes that arose through interviews were loneliness, bullying, confusion, homesickness, and suicide or self-harm. Talbot (2008) reported that 85% of offenders with an ID stated they had trouble reading information and understanding rules, compared to 0% of the comparison group. Further, 61% of prisoners in the comparison group stated they had a job during corrections, compared to 41% of offenders with an ID (Talbot, 2008). Prisoners with ID also struggled with daily living tasks.

Smith and colleagues (1990) found that offenders with an ID were three times as likely as the comparison group to receive hygiene violations as well as non-compliance with authority violations. Prisoners with an intellectual disability were less likely to be given a job (Talbot, 2008) or were given medial and poorly paid work (Cowardin, 1997).

Furthermore, offenders with intellectual disability are rarely provided specialized services and therapeutic intervention (Conley, Luckasson, & Bouthilet, 1992; McGee & Menolascino, 1992) and are more likely bullied (Gold, 1997; Reichard, Spenser, & Spooner, 1982). Talbot (2008) found that of prisoners with an intellectual disability were suffering from depression (52%) and anxiety (70%), describing their experience while incarcerated as lonely, bullied, confused, homesick, and suicidal or self-harm. Prisoners with intellectual disability were more likely to show maladaptive behavior (MacEachron, 1979) and twice as likely to receive violations for both assaults of other inmates and of correctional officers (Smith et al., 1990). Consequently, they were more likely to be reclassified to a higher security level (Hall, 1992).

Nichols, Bench, Morlok, and Liston (2003) surveyed 41 states in the U.S. regarding current conditions for offenders with intellectual disabilities, including programming and identifying procedures. Out of the 41 states, 44% said they had a special program for offenders with intellectual disability. In twenty-three states offenders with intellectual disability were grouped with offenders with mental health issues.

Finally, persons with intellectual disabilities were found to be less likely to experience early release or parole (Lampert, 1987), are considered a poor fit or risk for probation (Denkowski & Denkowski, 1985; Haskins & Friel, 1973), and consequently more likely to serve longer sentences (Santamour & Watson, 1982).

***Upon release,*** offenders with intellectual disabilities were less likely to be placed on specialized caseloads or given assistance or rehabilitation; and consequently, they were more likely to reoffend (Santamour, 1986, 1988). Stewart and colleagues (2016) demonstrated that levels of recidivism were higher for offenders with an intellectual disability, especially for those that have multiple or more severe needs. Young, van Dooren, Claudio, Cumming, and Lennox (2016) found that those being released from custody were unable to plan their lives without support and needed professionals to accurately recognize and understand the intellectual disability, and the challenges that occur in navigating the community systems and the complicated relationships with systems. Harley (2014) looked at the challenges that occur for offenders with intellectual disability when transitioning from a correctional institution and found that the most significant challenges were related to employment, medical services, and supports. Unruh and colleagues (2009) demonstrated that when persons with a dual diagnosis (intellectual disability and mental health need) were involved in a detention to community transition program that lower recidivism rates were evident.

## Recommended Practice

Given the rather dismal outcomes presented from the research for accused persons with intellectual disabilities within the criminal justice system, a critical question arises as to whether the system has provided appropriate support to accommodate the vulnerabilities experienced when they become involved as an accused. However, accommodations can only be provided if the individual's challenges and needs have been identified.

Baldry and colleagues (2013) noted that:

> Early intervention for this group is crucial to preventing the escalation in vulnerability as individuals with complex cognitive impairment move into and through the CJS. Lack of recognition of disability and supportive early education, early contact with police, contact with the juvenile justice system, and experience of out-of-home care are some key markers of ongoing and long-term enmeshment. It is speculated that there would be clear benefits of disability recognition and support at these early points in individuals' trajectories. (p. 228)

Often, people mistakenly think of persons with intellectual disabilities as a homogeneous group with variation only based on the relative rating on an IQ test; however, the disorder is not fixed or dichotomized. It can change depending on functional limitations and the environment, including level of supports. The challenge in providing supports is that different disabilities all present different challenges that make it difficult without a proper assessment to know not only if the person has a disability but what role it may have played in commission of an offense, and how can one best provide accommodations, supports, and even appropriate sentencing. "Etiology doesn't change the toolbox, it just gets you the right tool faster" (B. Finucane, personal communication, June 6, 2016). Thus, understanding the specifics of the disability enables there to be a more timely and appropriate response.

Pope, and Tarlov (1991) suggested that while pathology underlies the etiology of an impairment that produces a brain dysfunction that is typically measured by an IQ test, it only becomes a disability when it impacts on the person's social role. Thus, the nature of a disability can be modified by age and experience, emotional strengths and needs, health status, the environment, and the nature of the supports given (Schalock, 2002). Social ecologists suggest that we should create environments that maximize the individual's ability to function and participate (Ramey, Dossett, & Echols, 1996). Thus, using a "functional/ecological approach" the disability become defined "within the context of personal and social environment, and we will shift from what people are to what they need." (Schalock, 2002, p.57)

The social ecological approach to understanding intellectual disability can be translated into the notion of support and accommodations within the criminal justice system to allow accused persons with intellectual disability to be able to function to their potential by matching the needs of the individual with available supports. The intellectual disability may not only affect the person's understanding of the process in the case of fitness to stand trial but may be valuable in explaining the commission of the offense and/or questions of criminal responsibility, and in identifying appropriate accommodations that may be offered to allow the person to testify, successfully complete a diversion program, follow probationary terms, or better adapt to life in prison or successfully reintegrate into society after release.

As illustrated in *Figure 1: Inequities in Justice without Identification,* without identification at the time of arrest the individual with an intellectual disability is likely to experience challenges during the criminal interview that may lead to self-incrimination or false confessions. Furthermore, without appropriate support and advocacy, the path to charges being laid, even where they are not appropriate, are enhanced and thus involvement in court is likely. Without identification and access of appropriate supports the legal outcome is less likely to be equitable. Following a legal outcome, if there has not been identification, the person will be sent back to the community, again without an interjurisdictional plan to transition the person to re-enter the community with a plan that could potentially reduce recidivism.

## Figure 1: Inequities in Justice Without Identification

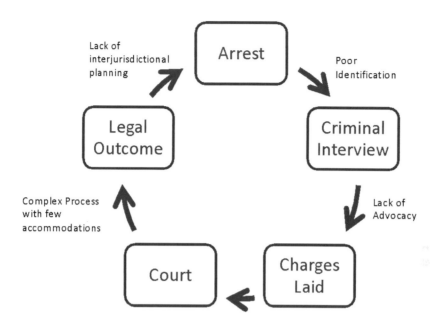

Research has also suggested that a tailored court response is effective in reducing recidivism rates and that unnecessarily restrictive responses may lead to higher incarceration rates. While comparing offenders with mental health who had been referred to a mental health court with those who had processed normally within the justice system, McNiel and Binder (2007) found that specialized mental health courts were successful in reducing future involvement in the justice system. This is congruent with research linking the appropriate allocation of services based on criminogenic risk levels to reduced recidivism rates. For instance, in a meta-analysis Gendreau, Goggin, Cullen, and Andrews (2000) concluded that providing intensive services to low-risk offenders may lead to higher incarceration rates by increasing administration of justice charges. While there is limited research addressing the impact that these services have on offenders with intellectual disabilities, it is apparent that this population may similarly benefit from identification and a tailored court response.

Many participants in Jones (2014) suggested that following the terms of a probation order may be very hard work for individuals with intellectual or developmental disabilities. In acknowledging these differences, both lawyers and mental health workers in Jones (2014) showed interest in adapting or providing accommodations for persons with IDD within the justice system. Some suggestions included teaching offenders lifestyle management tools, how to use a planner, and working with the school to identify learning strategies (Jones, 2014). Other participants noted challenges with the length of time between the offense and sentencing with respect to appreciating the consequences of one's actions, the length of the probationary period, the number of probational terms, or the language/descriptions of terms used on these legal forms (Jones, 2014).

Further, understanding the nature of the intellectual disability will ensure that the role the disability played, if any, in the commission of a crime, is appropriately evaluated. Petersilia (2000) suggested that offenders with intellectual disabilities might represent citizens who lack the education to function in a responsible way in society. Thus, identification of a person with an intellectual disability may provide valuable insights into issues of support, accommodation, and potential mitigating circumstances. For example, if examining criminal responsibility, one looks at criminal intent. An interview with a lawyer in Jones' (2014) research made the following point:

> You are describing a moderate disability affecting attention, language and memory skills. From my perspective that doesn't affect someone knowing right from wrong, and or like punching somebody. But if you said that he had a moderate intellectual disability that affected impulse control, judgement, that sometimes when he became excited the short circuit is thinking…Then I would give the disability a higher kind of focus because it would be saying, this is not all within his control, these are problems, I would be interested in checking out this theory with a probation officer who does risk-needs assessments, or talking to a defence counsel about it.
>
> It is a two-way sword if a person is compromised, if the compromise means that they are less able to make judgements of right and wrong and if they are more likely to repeat their behaviour then that becomes an aggravating circumstance opposed to a mitigating circumstance. (p. 50)

## Challenges and Risks to Identification

Although the case for identification of an intellectual disability has been strongly supported in the literature above, the identification of an intellectual disability in an accused person interacting with the criminal justice system may also pose risks and challenges.

First and foremost, the criminal justice system is designed to ensure law and order are protected; it is not designed to recognize or accommodate to the intellectual disability or potential comorbid mental health challenges (Baldry et al., 2013). Although the structure of the system has been adjusted to make space for persons with IDD, the system is, by its structure, able-bodied (Law Commission of Ontario, 2012).

Historically, people with intellectual disability have been linked to criminality. The Eugenics movement in the last century proposed that there were direct correlations between mental health challenges, intellectual disability, criminality, and a lack of morality (Scheerenburger, 1984). Baldry et al. (2013) suggested that some vestiges of the misguided views from the Eugenics movement may still prevail where some criminal justice professionals may believe that a person with an intellectual disability may have a greater propensity for criminal behavior.

As noted above, some individuals with an intellectual disability will don what is called a "cloak of competence" so that their disability is made less visible (Edgerton, 1967). The individual may attempt to hide their disability for fear of discrimination, stigmatization, or discriminatory treatment that has often accompanied the label.

This was demonstrated in Jones (2014), where one mental health worker who was interviewed reported the following comment:

> I am sure some of them are missed, you maybe have, say for example a 17 year old who may have a mild disability but he may also have… what we call like splinter skills, so, for example, you may get kids that can't read very well but they are always carrying around books and you kind of assume they are ok but he does have an issue with reading… Or he has really great verbal skills he could have a conversation with you about anything but, but he can't read so he has a you know great character, he shows appropriate emotions or those kind of things but he can't read or write, so umm I would assume some of those kids get missed. (p. 56)

The fear of stigmatization can in some cases be very real. McAfee, Cockram, and Wolfe (2001) found that police often held specific biases about persons with intellectual disabilities. When asked to provide a response to crime reports, they found that police officers reported that alleged offenders with an intellectual disability were labelled as less believable and identified their crimes to be more severe than scenarios involving nondisabled persons. Moreover, they reported that the actions they would take would be more severe. McAfee et al. (2001) suggested this bias may account for some of the inflated prevalence rates for this population in the criminal justice system.

Jones (2014) reported that some justice professionals held misconceptions about what an intellectual disability entailed, the associated risk/need factors, and the potential for rehabilitation. When risk-needs assessments are conducted on individuals with an intellectual disability, because the justice system is often geared to responsive and treatable solutions such as medication, a person with an intellectual disability, for whom no such solution would be possible might be viewed as 'risky' and as such be subject to greater sanctions. As noted above, offenders with intellectual disabilities were often seen as poor candidates for early probation, suggesting that this bias was the result of negative attitudes of the justice professionals towards the person with a disability (Haskins & Friel, 1973).

Additionally, if identified, a person with an intellectual disability, whose competence or fitness is in question, may be placed in a psychiatric facility pending evaluation or intervention (i.e. treatment or training for competence). The result is that the individual is often detained prior to any court proceeding for a prolonged period of time within the psychiatric facility, in some cases for a period of time that exceeds what they may have received had they been tried and sentenced for the offence(s). The assumption on which this diversion to the psychiatric facility is based rests on making a change that will allow the person to participate fully in the court process. However, the premise was founded on the idea that treatment would change the state that was rendering the person incompetent or unfit, as would be the assumption for some mental illnesses. For persons with intellectual disability, their cognitive challenges will remain regardless of length of hospitalization. There is no medication, as there might be with mental illness, that would change the functioning state of a person with an intellectual disability. As well, if the hope was based on training outcomes, Wall and Christopher (2012) cautioned training for fitness does not always result in the individual being able to meet the criteria to stand trial, and if they do it is likely in a lesser capacity.

An additional influence related to stigma has been found in how Crown or prosecuting attorneys might reflect on the perceived outcomes of prosecuting or diverting a case. In one case in which one of the coauthors was involved, the accused was allowed to stand trial for a sexual assault charge. The case was clearly one in which the person had touched a child inappropriately, but without sexual motivation; the act was an inappropriate method of communication that involved pointing to and touching things to which he was referring. The term 'counterfeit deviance' has been coined to describe this type of naïve offense in some people with intellectual disability (Griffiths, Hingsburger, Hoath, & Ioannou, 2013; Hingsburger, Griffiths, & Quinsey, 1991). Having become aware of this, it was likely the charge would have been withdrawn, however the Crown did not wish to appear to the community to be soft on sexual crimes. Although the Crown prosecutor reduced the charge from sexual assault to common assault, the individual remained involved in the criminal justice system for many years. Underlying some of the sentencing decisions are biases, such as whether the individual will be able to learn from the situation sufficient to ensure there is less likelihood of a reoffending. For persons with intellectual disabilities, this bias is a real concern and may result in individuals being placed in situations where supervision or confinement are recommended for extended periods of time for fear of a reoffense.

Bias against persons with intellectual disability can also have the opposite result, where the person is not sentenced to jail time because there is an assumption that the individual is not a serious threat or that the jail experience will not benefit them and may do them greater harm. McBrien and Murphy (2006) have suggested that there is often an assumption that persons with intellectual disabilities are already being cared for within social service systems, that they need to be provided understanding more than punitive approaches, and, as such, should not be charged or prosecuted. Although this assumption is based on compassionate grounds, it also leads to some intentional offenders learning that committing crimes has no punitive consequences (Griffiths, Hingsburger, Hoath, & Ioannou, 2013).

## Identifying Disabilities in the Criminal Justice System

In interviews with justice professionals Marinos et al., (2017) found that people who are accused with an intellectual disability are either not identified or insufficiently identified. As one judge noted "...you have to figure it out for yourself" (p. 89). Concern was expressed that because of a lack of identification some individuals may not be identified, and this lack of identification could affect their participation in the justice system. These professionals also reported that there was often reliance on physical features or behaviors as indicators of disability. Moreover, they relied on someone else identifying the disability and relaying this information to them; however, there was no clear jurisdiction as to who would make that identification or discriminate between intellectual disability and psychiatric illness. Additionally, it was reported that there is a lack of designated processes for screening; and there is no legal precedent for diagnosing an intellectual disability (Marinos et al., 2017).

Jones (2014) reported that justice professionals suggested that self-identification is preferential because it is quick and easy. There does not appear to be a systematic or consistent method of identification. Concern was expressed that because of a lack of identification some individuals may not be identified, and a lack of identification could affect their full and fair participation in the justice system. Jones (2014) similarly was told by a lawyer in in her research that there was no legal obligation either way to identify whether an individual had an intellectual disability.

One participant noted in Jones's (2014) research that unless there was involvement of parents or a social service professional, they were unable to get the whole picture. Without this additional support, counsel is often left to their own creative devices, such as investigating previous learning accommodations in school or involvement in community social services. Marinos et al. (2017) found some lawyers reported that they felt confident on their own and the system's ability to identify persons with disabilities (Marinos et al., 2017). However, since most defense lawyers are not trained in this area, they reported that they relied on intuition and informal screening procedures and application of their limited understanding of the disability to aid in identification (Jones, 2014). Furthermore, forensic psychiatrists and psychologists who are the majority called to inform the court of mental health diagnoses are not uniformly aware of the criteria for confirming intellectual disability (Jones, 2004). A mental health worker in the Jones (2014) study suggested that since there is no access to a screening tool, probing questions can be used to identify a potential disability such as specific questions for uncovering a previous diagnosis including "do you struggle in school, how big is your classroom, how many kids are in your class, are there more teachers in the class or is there just one teacher in your class?" (p. 57-58)

## Overcoming the Roadblocks to Identification within the Criminal Justice System

There appear to be three major roadblocks to identification of intellectual disability within the criminal justice system. First is a lack of training within the criminal justice system at all levels, from police, lawyers, judges, and within the jails and parole system. Second, even with awareness training, there is no way that the criminal justice system can take on the responsibility for identifying the needs of the vastly heterogeneous group of persons who have intellectual disabilities or for providing the supports necessary for the system to be able to respond to the needs of the person. To enable this to occur, a connection with the community support systems is vital. Third, to enable this connection to be made, an easy method of screening needs to be instituted in protocol and policy established for there to be ease of communication between the criminal justice system and the developmental services sector that exist for persons with intellectual disabilities.

In *Table 2: Interjurisdictional Connections and the Benefits of Screening and Identification*, the authors have illustrated how the process of screening and identification has a facilitating role throughout the stages from arrest, trial, sentencing, and jail (where appropriate), and through re-entry. Moreover, it visually illustrates how screening and identification processes can create valuable links to community agencies which can facilitate resources to aid the criminal justice system at various stages to support appropriate justice for the individual and reduce the potential of recidivism.

## Table 2: Interjurisdictional Connections and the Benefits of Screening and Identification

| Timeframe within the Criminal Justice System | Benefits of Identification | Involvement of Community Supports (CS) |
|---|---|---|
| At arrest | If police have been provided training and protocols developed with the community support person may be available during interviews Protection against cloak of competence providing misleading impression of ability | Protection of rights during interviews Possible diversion which might result in community placement with services |
| Pre-trial | Differential diagnosis of possible conditions that prevent unwarranted care in psychiatric facility pretrial | Preparation for court both in regard to the person and for the lawyers involved Fitness training where needed Accessing legal services |
| During trial | Access to required accommodations and conditions conducive to participation of accused | Support during the trial |
| When sentencing | Opens options for appropriate sentencing consistent with the person's disability and crime | Liaison for possible diversion |
| While in jail or if acquitted | Access to services that are appropriate to the nature of the disability | Relationship building with community partners for after jail or upon acquittal services |
| Probation and re-entry | Early planning for re-entry into the community consistent with the overall biopsychosocial needs of the individual to promote long term resilience | Planning for residence, job, and possible therapeutic services where indicated (i.e. AA, counselling) to create a full life that will reduce opportunity and need for reoffence Assistance in ensuring that probation requirements are met (i.e., attending meetings etc.) |

In summary of Table 2 the following connections and benefits to screening and identification emerge:

If police, at the time of arrest, have been provided training and there is an identified protocol for screening and liaison with the community services for persons with an intellectual disability, the police are then able to engage with the community to understand the disability, which may lead to a diversion or may ensure their interview is in a manner that is conducive to justice. If the interview results in an individual being charged, then identification can result in an appropriate community liaison person to prepare the person for court and also provide invaluable information for the lawyers and the court with regard to the disability and potential areas of accommodation. This information may be helpful in the judge's verdict or sentencing. Additionally, the involvement of the community services could provide ongoing support to the individual through the process. Lastly, if the person is sentenced to jail, the identification allows for the opportunity for the guards to be made aware of the individual's challenges. If acquittal or after sentencing, on probation, the identification can result in the community support being available to develop an appropriate support plan for the individual that can provide the types of supports necessary to create a new life that can potentially reduce recidivism or administration of justice charges.

## Summary

In summary, there are obvious benefits to ensuring there is a formal identification process within the criminal justice system; however, identifying an intellectual disability without appropriate training of criminal justice system personal and creating appropriate links to the community developmental services to support the criminal justice professionals could potentially be harmful and lead to tricter sentencing. It is important that professionals working within the justice system have a more in-depth understanding of intellectual disability to ensure that equitable justice is carried out. However, the schedules and pressures within the justice system cannot accommodate this level of expertise, and collaboration with professionals in the community to provide the needed information and supports is a vital resource for the criminal justice system. The key to ensuring this collaboration occurs is, however, based in early screening and identification and a protocol with the community services to activate supports at the first stage of police involvement through transition from the criminal justice system to the community at whatever stage that may be.

## References

Aiken, L. R. (1994). *Psychological testing and assessment* (8$^{th}$ ed.). Needham Heights, Mass: Allyn & Bacon.

Ali, A., Ghosh, S., Strydom, A., & Hassiotis, A. (2016). Prisoners with intellectual disabilities and detention status: Findings from a UK cross sectional study of prisons. *Research in Developmental Disabilities*, 53, 189 - 197. https://doi.org/10.1016/j.ridd.2016.02.004

American Psychiatric Association (APA). (2013). *Diagnostic and statistical manual of mental disorders: DSM-5*. Washington, DC: Author.

American Association for Intellectual and Developmental Disabilities (AAIDD) (2017). What is intellectual disability? Retrieved from http://aaidd.org/intellectual-disability/definition/faqs-on-intellectual-disability#.WVpT2bpFyUl

ARC. (2017, December 12). *Intellectual Disability*. Retrieved from http://www.thearc.org/learn-about/intellectual-disability.

Baldry, E., Clarence, M., Dowse, L., & Trollor, J. N. (2013). Reducing vulnerability to harm in adults with cognitive disabilities in the Australian criminal justice system. *Journal of Policy and Practice in Intellectual Disabilities*, 10(3), 222-229.

Bonnie, R. J. (1992). The competency of defendants with mental retardation to assist in their own defense. In R. W. Conley, R. Luckasson, & G. N. Bouthilet (Eds.), *The criminal justice system and mental retardation* (pp. 97-120), Baltimore MD: Paul H, Brookes.

Canadian Criminal Code (R.S.C., 1985, c. C-46.

Carulla, L. S., Reed, G. M., Vaez-Axisi, L. M., Cooper, S., Martinez Leal, R., Bertelli, M., Adnams, C., ... Saxena, S. (2011). Intellectual developmental disorders: Towards a new name, definition and framework for "mental retardation/intellectual disability" in ICD 11. *World Psychiatry*, 10(3), 175-180.

Cockram, J. (2005). Justice or differential treatment? Sentencing of offenders with an intellectual disability. *Journal of Intellectual and Developmental Disability*, 30(1), 3–13.

Cockram, J. (2000). *Adult offenders with an intellectual disability in the criminal justice system* (Unpublished doctoral dissertation). Edith Cowan University, Joondalup, Australia.

Cockram, J., Jackson, R., & Underwood, R. (1992). Perceptions of the judiciary and intellectual disability. *Australia and New Zealand Journal of Developmental Disability, 18*, 189-200.

Cockram, J., Jackson, R., & Underwood, R. (1998). People with an intellectual disability and the criminal justice system: The family perspective. *Journal of Intellectual & Developmental Disability, 23*(1), 41-56.

Conley, R. W., Luckasson, R., &. Bouthilet, G. N. (1992). *The criminal justice system and mental retardation: Defendants and victims.* Baltimore, MD: Brookes Publishing Company.

Cowardin, N. (1997). Advocating for learning disability accommodations in prisons. *Wisconsin Defender, 5*, 1-14.

Crocker, A.J., Cote, G., Toupin, J., & St.-Onge, B. (2007). Rate and characteristics of men with an intellectual disability in pre-trial detention. *Journal of Intellectual & Developmental Disability, 32*(2), 143 – 152.

Denkowski, G., & Denkowski, K. (1985). The mentally retarded offender in the state prison system: Identification, prevalence, adjustment and rehabilitation. *Criminal Justice and Behavior, 12*, 55-70.

Day, K. (1994). Male mentally handicapped sex offenders. *The British Journal of Psychiatry, 165*(5), 630-639.

Eadens, D. M., Cranston-Gingras, A., Dupoux, E., & Eadens, D. W. (2016). Police officer perspectives on intellectual disability. *Policing: An International Journal, 39*(1), 222–235.

Edgerton, R. B. (1967). The cloak of competence: Years later. *American Journal of Mental Deficiency, 80*, 485-497.

Edwards, W. & Reynolds, L. (1997). Defending and advocating on behalf of individuals with mild mental retardation in the criminal justice system. *IMPACT, 10*(2). Minneapolis, MI: University of Minnesota College of Education and Human Development.

Einfeld, S. L., Piccinin, A. M., Mackinnon, A., Hofer, S. M., Taffe, J., Gray, K. M., . . . Tonge, B. J. (2006). Psychopathology in young people with intellectual disability. *Journal of the American Medical Association, 296*, 1981–1989.

Ellis, J. W. & Luckasson, R. A. (1985). Mentally retarded criminal offenders. *George Washington Law Review, 53*, 414-493.

Ericson, K. I., & Perlman, N. B. (2001). Knowledge of legal terminology and court proceedings in adults with developmental disabilities. *Law and Human Behavior, 25*(5), 529-545.

Everington, C., & Fulero, S. M. (1999). Competence to confess: Measuring understanding and suggestibility of defendants with mental retardation. *Mental Retardation, 37*(3), 212–220.

Fedoroff, J. P., Griffiths, D., Marini, Z, & Richards, D. (2000). One of our clients has been arrested for sexual assault: Now what? The interplay between developmental and legal delay. In A. Poindexter (Ed.), *Bridging the Gap - Proceedings 17th Annual NADD Conference. Kingston,* (pp. 153-160). NY: NADD.

Fraser, M. (2017). Individuals with intellectual disabilities and their experiences within the criminal justice system (Unpublished Honours Thesis). Brock University: St. Catharines, Canada.

Gendreau, P., Goggin, C., Cullen, F. T., & Andrews D. A. (2000). The effects of community sanctions and incarceration on recidivism. *Forum on Corrections Research, 12*(3), 10-13.

Gold, S. (1997). Amicus Curiae Brief, Pennsylvania Department of Corrections vs. Yeskey, US Supreme Court, No 97-634, October.

Greenspan, S. (2006). Functional concepts in mental retardation: Finding the natural essence of an artificial category. *Exceptionality, 14*(4), 205–224.

Griffiths, D., & Fedoroff, P. (2008) Persons with intellectual disabilities who sexually offend. In F. M. Saleh, A. J. Grudzinskas, J. M., Bradford, & D. J. Brodsky (Eds.), *Sex offenders: Identification, risk, assessment, treatment, and legal issues (pp. 352-374)*. New York: Oxford University Press.

Griffiths, D., Hingsburger, D., Hoath, J., & Ioannou, S. (2013). 'Counterfeit deviance' revisited. *Journal of Applied Research in Intellectual Disabilities, 26*, 471-480.

Griffiths, D., Hingsburger, D., Ioannou, S., & Hoath, J. (2018). Ethical considerations in working with people with intellectual disabilities who have offended. In B. Lindsay & J.L. Taylor (Eds.). *The Wiley handbook on offenders with intellectual and developmental disabilities: research, training and practice* (pp. 105-122). Chichester, UK: Wiley.

Griffiths, D., & Marinos, V. (2005). *People with intellectual disabilities and the courtroom: A guide for judges* (National Judicial Institute). Brock University, St. Catharines, Canada.

Griffiths, D., Watson, S., Lewis, R., & Stoner, K. (2004). Sexuality research and persons with intellectual disabilities. In E. Emerson, C. Hatton, T. Thompson & T. R. Parmenter (Eds.), *International handbook of applied research in intellectual disabilities* (pp. 311-334). London, UK: John Wiley & Sons.

Gudjonsson, G. H. (1990). The relationship of intellectual skills to suggestibility, compliance, and acquiescence. *Personality and Individual Differences, 11*, 227-231.

Hall, J. N. (1992). Correctional services for inmates with mental retardation: Challenge or catastrophe? In R. W. Conley, R. Luckasson, & G. N. Bouthilet (Eds.), *The criminal justice system and mental retardation* (pp. 67-190). Baltimore MD: Paul H, Brookes.

Harley, D. A. (2014). Adult ex-offender population and employment: A synthesis of the literature on recommendations and best practices. *Journal of Applied Rehabilitation Counseling, 45*(3), 10 - 21.

Hartford, K., Carey, R., & Mendonca, J. (2004). Pre arrest diversion of people with mental illness: Literature review and international survey. *Behavioral Sciences & the Law, 24*(6), 845-856.

Haskins, J. R. & Friel, C. (1973). A national survey of the diagnosis and treatment of mentally retarded offenders in an adult correctional institution project CAMIO, Volume 8. Retrieved from https://files.eric.ed.gov/fulltext/ED089494.pdf

Hayes, S. (2007). Missing out: Offenders with learning disabilities and the criminal justice system. *British Journal of Learning Disabilities*, (3), 146-153.

Hingsburger, D. (2013). Counterfeit criminality: Cautions in community living. *The Direct Support Worker Newsletter, 1*(6), 1-5. Retrieved from http://www.thefamilyhelpnetwork.ca/wp-content/uploads/2013/03/counterfiet-criminality.pdf

Hingsburger, D., Griffiths, D., & Quinsey, V. (1991). Detecting counterfeit deviance: Differentiating sexual deviance from sexual inappropriateness. *The Habilitative Mental Healthcare Newsletter, 10*, 51-54.

Holland, A. J. (1991). Challenging and offending behaviour by adults with developmental disorders. *Australia and New Zealand Journal of Developmental Disabilities, 17*(2), 119-126.

Hyun, E., Hahn, L., & McConnell, D. (2014). Experiences of people with learning disabilities in the criminal justice system. *British Journal of Learning Disabilities,* (4), 308-314.

Jones, A. (2014). *Bridging the conceptualization of youth with intellectual disabilities to sentencing under the YCJA* (Unpublished Master's thesis). Brock University, St. Catharines, Canada.

Jones, J. (2007). Persons with intellectual disabilities in the criminal justice system. *International Journal of Offender Therapy and Comparative Criminology, 51*(6), 723-733.

Lampert, R.O. (1987). The mentally retarded offender in prison. *Justice Professional, 2*, 60-69.

Laski, F.J. (1992). Sentencing the offender with mental retardation: Honoring the imperative for immediate punishments and probation. In R. W. Conley, R. Luckasson, & G. N. Bouthilet (Eds.), *The criminal justice system and mental retardation* (pp. 137-1520). Baltimore, MD: Paul H. Brookes.

Law Commission of Ontario (2012). *A framework for the law as it affects persons with disabilities: Advancing substantive equality for persons with disabilities through law, policy and practice.* Toronto: Author.

Leo, R. & Ofshe, R. (1998). The consequences of false confession: Deprivations of liberty and miscarriages of justice in the age of psychological interrogation. *The Journal of Criminal Law and Criminology, 88*, 1-68.

Lindsay, W. R. (2009). *The treatment of sex offenders with developmental disabilities: A practice workbook.* Chichester, UK: Wiley-Blackwell.

Lindsay, W., Carson, D., O'Brien, G., Holland, A. J., Johnston, S., Taylor, J. L., ... Price, K. (2010). The relationship between assessed risk and service security level for offenders with intellectual disability. *The Journal of Forensic Psychiatry and Psychology, 21*(4), 537-545.

Loucks, N. (2007). *No one knows: Offenders with learning difficulties and learning disabilities: Review of prevalence and associated needs.* London, UK: Prison Reform Trust.

MacEachron, A. E. (1979). Mentally retarded offenders: Prevalence and characteristics. *American Journal of Mental Deficiency, 84*, 165-176.

Mallett, C. A. (2009). Disparate juvenile court outcomes for disabled delinquent youth: A social work call to action. *Child and Adolescent Social Work Journal, 26*(3), 197-207.

Marinos, V., Griffiths, D., Fergus, C., Stromski, S., & Rondeau, K. (2014). Victims and witnesses with intellectual disability in the criminal justice system. *Criminal Justice Quarterly.* 517-30.

Marinos, V., Griffiths, D., Robinson, J., Gosse, L., Fergus, C., Stromski, S., & Rondeau, K. (2017). Persons with intellectual disabilities and the criminal justice system: A view from criminal justice professionals in Ontario, Canada. *Criminal Justice Quarterly, 64*(1&2), 83-107.

McAfee, J. K., Cockram, J. & Wolfe, P. S. (2001) Police reactions to crimes involving people with mental retardation: A cross-cultural experimental study. *Education and Training in Mental Retardation and Developmental Disabilities*, 36 (2), 160-171.

McAfee, J., & Gural, M. (1988). Individuals with mental retardation and the criminal justice system: The view from the state attorney's general. *Mental Retardation, 6*, 5-12.

McBrien, J., & Murphy, G. (2006). Police and carers' views on reporting alleged offences by people with intellectual disabilities. *Psychology, Crime & Law, 12*(2), 127-144.

McGee, J. & Menolascino, F. J. (1992). The evaluation of defendants with mental retardation in the criminal justice system. In R. W. Conley, R. Luckasson, & G. N. Bouthilet (Eds.), *The criminal justice system and mental retardation* (pp. 55-77). Baltimore, MD: Paul H. Brookes.

McNiel, D. E., & Binder., R. L. (2007). Effectiveness of a mental health court in reducing criminal recidivism and violence. *The American Journal of Psychiatry,164* (9), 1395-1403.

Murphy, W. D., Coleman, E. M., & Haynes, M. R. (1983). Treatment and evaluation issues with the mentally retarded sex offender. In J. G. Greer & I. R. Stuart (Eds.), *The sexual aggressor: Current prospective on treatment* (pp. 22–41). Van Nostrand: Reinholt Company.

Murphy, G. H., Harnett, H., & Holland, A. J. (1995). A survey of intellectual disabilities amongst men on remand in prison. *Mental Handicap Research, 8*(2), 81–98.

Nezu, C. M., Nezu, A. M., & Gill-Weiss, M. (1992). *Psychopathology in persons with mental retardation: Clinical guidelines for assessment and treatment.* Champaign, Il: Research Press.

Nichols, M., Bench, L. L., Morlok, E., & Liston, K. (2003). Analysis of mentally retarded and lower-functioning offender correctional programs. *Corrections Today,* (2), 119.

O'Connell, M. J., Garmoe, W., & Goldstein, N. E. S. (2005). Miranda comprehension in adults with mental retardation and the effects of feedback style on suggestibility. *Law and Human Behavior, 29*(3), 359-369.

Pennsylvania Department of Corrections v. Yeskey, 524 U.S. 206, 118 S. Ct. 1952, 141 L. Ed. 2d 215 (1998).

Perske, R. (2004). Understanding persons with intellectual disabilities in the criminal justice system: Indicators of progress? *Mental Retardation, 42*(6), 484–487.

Pertersila, J. (2000). *Doing justice? The criminal justice system and offenders with developmental disabilities.* Irvine, CA: Mental Retardation/Developmental Disabilities Research Center UCLA Medical Center University of California.

Pope, A.M. & Tarlov, A.R. (Eds.). (1991). *Disability in America: Toward a national agenda for prevention.* Washington D.C.: National Academy Press.

R. v. Demers [2004], S.C.R.2 489, 2004 S.C.C. 46 (2004).

Ramey, S. L., Dossett, E., & Echols, K. (1996). *The social ecology of mental retardation.* In J. W. Jacobson, & J. A. Mulick (Eds.), *Model of diagnosis and professional practice in mental retardation* (pp. 55-65). Washington D.C.: American Psychological Association.

Reichard, C. L., Spenser, J., & Spooner, F. (1982). The mentally retarded defendant-offender. In M. Santamour & P. Watson (Eds.), *The retarded offender,* (pp. 121-139). New York: Praeger.

Reynolds, T, Zupanick, C. E., & Dombeck, M. (2013a). *Diagnostic criteria for intellectual disabilities: DSM-5 Criteria.* Retrieved from https://www.mentalhelp.net/articles/diagnostic-criteria-for-intellectual-disabilities-dsm-5-criteria/

Reynolds, T, Zupanick, C. E., & Dombeck, M. (2013b). *The American Association on Intellectual and Developmental Disabilities (AAIDD) diagnostic criteria for intellectual disability.* Retrieved from https://www.mentalhelp.net/articles/diagnostic-criteria-for-intellectual-disabilities-dsm-5-criteria/

Reynolds, T, Zupanick, C. E., & Dombeck, M. (2013c). *Comparing the APA and the AAIDD diagnostic criteria for intellectual disabilities.* Retrieved from https://www.mentalhelp.net/articles/diagnostic-criteria-for-intellectual-disabilities-dsm-5-criteria/

Reynolds, T, Zupanick, C. E., & Dombeck, M. (2013d). *Intellectual disability and severity codes.* Retrieved from https://www.mentalhelp.net/articles/diagnostic-criteria-for-intellectual-disabilities-dsm-5-criteria/

Santamour, M. (1986). The offender with mental retardation. *The Prison Journal, 66,* 3-18.

Santamour, M. (1988). *The mentally retarded offender and corrections.* Laurel, MD: American Correctional Association.

Santamour, M. & Watson, P. (Eds.) (1982). *The retarded offender.* New York, NY: Prager.

Santamour, M. & West, B. (1977). *The mentally retarded offender and corrections.* Washington, DC: Law Enforcement Assistance Administration, Department of Corrections.

Schalock, R. L. (2002). Definitional issues. In. R. L. Schalock, P.C. Baker, & D. Croser (Eds.), *Embarking on a new century: Mental retardation at the end of the 20$^{th}$ century* (pp. 45-66). Washington, D.C.: American Association of Mental Retardation.

Scheerenburger, R. C. (1984). *The history of mental retardation.* Baltimore, MD: Paul H. Brookes.

Schilit, J. (1989). The mentally retarded offender and criminal justice personnel. *Exceptional Children, 56,* 16-22.

Simpson, M. K., & Hogg, J. (2001). Patterns of offending among people with intellectual disability: A systematic review. Part I: Methodology and prevalence data. *Journal of Intellectual Disability Research, 45*(5), 384–396.

Smith, C., Algozzine, R., & Schmid, R. E. (1990). Prison adjustment of youthful inmates with mental retardation. *Mental Retardation, 28*(3), 177–181.

Smith, S. A. & Broughton, S. F. (1994). Competency to stand trial and criminal responsibility: An analysis in South Carolina. *Mental Retardation, 28,* 177-181.

Statistics Canada. (2011). *Trends in the use of remand in Canada.* Retrieved from http://www.statcan.gc.ca/pub/85-002-x/2011001/article/11440-eng.htm

Statistics Canada (2015a). *Adult criminal court statistics in Canada, 2013/2014.* Retrieved from http://www.statcan.gc.ca/pub/85-002-x/2015001/article/14226-eng.htm

Statistics Canada. (2015b). Trends in offences against the administration of justice. Retrieved from http://www.statcan.gc.ca/pub/85-002-x/2015001/article/14233eng.htm

Statistics Canada. (2016). *The Youth Criminal Justice Act summary and background.* Retrieved from http://www.justice.gc.ca/eng/cj-jp/yj-jj/tools-outils/back-hist.html.

Steadman, H. J., Redlich, A., Callahan, L., Robbins, P. C., & Vesselinov, R. (2011). Effect of mental health courts on arrests and jail days: A multisite study. *Archives of General Psychiatry, 68*(2), 167–172.

Steiner, J. (1984) Group counselling with retarded offenders. *Social Work*, 29, 181–182.

Stewart, L. A., Wilton, G., & Sapers, J. (2016). Offenders with cognitive deficits in a Canadian prison population: Prevalence, profile, and outcomes. *International Journal of Law and Psychiatry*, 7-14.

Talbot, J. (2008). *No One Knows*. Retrieved from: http://www.prisonreformtrust.org.uk/Portals/0/Documents/No%20One%20Knows%20report-2.pdf

Toberg, M. A. (1992). *Pretrial release: A national evaluation of practice and outcomes*. McLean, VA: Lazar Institute.

Unruh, D. K., Gau, J. M., & Waintrup, M. G. (2009). An exploration of factors reducing recidivism rates of formerly incarcerated youth with disabilities participating in a re-entry intervention. *Journal of Child & Family Studies*, 18(3), 284–293.

Valenti-Hein, D., & and Schwartz, L. D. (1993). Witness competency in people with mental retardation: Implications for prosecution of sexual abuse. *Sexuality and Disability*, 11 (4), 287–294.

Wall, B. W. & Christopher, P. P. (2012). A training program for defendants with intellectual disabilities who are found incompetent to stand trial. *Journal of the American Academy of Psychiatry and the Law*, 40 (3) 366-373.

White, A. J., Batchelor, J., Meares, S., Pulman, S., & Howard, D. (2016). Fitness to stand trial in one Australian jurisdiction: The role of cognitive abilities, neurological dysfunction and psychiatric disorders. *Psychiatry, Psychology & Law*, 23(4), 499–511.

White, A.J., Batchelor, J., Pulman, & Howard, D. (2015). Fitness to stand trial: Views of criminal lawyers and forensic mental health experts regarding the role of neuropsychological assessment. *Psychiatry, Psychology and Law*, 22(6), 880-889.

White, B. L. & Wood, H. (1988). The Lancaster county mentally retarded offenders program. In J. A. Stark, F. J. Menolascino, M. H. Albarelli, & C. C. Gray (Eds.), *Mental retardation and mental health: Classification, diagnosis, treatment, services* (pp. 434-444. New York: Springer-Verlag.

Young, J., van Dooren, K., Claudio, F., Cumming, C., & Lennox, N. (2016). *Transition from prison for people with intellectual disability: A qualitative study of service professionals*. Retrieved from https://aic.gov.au/publications/tandi/tandi52

# Part II:

# Persons with IDD in the Justice System

*Chapter 3*

# Accommodations and Supports to Participate in the Criminal Courts: The Case of Ontario

*Voula Marinos, Mihael Cole & Samantha Stromski*

**Introduction:**

*The cognitively challenged are before our courts in unknown numbers. We prosecute them again and again and again. We sentence them again and again and again. We imprison them again and again and again. They commit crimes again and again and again. We wonder why they do not change. The wonder of it all is that we do not change (R. v Harris, 2002; as cited in Goldberg, 2011, p. 65).*

Justice Trueman stated the above-mentioned quote in 2002 to highlight the challenges courts face when a person with an intellectual disability is involved in the justice system and not much has changed. Persons with intellectual and developmental disabilities (IDD) continue to enter and re-enter the system because the underlying reasons for their offending behaviors have not improved. Justice Trueman's remarks also shift our attention towards the responsibility of the justice system and its responses.

This chapter addresses the ways in which the courts respond to persons with IDD to ensure their participation. We describe some of the structural changes in the criminal justice system in Canada and the United States, including changes to the law and policies to accommodate the needs of persons with IDD. We are witnessing a shift away from 'fixing' the individual with a disability to be able to participate, towards a focus on modifying the policies within the justice system to benefit individuals with varying ability levels to participate in more meaningful ways. We argue that while some important developments have taken place, their access to justice and participation need to be maximized in humane ways.

This chapter begins by outlining a multidisciplinary and multidimensional perspective – one that is person-centered, focused on human rights, and integrates elements of the biopsychosocial model that can be used as a lens through which to understand developments in the participation of persons with IDD in the criminal justice system. We focus on the province of Ontario as a case study to understand how and why changes have been made and future directions that need to take place. In writing this chapter, we acknowledge that the more we do within systems to identify persons with IDD, the more we reinforce the regulation of people with disability. We risk reinforcing biomedical assumptions about disability, to the extent that people with disability are involved in the justice system. We call for continued efforts towards an inclusive and participatory model of persons with intellectual disabilities in the criminal justice system.

## Challenges for Persons with Intellectual Disability and the Criminal Courts

*Lawrence has fetal alcohol syndrome (FAS), characterized by poor judgment (rendering him easily victimizable), difficulty with abstraction (which means he does not understand consequences), and disorientation in time and space (which means he has difficulty perceiving social cues). Peers convince him that one of the girls at school has a crush on him and that he should steal some candy for her as a gift. He steals the candy without appreciation of the consequences, the fact that the girl did not in fact have a crush on him, or the fact that his peers were just setting him up.[1]*

As you can see from this example, the underlying reasons why persons with IDD engage in a crime can be similar to the challenges they face during participation in the justice system. There are a number of different ways in which they may not be able to participate meaningfully within the courts as accused, victims, or witnesses. They may not fully comprehend questions or the implications of their statements; they may seek approval of authority figures by giving what they believe are correct answers. In addition, persons with IDD may not always appear "disabled" in their outward appearance, and they may not be easily identified as having significant impairments by criminal justice professionals. They may not want to be identified as a person with a disability because of the desire to fit in to mainstream society and avoid the stigma of being impaired. Finally, they may lack understanding why identification might be important (to access diversion, supports and accommodations) (Marinos, Griffiths, Fergus, Stromski & Rondeau, 2014).

## Conceptualizations of Persons with Intellectual Disability

There are varying conceptualizations of individuals with intellectual disabilities and their role within society that tend to view them as either passive or active members within the community. Both biomedical and social models produce varying conceptualizations of persons with intellectual disability. The biomedical model reinforces a biological understanding of disability whereby IDD is the result of physical or mental inadequacy that has placed individuals at a disadvantage position within society (Kirby 2004). This has led to persons with IDD experiencing difficulties in accessing their human rights in many areas of their lives including medical, educational, sexual, and legal spheres (Griffiths, Owen & Watson, 2012). Historically, the human rights that everyone is entitled to have been ignored for people with IDD due to their mental or physical 'inadequacies,' making them more vulnerable to experiencing inequality

---

[1]From *People with Intellectual Disabilities and the Courtroom: A Guide for Judges* (p.16), by D. Griffiths and V. Marinos, 2005, Ottawa, ON: National Judicial Institute. Reprinted with permission.

within their everyday lives (Owen & Griffiths, Tarulli, & Murphy, 2009). Furthermore, the traditional biomedical model of disability does not take into account the environment in which individuals with IDD live and the role that the broader social world can have in supporting them through the development of services that can aid them in accessing their rights as citizens.

Many Westernized societies such as Canada and the United States have created dichotomies whereby groups and individuals are classified as either abled/disabled or normal/abnormal (Kirby, 2004). In practice, individuals and groups are more complex than these binaries suggest. The result of these binaries has been the stigmatization and exclusion of individuals who do not meet the 'normalized standards' constructed by the social world. In order for individuals with IDD to exercise their right to be active participants within the various service delivery systems such as the criminal justice system, persons with disabilities should be seen as agents in their own lives as opposed to passive and dependent individuals (Stromski, 2015).

'Disability' is a powerful discourse that frames individuals as abnormal, passive, inadequate, irrelevant, and needy. Consistent with the biological model where individuals with IDD are identified according to their deficits and 'inadequacies,' these individuals are also marginalized due to social spaces and service delivery systems remaining inaccessible (Tisdall, 2012). This is achieved by individuals being reduced to their disability as a defining characteristic, rather than individuals with agency, in addition to various strengths as well as weaknesses. Accordingly, the biomedical discourse encourages responses to IDD that seek to 'repair' or 'fix' the characteristics of individuals on an individual level often through medical treatment.

Compared to the biomedical model, the social model examines the role of the social world, including social institutions and language, in shaping the discourse about IDD (Kirby, 2004). The social model of disability focuses on the role of the environment, such as social service delivery systems, in supporting individuals with intellectual disability (Owen et al., 2009). The social model is focused on the ways society and its delivery systems can be improved and structured in order to support individuals with IDD in accessing their human rights in a fair way. This model also puts more onus on society to provide services and support to ensure persons with IDD are able to exercise autonomy within their own world, compared to their biological and physical attributes (Kirby, 2004; Owen et al., 2009).

More recent, applied conceptualizations of intellectual disability have merged the biological model and social model to create a more holistic understanding of IDD. Known as the biopsychosocial model, it takes into account the biological factors associated with an individual as well as the influence of psychological and external factors (Wicks-Nelson & Israel, 2009). That is, while this approach recognizes the importance of an individual's biological and genetic differences as well as the role of society in supporting those differences, the biopsychosocial model provides a more integrative and cohesive framework for advocating for the human rights of persons with IDD. When considering the role of disability in a person's life, the biopsychosocial perspective is mindful that a variety of services are required to holistically support the biological characteristics and emotional and social aspects that affect an individual's life (Dart, Gapen & Morris, 2002; Griffiths & Gardner, 2002).

The next section addresses how the biopsychosocial approach is conducive to meaningful legislation and policies that move towards advancing the needs and human rights of persons with IDD who participate within the criminal justice system.

## Creating Space: Advancements in Law and Practice to Recognize Persons with Intellectual Disabilities as Full Participants in the Criminal Justice System

The principles of social inclusion hold that all individuals have the right to have personal relationships and to participate in their community (Simplican, Leader, Kosciuklek, & Leahy, 2015). It assumes that we should make changes to our physical environment and our ableist attitudes in order to create space for the full participation of everyone. Social inclusion is aligned with a biopsychosocial perspective of persons with disabilities. When legislation and strategies are socially inclusive, they attempt to ensure that persons with IDD have access to the community and everyday living activities, in addition to placing the onus on society to make adjustments rather than the individual. For example, the *Accessibility of Ontarians with Disabilities Act* (AODA) (2005) is a major breakthrough in shifting away from ableism. The legislation, described later in more detail, represents a commitment of the Ontario government to create standards for accessibility and to enforce these requirements for public places, including employment, education, and other public services. Similarly, in 1990 the United States enacted the Americans with Disabilities Act that outlines provisions to ensure that those with disabilities have access to accommodations and non discrimination in various areas of their lives such as employment, criminal justice and other community services (United States Department of Justice and Civil Rights Division, 2010). This change in approach is in direct contrast to the historical practices that defined persons with disability as either 'unfixable,' or in need of being 'fixed,' leading to their exclusion through institutionalization.

The law can play a critical role in promoting social inclusion. As Timothy Endicott (2012) explained, the law is a critical foundation for addressing the needs of persons with intellectual disabilities:

> The law cannot do everything, and when you hope and work for good things for people with intellectual disabilities, you shouldn't expect everything from the law. But it is crucial to get the law right. It is crucial to treat a person with a disability as the subject of human rights – that is, as a person who has a right, and who can claim it. Crucial, too, to make sure that those who cannot do any claiming are respected, in just the same ways that you and I are (p. 18).

Endicott (2012) rightly argued that while there are limits to what the law can accomplish, it is nonetheless important to consider what the law can do for persons with IDD. Within the context of disability, the hope is that rights are interconnected – including human, legal, health, and others– and the principles of equality and social inclusion can be infused into everyday activities including criminal justice system participation as accused, victims, and witnesses.

Historically, legal rights have been awarded to individuals based on their capacity to understand the legal process, communicate with counsel, and know their rights and responsibilities within the court process (Flynn & Arstein-Kerslake, 2014). This link between capacity and 'legitimate' legal rights has resulted in persons with IDD being excluded from the justice system, leading to barriers in accessing fundamental rights, such as maintaining counsel or communicating with justice professionals in a way that is meaningful (Flynn & Arstein-Kerslake, 2014). In recent years, however, the creation of legislation such as the United Nations Convention on the Rights of Persons with Disabilities (CRPD; United Nations, 2006) has begun to address both the human and legal rights of persons with IDD.

Article 13 (Access to justice) of the UN Convention on the Rights of Persons with Disabilities (2006) states:

1. States Parties shall ensure effective access to justice for persons with disabilities on an equal basis with others, including through the provision of procedural and age-appropriate accommodations, in order to facilitate their effective role as direct and indirect participants, including as witnesses, in all legal proceedings, including at investigative and other preliminary stages.
2. In order to help to ensure effective access to justice for persons with disabilities, States Parties shall promote appropriate training for those working in the field of administration of justice, including police and prison staff.

In essence, the Convention on the Rights of Persons with Disabilities guarantees persons with disabilities full access and participation in the criminal justice system, regardless of age, role (i.e., accused, victim, witness) or the stage of the process (i.e., police investigation to corrections). Secondly, it ensures that governments must provide training about disabilities to justice professionals responsible for administering justice so that access is meaningfully accomplished. Moreover, in Article 12, the Convention on the Rights of Persons with Disabilities guarantees equal recognition before the law, including an assumption about the same level of legal capacity with others; however, it is recognized that it may be necessary to provide any appropriate measures or supports to the person with IDD to exercise their legal capacity (United Nations, 2006). For example, a person may require a support person in court to assist with understanding procedures and testifying.

A combination of legal, policy, and academic initiatives represent a tremendous commitment towards accessibility within the justice system within the last two decades in the province of Ontario. For example, The Ontario Human Rights Code (1990) provides that services must be provided equally:

> 1. Every person has a right to equal treatment with respect to services, goods and facilities, without discrimination because of race, ancestry, place of origin, colour, ethnic origin, citizenship, creed, sex, sexual orientation, gender identity, gender expression, age, marital status, family status or disability.

In 2005, Ontario implemented the *Accessibility of Ontarians with Disabilities Act* (AODA). Its stated purpose was to recognize "the history of discrimination against persons with disabilities in Ontario", by "developing, implementing and enforcing accessibility standards" for Ontarians with disabilities as well as to "provide involvement" in the Government of Ontario, industries and various sectors of the economy in the development of accessibility standards (S.O., 2005). The Accessibility of Ontarians with Disabilities Act (2005) further put in place a process for the development of standards, inspections of the implemented standards, enforcement mechanisms for failure to comply, and tribunals to adjudicate disputes. The Accessibility of Ontarians with Disabilities Act (2005) passed in a bipartisan manner and is expected to be fully implemented by 2025 (*Accessibility of Ontarians with Disabilities Act,* 2005, section 1(a)).

Within Ontario, steps have been taken to ensure courts within the province are fully accessible for individuals with disabilities by the year 2025. In concert with human rights legislation and the Accessibility of Ontarians with Disabilities Act, the review *Making Ontario's Courts Fully Accessible to Persons with Disabilities* (Government of Ontario, 2006) provides a framework that attempts to address the barriers to accessibility that individuals with disabilities experience and offers recommendations to ensure they are active participants within the court process. This document conceptualizes individuals with disabilities as capable of being active participants within the justice system and worthy to receive legal rights on an equal basis as others (Government of Ontario, 2006). Rather than viewing individuals with IDD as passive actors within the justice system, the legislation and policy address the supports and services that must be made available to ensure individuals with disabilities can participate fully within their own court experiences.

Finally, the review suggests there is a need for specific court officials that are responsible for ensuring individuals with disabilities are connected with the appropriate accommodations necessary to support them through the court process, such as accessing legal aid or appropriate legal counsel. They also identify that mandatory training for justice professionals on how to communicate and support persons with ID effectively is also essential (Government of Ontario, 2006).

## The Canadian Criminal Code: Progress and Gaps

### *The Definition of Mental Disorder*

In Section 2 of the *Criminal Code of Canada* (CCC), "mental disorder" is defined as a 'disease of the mind' (1985). In *R. v. Cooper* (1980) the Supreme Court of Canada defined 'disease of the mind' as "…any illness, disorder or abnormal condition which impairs the human mind and its functioning, excluding, however, self-induced states caused by alcohol or drugs, as well as transitional mental states such as hysteria or concussion" (p. 144). Under section 16 of the Criminal Code of Canada, an individual can be found *not criminally responsible on account of mental disorder* and then diverted to a provincial or territorial review board.

The definition of mental disorder is deliberately broad, making space to include a wide range of conditions that are not limited to precise definitions within the mental health or developmental disability fields. In addition, case law has added to the range of eligible conditions. For example, in *R. v. Rouse* (1986), an Ontario General Division court found that 'mental retardation' constitutes a mental disorder under section 2; and in *R. v. Malcolm* (1989), delirium tremens was also found to fall within the scope of a mental disorder (see Schneider 2004, p. 2).

Typically, intellectual and developmental disabilities, mental health issues, or dual diagnosis are legally relevant, beginning with the *standard of fitness to stand trial,* the test of whether one is of "limited cognitive capacity" (*R. v. Taylor,* 1992). The *Taylor test* is typically used within the context of forensic decision-making, particularly in mental health diversion courts. The fitness assessment ultimately focuses on whether the individual can understand the court processes (e.g., oath, perjury), the roles of the court actors (e.g., judge, Crown attorney, and defence attorney), and whether the individual can communicate their desires with counsel. Despite this involved knowledge of the processes involved in the criminal justice system, the individual requires "...only a rudimentary factual understanding of his legal predicament" (Bloom & Schneider, 2006, p. 76). This leaves persons with intellectual limitations, the bulk of those who suffer from mild to moderate impairments (Jones, 2007), or who may have limits on their "analytical capacity" (R. v. *Taylor*, 1992) to be at higher risk of not being able to make decisions within their best interests, nor to appreciate the implications of processes and decisions at trial (Bloom & Schneider, 2006, pp. 76-78). As Bloom and Schneider (2006) pointed out:

> The test is not whether the accused *knows* his legal situation etc. but whether he is *able* to understand the concepts and communicate with counsel. The accused's capacity is the central concern. Simple ignorance does not render an accused unfit (p. 72).

Furthermore, a stay of proceedings is also available for permanently unfit accused, when someone is not likely ever to become fit, does not pose significant danger to public, and is in interest of administration of justice (*R. v. Demers*, 2004).

## *Participating in Court*

A judge or justice, on an application of the prosecutor or a witness with an IDD, can order a support person of the witness's choosing to be permitted to be present and close to the person while testifying (Part XV Criminal Code of Canada s. 486(1.2)). In addition, section 486 (1.4) allows the court to sanction this communication. A complainant or witness who has difficulty communicating evidence due to a mental disability can testify outside the courtroom or behind a screen or other device that would allow the complainant or witness not to see the accused (Part XV Criminal Code of Canada s. 486(2.1)) (Hamelin, Marinos, Robinson, & Griffiths, 2012).

For sexual offences, a videotape of the complainant's testimony can be entered as evidence (Criminal Code of Canada s. 715.2). The use of videotaped evidence as an accommodation exists at the trial stage but requires a submission to the judge to occur. Another accommodation can be found in the *Canada Evidence Act* (1985), section 16.(1). This accommodation provides that, with a witness whose mental capacity is in question, the court must inquire into whether the person understand the nature of an oath or solemn affirmation and is able to communicate the evidence. However, many individuals with intellectual disabilities may well be able to communicate the evidence without understanding the concept of oath or solemn affirmation. Therefore, section 16.(3) provides for accommodation for individuals who can communicate evidence but lack the understanding of an oath by allowing them to give unsworn testimony on the condition that they promise to tell the truth.

## *Court Diversions*

Within Canada there are several mental health courts (Bloom & Schneider, 2006) that can accommodate persons with IDD if there is reason to believe there is a disability or the person has been identified as having an IDD. These specialized courts are better able to deal with the underlying issues related to the offense, and usually requires the individual to take responsibility for the offense or plead guilty. Once a program or conditions are developed and have been followed and monitored for an established period of time, the charge(s) will be withdrawn.

These supports and accommodations practiced within Canadian courts are not unlike the ones found in other countries and jurisdictions, except for a few small differences. For example, some jurisdictions, such as those found in Western Australia have more specialized diversionary streams. The Magistrates Court in Perth, Western Australia has a specific Intellectual Disability Diversion Program. As such, this jurisdiction does not treat this population within a mental health court or under the umbrella of mental disorder (Government of Western Australia, 2014).

While it is clear that Canadian law is working towards the ability to accommodate persons with intellectual disabilities, there are a number of key gaps to consider. First, while mental disorders are addressed within the Canadian Criminal Code to ensure that persons with a wide variety of impairments are considered, in terms of practicality, it has likely contributed to a lack of understanding regarding the differences between mental illness and intellectual or cognitive disability. In a small study of criminal justice professionals within Ontario (Marinos, Robinson, Gosse, Fergus & Griffiths, 2017), several of the participants could not define what constitutes an intellectual disability accurately, and many conflated it with a mental illness. It is critical for front-line professionals to understand the strengths and challenges of this population to be able to interact and refer them for identification and appropriate specialized supports that may be distinct from a person with a mental illness. Second, as mentioned earlier, the *Taylor test* (*R. v. Taylor*, 1992) of fitness to stand trial provides a low threshold for participation in the justice process. This may lead to the possibility that persons with impairments will be participating in court proceedings they do not understand and may not be making decisions in their best interests. This risk could be further compounded with pressure on the system to expedite cases. Lastly, given the distinct needs of persons with IDD, it is critical that specialized and individualized supports are given based on individual need and using expertise from the developmental sector.

## Ontario, Canada as a Case Study

The criminal justice system has recognized the need for a more enlightened approach to the treatment of the mentally ill. As noted in a speech by Chief Justice Beverly McLachlin (2007):

> A few years ago, I found myself at a dinner at government house. Next to me sat the chief of one of Toronto's downtown precincts. I asked him what his biggest problem was. I thought he would say the *Charter* and "all those judges who pronounce on rights." But he surprised me. "Mental illness," was his reply. He then told me a sad story, one I have heard throughout the country in the years since. Every night, his jails would fill up with minor offenders or persons who had created a nuisance – not because they are criminals, but because they are mentally ill. They would be kept overnight or for a few days, only to be released – the cycle inevitably to repeat itself.

Such people are not true criminals, not real wrong-doers in the traditional sense of those words. They become involved with the law because they are mentally ill, addicted or both. Today, a growing awareness of the extent and nature of mental illness and addiction is helping sensitize the public and those involved in the justice system. This sensitization and knowledge is leading to new, more appropriate responses to the problem.

With this perspective in mind and following the introduction of Accessibility of Ontarians with Disabilities Act to the province, both Crown Attorneys and judges were given increased training on the best approach to interacting with individuals with disabilities (Best, 2018). For Crown Attorneys, this included comprehensive "webinars" designed to teach best practices in a variety of different scenarios and more traditional discussions at Crown Attorney educational conferences. Furthermore, the Victim/Witness Assistance Program (Ministry of the Attorney General [Ontario]), who are responsible for assisting victims with IDD to prepare and deliver their testimony became responsible, in part, for addressing modifications of the "regular" court system to make it more accessible for victims and witnesses with IDD, including the use of screens, pre-taped testimony, and the use of a support person (Ministry of the Attorney General, 2016).

Most courthouses within Ontario now have an Accessibility Coordinator that can assist individuals. The Ontario Court of Justice has developed a *Guide for Accused Persons in Criminal Trials* including instructions for how to contact an Accessibility Coordinator at the courthouse in addition to further updates on their website about accessibility (Ontario Court of Justice, 2012). Many courthouses in Ontario also have a Dual Diagnosis Justice Case Manager who offers assistance to persons who have an intellectual disability and a mental illness. For example, in the case of Joel, a 31-year-old man diagnosed with a developmental disability and charged with arson, the Dual Diagnosis Case Manager:

- Remained with him throughout the court process
- Attended all court dates with him
- Assisted him in accessing Legal Aid
- Liaised between the defense counsel and Joel and his support network about the services and supports he is involved with.
- Referred Joel to other services and supports that could assist him in being an active participant in his community and reduce the risk of recidivism.
- At Joel's sentencing hearing, provided a letter outlining the supports he was involved with in the community.

The outcome of this process was that Joel was sentenced to three years' probation. Furthermore, following court, the case manager assisted Joel in checking in at the probation office and reviewed the expectations of his probation order to ensure understanding.

In addition, in recent years there has been an increase in the use of information gathering tools such as pre-sentence reports and mental health assessments to provide all parties with a greater understanding of the needs of individuals with both IDD and physical disabilities (Ontario Court of Justice, 2012). It is therefore not surprising that case law has similarly recognized the need to support and understand the needs of those with IDD. Two Ontario case examples are demonstrative.

The first case example demonstrates there is often a misunderstanding that a person's intellectual disability implies a lack of capacity to participate in the judicial system. In R. v. *D.A.I.* (2012) the Supreme Court of Canada dealt with the issue of capacity to testify. Here, the accused was charged with sexual assault. The complainant was a 22-year-old woman who was described as having "the mental age of a three to six-year-old." The court entered into a *voir dire* in order to determine whether she was competent to testify. The trial court found that while the complainant was able to understand the difference between telling the truth and lying in concrete situations, she was unable to articulate her understanding of the nature of telling the truth and lying, moral and religious duties, and the legal consequences of telling a lie in court. Accordingly, the court did not allow her to testify.

In overturning the trial judge's ruling, the Supreme Court of Canada ruled that there is no requirement that adults with mental disabilities are to be questioned on the obligation to tell the truth. The underlying policy concerns here emphasize the need to support adults with mental disabilities to testify. To require an added step of necessitating complainants to explain the nature of their obligation to tell the truth would "immunize" an entire category of offenders from criminal responsibility and further marginalize the already vulnerable victims of sexual predators. If a witness with ID agreed to tell the truth, the introduction of the evidence at this stage would therefore meet the criteria of threshold reliability. It would then be up to the trier of fact to determine ultimate reliability and whether the Crown has proven its case beyond a reasonable doubt.

In the second illustrative case study, R. v. *Conception* (2014), the accused was charged with sexual assault. When he appeared in court he was found to be in a psychotic state, failed the Taylor test, and was declared unfit to stand trial. The Crown recommended a treatment order noting that a bed in a psychiatric hospital would be ready six days after the hearing due to a high demand of residential treatment for the mentally ill and a limited number of beds. Nonetheless, the hearing judge issued an order that the treatment be conducted "forthwith" at a second hospital or its designate if no bed was available at the first hospital. Having no bed to take the accused to, court services delivered the accused to the first hospital and left him in the hallway.

The hospital appealed the ruling to the Ontario Court of Appeal who ruled that the hearing judge had erred by acting on the basis that the hospital's consent had been given irrespective of timing. They also determined that the applicable sections of the Criminal Code engage the rights to liberty and security of the person under section 7 of the Charter of Rights, but do not violate the principles of fundamental justice.

On further appeal, the Supreme Court of Canada came to a different conclusion. Here, the Court held that the hospital's consent is not required to all the terms and conditions of the treatment order. The only requirement is for the hospital to consent to the treatment itself. Bed shortages do not permit a hospital to refuse or defer consent. Consent can only be withheld for medical reasons rather than on the basis of efficient hospital resources.

The Court continued to recognize that the purpose of treatment orders is to render the accused fit to stand trial in order to protect the accused's rights to a timely trial and the public interest in its right to a fair trial. Therefore, the requirement for consent only relates to a hospital's willingness to provide a particular treatment. Requiring a hospital to consent to all terms of a court disposition would effectively give them a broad veto over an accused's legal interests. Only judges are able to assess the balance between an individual's legal rights and the pragmatic realities of ability to provide treatment.

Accordingly, while bed shortages are not a basis for a hospital to independently refuse consent, they are part of the circumstances in which the judge considers in exercising their discretion for the start date of treatment. If a bed is unavailable a discussion should take place before the judge about triage in the intervening period. The hospital may always exercise its statutory right of appeal and benefit from an automatic stay until the hearing is heard. In the present case, the Supreme Court held that the trial judge erred by failing to consider the totality of the circumstances and not engaging in the triage with the hospital about alternative courses of action to fulfill the order. The Ontario Court of Appeal's decision was therefore upheld.

While both of these two cases differ in the nature of the issues covered, they similarly reflect an increased focus on the needs of individuals with IDD. As the law evolves and continued progressive measures are introduced in the criminal justice sphere, our highest courts will advance and refine legal norms in the treatment of those individuals with the unique and often substantial needs related to IDD.

## Conclusions: Advancements and Gaps in the Legal Context

Although legislation has been put in place to ensure persons with IDD experience equality within the law, they continue to experience challenges within the criminal justice system. Some of the challenges include understanding abstract concepts, communicating with justice professionals, or remembering the details of the criminal act they took part in (Brown, Gudjonnson & Connor, 2011; Fast & Conry, 2009; Moore & Green, 2004). When developing unique and specialized supports to assist individuals with IDD in accessing justice it is important to keep in mind that those with disabilities may be differently circumstanced. Therefore, it is critical that the supports and accommodations implemented are individualized to address a range of abilities. For example, some individuals may require a single visit to an empty courtroom to understand the expectations of court, while others may require multiple visits to both empty and working courtrooms in order to fully comprehend what is expected of them, where to sit, and who will be present during the upcoming trial (Pathak, 2010). According to the Law Commission of Ontario (2012) there is often more of a focus on the functional aspects of a disability rather than a broader human rights approach.

This chapter shows that in many jurisdictions that the law has been changed to make space – both conceptually and physically -- for persons with IDD to participate as accused, victims, and witnesses and that we have moved in positive directions in meeting the needs of persons with IDD. Furthermore, instead of suggesting ways to 'fix' the individual with a disability, we must continue to identify and provide accommodations that will assist individuals with disabilities in accessing their rights to justice, and to be treated with respect and have their needs addressed if they find themselves in the criminal justice system. At the same time, it is critical that the changes made do not cause an onerous responsibility on justice professionals nor persons with IDD.

## References

Accessibility for Ontarians with Disabilities Act (S.O., 2005, c. 11).

Best, S. (2008). May I Help You? Understanding Ontario's New Regulation on Accessible Customer Service. Retrieved from: https://www.canadaone.com/ezine/sept08/accessible_customer_service.html

Bloom, H., & Schneider, R. D. (2006). *Mental disorder and the law: A primer for legal and mental health professionals.* Toronto: Irwin Law

Brown, N. N., Gudjonsson, G., & Connor, P. (2011). Suggestibility and fetal alcohol spectrum disorders: I'll tell you anything you want to hear. *The Journal of Psychiatry & Law, 39*(1), 39-71.

Canadian Criminal Code (R.S.C., 1985, c. C-46).

Dart, L., Gapen, W., & Morris, S. (2002). Building responsive service systems. In D. M. Griffiths, C. Stavrakaki, & J. Summers. (Eds.), *Dual diagnosis: An introduction to the mental health needs of persons with developmental disabilities* (pp. 282-323). Sudbury, ON, Canada: Habilitative Mental Health Resource Network.

Endicott, O. (2012). Introduction: A rights agenda. In D. Griffiths, F. Owen, & S. L. Watson (Eds.), *The Human Rights Agenda for Persons with Intellectual Disabilities* (pp. 219 – 236). Kingston NY: NADD Press.

Fast, D. K., & Conry, J. (2009). Fetal alcohol spectrum disorders and the criminal justice system. *Developmental Disabilities Research Reviews, 15*, 250-257.

Flynn, E., & Arstein-Kerslake, A. (2014). Legislating personhood: Realising the right to support in exercising legal capacity. *International Journal of Law in Context, 10*(1), 81-104.

Goldberg, S. (2011). Problem-solving in Canada's courtroom: A guide to therapeutic jurisprudence. Retrieved from: https://www.nji-inm.ca/index.cfm/publications/problem-solving-in-canada-s-courtrooms-a-guide-to-therapeutic-justice-2nd-edition/?langSwitch=en

Government of Ontario. (2006). Making Ontario's courts fully accessible to persons with disabilities [Report of courts disabilities committee]. Retrieved from: http://www.ontariocourts.ca/accessible_courts/en/report_courts_disabilities.htm

Government of Western Australia. (2014). Intellectual Disability Diversion Program (IDDP). Retrieved from: http://www.magistratescourt.wa.gov.au/I/intellectual_disability_diversion_program_iddp.aspx?uid=7942-2328-8603-7948.

Griffiths, D. M., & Gardner, W. I. (2002). The integrated biopsychosocial approach to challenging behaviours. In D. M. Griffiths, C. Stavrakaki, & J. Summers (Eds.), *Dual diagnosis: An introduction to the mental health needs of persons with developmental disabilities* (pp. 387 – 418). Sudbury, ON: Habilitative Mental Health Resource Network.

Griffiths, D., & Marinos, V. (2005). *People with intellectual disabilities and the courtroom: A guide for judges* (National Judicial Institute). Brock University, St. Catharines, Canada.

Griffiths, D. M., Owen, F., & Watson, S. (2012). Introduction: A rights agenda. In D. Griffiths, F. Owen, & S. L. Watson (Eds.), *The Human Rights Agenda for Persons with Intellectual Disabilities* (pp. 1 – 8). Kingston, NY: NADD Press.

Hamelin, J., Marinos, V., Robinson, J., & Griffiths, D. (2012). Human rights and the justice system. In D. Griffiths, F. Owen, & S. L. Watson (Eds.), The human rights agenda for persons with intellectual disabilities (pp. 169 – 194). Kingston, NY: NADD Press.

Jones, J., (2007). Persons with intellectual disabilities in the criminal justice system. *International Journal of Offender Therapy and Comparative Criminology, 651*(6), 723-733.

Kirby, J. C. (2004). Disability and justice: A pluralistic account. *Sociology Theory Practice, 30*(2), 229- 246.

Law Commission of Ontario (2012). *A framework for the law as it affects persons with disabilities: advancing substantive equality for persons with disabilities through law, policy and practice*. Retrieved from: https://www.lco-cdo.org/wp-content/uploads/2012/12/disabilities-framework.pdf

Marinos, V., Griffiths, D., Fergus, C., Stromski, S., & Rondeau, K. (2014). Victims and witnesses with intellectual disability in the criminal justice system. *Criminal Law Quarterly, 61*(4), 517-530.

Marinos, V., Robinson, J., Gosse, L., Fergus, C., & Griffiths, D. (2017). Persons with Intellectual Disabilities and the Criminal Justice System: A View from Criminal Justice Professionals in Ontario. *Criminal Law Quarterly, 64*(1 & 2), 83-107.

McLachlin, B. (2007, March 8). *The challenges we face: Remarks to the Empire Club of Canada. Toronto, ON, Canada*. Retrieved from: https://www.scc-csc.ca/judges-juges/spe-dis/bm-2007-03-08-eng.aspx

Ministry of the Attorney General. (2016). *The victim/witness assistance program*. Retrieved from: https://www.attorneygeneral.jus.gov.on.ca/english/ovss/VWAP-English.html

Moore, T. E., & Green, M. (2004). Fetal alcohol spectrum disorder (FASD): A need for closer examination by the criminal justice system. *Criminal Reports*, 19(1), 1-9.

Ontario Court of Justice. (2012). *Guide for accused persons in criminal trials*. Retrieved from: http://www.ontariocourts.ca/ocj/files/guides/guide-criminal.pdf

Ontario Human Rights Code (R.S.O. 1990, c. H-19).

Owen, F., Griffiths, D., Tarulli, D., & Murphy, J. (2009). Historical and theoretical foundations of rights of persons with intellectual disabilities: Setting the stage. In F. Owen & D. Griffiths. (Eds.), *Challenges to the human rights of people with intellectual disabilities* (pp. 23- 42). London, UK: Jessica Kingsley Publishing.

Pathak, M. (2010, April). *"Witness support, preparation and profiling" (or, putting it another way) "Let's learn from the other side"*. Paper presented at Human Rights and Persons with Intellectual Disabilities Conference, Niagara Falls, ON, Canada.

R. v. Conception (2014), SCC 60, [2014] 3 S.C.R. 82

R. v. Cooper (1980), 1 S.C.R. 1149, 51 C.C.C. (2d) 129 (S.C.C.).

R. v. D.A.I. ([2012] 1 S.C.R. 149

R. v. Demers, [2004] 2 S.C.R. 489, 2004 SCC 46

R. v. Malcolm (1989), 50 C.C.C. (3d) 172, 71 C.R. (3d) 238 (Man. C.A.).

R. v. Rouse (1986), 112 C.C.C. (3d) 406, 19 O.T.C. 155 (Ont. Gen. Div.).

R. v. Taylor (1992), 77 CCC (3d) 551.

Schneider, R. D. (2004). *The mentally disordered accused*. Ontario: Bar Admission Course, Law Society of Upper Canada.

Simplican, S. C., Leader, G., Kosciulek, J., & Leahy, M. (2015). Defining social inclusion of people with intellectual and developmental disabilities: An ecological model of social networks and community participation. *Research in developmental disabilities, 38*, 18-29.

Stromski, S. (2015). *Searching for accommodations within the Ontario criminal justice system for persons with fetal alcohol spectrum disorder: Views of social service agency and justice professionals* (Unpublished master's thesis). Brock University: St. Catharines, ON.

Tisdall, E. K. M. (2012). The challenge and challenging of childhood studies? Learning from disability studies and research with disabled children. *Children & society, 26*(3), 181-191

United Nations (2006). *Convention on the Rights of Persons with Disabilities.* Retrieved from:http://www.un.org/disabilities/convention/conventionfull.shtml

United States Department of Justice and Civil Rights Division. (2010). *The Americans with Disability Act of 1990 and Revised ADA Regulations Implementing Title II and Title III.* Retrieved from: https://www.ada.gov/2010_regs.htm.

Wicks-Nelson, R., Israel, A. C., & Wicks-Nelson, R. (2009). *Abnormal child and adolescent psychology.* Upper Saddle River, NJ: Pearson Prentice Hall.

*Chapter 4*

# Forensic Inpatient Involvement of Persons with Intellectual and Developmental Disabilities

## *Lisa Whittingham*

There is consensus internationally that it is unfair to punish people for a criminal act when there are extenuating circumstances that inhibit their ability to appreciate the nature or the consequences of their actions. As such, most countries have developed legislation to protect defendants with mental disabilities; and if a defense lawyer, public prosecutor, or judge (collectively known as court professionals or court actors in this chapter) believes that a mental disability is a factor contributing to the offense or may inhibit the person's ability to participate in the criminal proceeding, they may refer an individual to the forensic mental health system for an assessment. One assessment that may be requested is to determine the individual's ability to participate in the court process, whereas, the other assessment establishes the role that mental disability played in the criminal offense or for treatment that will decrease the risk of the individual reoffending in the future (Barroff, Gunn, & Hayes, 2004). That is, the forensic mental health system has developed as a complementary system to the criminal justice system to ensure that people with mental disabilities in contact with the law have a place to address mental illness related variables associated with their offense (Bettridge & Barbaree, 2008).

Though most legislation internationally uses the language of *mental disability* to identify individuals who may need to be assessed and treated in a forensic inpatient setting, it is important to recognize that this is not a homogenous group, and persons with intellectual and developmental disabilities (IDD) represent but one type of individual protected by these laws. Furthermore, it is important to recognize how persons with IDD are different than persons diagnosed with a mental illness. As identified in Chapter 2, persons with an intellectual disability are characterized by significant limitations in cognitive skills (such as verbal skills or problem-solving) and adaptive skills (such as social skills) (American Association of Intellectual and Developmental Disabilities, 2018); while mental illness is typically used to describe "changes in emotions, thoughts, or behaviour (or a combination of these)" (Parekh, 2018). While it is broadly recognized that there are social determinants (e.g., homelessness, poverty) which influence the severity and individual experiences of mental illness, typically what constitutes a mental illness or an intellectual disability is usually based on criteria laid out in the *Diagnostic and Statistical Manual* (DSM-5) or *International Classification of Disorders* (ICD-11) (American Psychological Association, 2013; World Health Organization, 2018). Furthermore, research has demonstrated that many individuals with IDD accused of a criminal offense may also be experiencing a mental illness and therefore will be labeled as having a *dual diagnosis*[1] (Bettridge & Barbaree, 2008; Lunsky et al., 2011). Given the differences between persons with IDD and mental illness, it is important to recognize that the accommodations required by each of these groups are different and that failure to recognize these differences may create unique barriers and challenges when they are transferred to the forensic inpatient system. This may be in part due to forensic professionals' beliefs about the role that the disability played in the individual's offense, beliefs about the person with IDD's ability to be rehabilitated, and beliefs about the importance of treatment responsivity (Bettridge & Bararabee, 2008; Heerema, 2005).

The goal of this chapter is to describe the characteristics of individuals with IDD who are being transferred to forensic inpatient settings, to describe how persons with IDD end up in inpatient forensic settings, and to summarize the forensic assessments and interventions currently used with persons with IDD. More information regarding community-based forensic interventions are included in chapter 7 in this book, *Challenges in Community Support for Offenders with Intellectual Disabilities Who Have Offended*. I argue that there appears to be significant gaps in our knowledge and understanding of persons with IDD in forensic inpatient settings in Canada, the US, and internationally. It appears that more attention and research is needed to understand the contributing factors influencing their involvement in the forensic inpatient system, the supports needed to be successful in a forensic inpatient system (including dual diagnosis specialists), and systemic supports and resources needed for their return to the community or towards diversion to prevent involvement in the forensic system.

## Prevalence and Characteristics of Persons with Intellectual and Developmental Disabilities in Inpatient Forensic Settings

### Prevalence

Prevalence studies of persons with IDD have largely focused on incarcerated persons with IDD or individuals in non-forensic hospital settings. The little research to date has indicated that similar to in the criminal justice system, persons with IDD are overrepresented in forensic inpatient settings. Furthermore, researchers have identified that the prevalence of persons with IDD in the forensic inpatient setting are estimates and may vary depending on whether a person is identified as having an intellectual or developmental disability in addition to the similar variance found in incarceration data (e.g., how intellectual and developmental disability is defined or measurements or assessments used) (Jones, 2007; Murphy, 2015). Several Ontario-based studies of prevalence have estimated that persons with IDD represent between 12% and 19% of

---

[1] Dual diagnosis may also be used in some countries to describe persons with both a mental health and substance use disorder (also known as a concurrent disorder).

persons in forensic inpatient settings (Lin et al., 2017; Maulik, Mascarenhas, Mathers, Dua, & Sexena, 2011; Woodbury-Smith, Furimsky, & Chaimowitz, 2018). It is important to note that this figure is considerably higher than the proportion of persons with IDD in the general population (1.6%) and persons without DD in forensic settings (0.8%) (Lin et al., 2017; Maulik et al., 2011; Woodbury-Smith et al., 2018).

## *Characteristics of Persons with Intellectual and Developmental Disabilities in Forensic Inpatient Settings*

Evidence-to-date indicates that persons with IDD are amongst the most complex individuals being supported in forensic inpatient settings. While it is important to recognize that persons with IDD are a heterogenous group, research has noted some trends regarding the characteristics of persons with IDD in forensic inpatient settings.

*Cognitive and Intellectual Impairments.* With the exception of autism spectrum disorder (ASD), persons with IDD tend to be represented as a homogenous group in the criminal justice system with little consideration for the diversity of diagnoses including genetic disorders, fetal alcohol spectrum disorder, and traumatic brain injury. In one US study, participants with traumatic brain injuries (TBI), fetal alcohol syndrome (FAS), and pervasive developmental disability (PDD) were classified as a mutually exclusive group from other participants classified according to their IQ (Stinson & Robbins, 2014). They found that of 235 persons with IDD, 52 individuals were diagnosed with a traumatic brain injury, 18 individuals were diagnosed with fetal alcohol syndrome, and 35 individuals were diagnosed with pervasive developmental disorder.

In addition, less is known about the range of cognitive impairment or the range of IQ scores for persons with IDD in inpatient forensic settings. Jones (2007) suggested that the likelihood of criminal justice system involvement decreases as the level of cognitive impairment increases. Stinson and Robbins (2014) found that 55 individuals fell within the borderline IQ score range, 55 individuals fell within the mild IQ range, and 20 individuals fell in the moderate IQ range.

*Presence of Psychiatric Symptoms.* As stated previously, persons with IDD are also likely to experience a mental illness, with estimates of dual diagnosis being approximately 50% (Alexander et al., 2010; Glaser & Florio, 2004; Stinson & Robbins, 2014). Several studies have examined the prevalence of psychiatric illnesses comorbid with intellectual and developmental disabilities and have suggested a wide range of psychiatric diagnosis. Some of the comorbid psychiatric diagnosis identified in persons with IDD confined in forensic inpatient settings, included psychotic disorders (Gralton, James, & Crocombe, 2000; Puri, Lekh, & Treasaden, 2000; Raina & Lunksy, 2010; Thomas et al., 2004), mood disorders (Alexander et al., 2010), and impulse control disorders (Raina & Lunsky, 2010; Stinson & Robbins, 2014).

Particular attention has been given to the comorbidity between personality disorders and intellectual and developmental disabilities given the potential increased risk for violent offending, substance abuse, and multiple offences (Lindsay & Ansari, 2019). Several researchers identified that there is a high prevalence of personality disorders in persons with IDD in forensic inpatient settings (e.g., Alexander et al., 2010; Lunksy et al., 2011; Stinson & Robbins, 2014). Research has indicated that persons with IDD are more likely to be diagnosed with antisocial personality disorder (Hogue et al., 2007; Reed, Russell, Xenitidis, & Murphy, 2004; Stinson & Robbins, 2014). Evidence has also indicated that persons with IDD in a forensic inpatient unit were more likely than individuals in other hospital units to be diagnosed with borderline personality disorder (Raina & Lunsky, 2010; Stinson & Robbins, 2014). Lindsay and colleagues (2017) suggested that one of the possible reasons for high rates of personality disorder in forensic populations is due to the comfortability of forensic professional to make a diagnosis of personality disorder, particularly antisocial personality disorder.

***Nature of Offenses.*** In an earlier study of the offenses committed by persons with IDD in forensic inpatient settings, results indicated that persons with IDD tended to commit more arson-related (15%) and sexual offenses (28%) than patients without IDD (Walker & McCabe, 1973). Subsequent research has found similar results, with arson, physical assault, and sexual offences making up the majority of the offenses committed by persons with IDD in forensic inpatient settings, and at rates considerably higher than what is observed in patients without IDD (Lunsky et al., 2011; Mannynsalo, Putkonen, Lindberg, & Kotilainen, 2009; Palucka, Raina, Liu, & Lunsky, 2012; Thomas et al., 2004).

***Length of Stay.*** Several studies have examined the amount of time that persons with IDD have spent in forensic inpatient settings and have found that when compared to persons without IDD, they spend more time in hospitals (Butwell, Jamieson, Leese, & Taylor, 2000; Palucka et al., 2012; Raina & Lunsky, 2010; Thomas et al., 2004). For example, Lin and colleagues (2017) found that in Ontario, persons with IDD remained in forensic inpatient settings for 32 weeks (8 months) longer than patients without IDD; while Thomas and colleagues (2004) found in a UK study, that 32% of persons with IDD in a secured setting could have been transferred to a lower security setting had it been available. It is possible that length of stay may contribute to the high numbers of persons with IDD found in forensic inpatient settings.

Researchers have proposed that the extended length of stay on forensic inpatient units is the result of the complexity of the behaviors observed (e.g., index offense and behavior while inpatient) and the supervision and support needed to reduce the risk of reoffending (Lin et al., 2017; Thomas et al., 2004). For example, Thomas and colleagues (2004) found that some of the barriers that prevented individuals with IDD from moving from high security settings included professional and staff perceptions regarding higher treatment and security needs, the presence of on-going aggressive behavior, and the risk associated with the nature of the index offense. Similarly, Lunsky and colleagues (2011) identified that forensic patients with IDD required higher levels of residential and therapeutic care compared to other inpatient groups, creating challenges for finding required supports within the community.

## How Do Persons with Intellectual and Developmental Disabilities End Up in Inpatient Forensic Settings

### *Fitness to Stand Trial or Competency*

As stated previously, many countries have legislation that protects individuals from being tried for an offense if there is reason to believe that the individual is not able to participate in the criminal proceedings. Central to the constitutional right to a fair trial under section 11(d) of the Canadian Charter of Rights and Freedoms and the Sixth Amendment to the United States Constitution, all defendants must be a participant to the proceedings against them. While Canadian law considers the question of "fitness," the U.S. uses the language of "competency." While it is unlikely an issue of semantics, the language of 'fitness' in the Canadian context is meant to communicate a neutral tone around one's capacity to participate without judgment about ability. Nonetheless, court actors may request an assessment of *competency or fitness to stand trial* when they believe that an individual is not able to understand the crime that they are being charged with, is unaware of the court proceedings, is not knowledgeable about the role of court actors, and/or is not able to assist in their own defense (Baroff et al., 2004; Griffiths, Taillon-Wasmund, & Smith, 2002). It is important to note that competency or fitness to stand trial is not the same as criminal responsibility described below.

It has been suggested that some forensic and legal professionals may still subscribe to the belief that persons with IDD are not capable of understanding court procedures or participating in their own defense (e.g., making a plea) (Craig, Stringer, & Hutchinson, 2017; Puri et al., 2000; Sakdalan & Egan, 2014). Despite these long-held beliefs, research has demonstrated that most persons with IDD are competent to stand trial. For example, Baroff and colleagues (2004) reported that 78% of persons with mild IDD (i.e., an IQ between 50 – 55 and 70) were competent to stand trial, as were 68% of persons with a moderate IDD (i.e., an IQ between 35 and 50 – 55). Similarly, Petrella (1992) found that only one-third of persons with IDD were found unfit to stand trial. The reasons cited for why these individuals with IDD were unfit were primarily centered around communication. For example, Petrella (1992) indicated that reasons why persons with IDD were found unfit included their inability to coherently describe their offense or to identify the consequences if they were convicted of an offense, while James, Duffield, Blizard, and Hamilton (2001) found that persons with IDD were found unfit to stand trial if the individual could not participate in the trial procedure (e.g., instruct their lawyer). Little attention has been given to the competency and fitness of individuals with severe and profound developmental disabilities, likely given they are often excluded from participation in the criminal justice system as a whole (Griffiths et al., 2002).

When an individual has been judged or deemed incompetent or unfit to stand trial, the individual may be committed to a forensic inpatient setting to address the competency of that individual with the goal of releasing and returning the accused to court to face prosecution. Fitness or competence, then, is meant to be time-limited until the individual returns to a state in which they are able to understand the charges and/or processes necessary to participate. As Woodbury-Smith and colleagues (2018) identified, this poses a serious risk to persons with IDD, who may be detained indefinitely in a forensic inpatient unit without being convicted and sentenced for an alleged offense. One barrier that may need to be overcome in order to reduce this risk of indefinite detention is the recognition of the difference between the intended goals for persons with IDD and persons with mental illness. Several researchers have identified that while the intended goal for persons with mental illness is rehabilitation, the goal for persons with IDD is habilitation (Baroff et al., 2004; Griffiths et al., 2002). As Griffiths and colleagues (2002) pointed out, rehabilitation implies that there is a previous state that the individual is being returned to, whereas habilitation recognizes that due to psychological and social conditions, the individual did not have the ability to begin with. For example, if a person is experiencing active hallucinations, it might inhibit their ability to participate in court processes or to effectively communicate with their lawyer. Therefore, the goal of the forensic inpatient treatment is to address these hallucinations, so they are able to return to court. For persons with IDD who may not have had the opportunity to learn about the legal system, the goal of forensic inpatient treatment is to teach knowledge to enable participation in the court processes. It is important to note that any treatment provided at this stage in the process is intended to increase the individual's ability to participate in the court processes and may not have a long-term impact on the individual.

One of the challenges that faces forensic professionals responsible for assessing the competency or fitness to stand trial is determining what exactly constitutes fitness or competency for persons with IDD. That is, forensic professionals must identify whether a person is fit or competent without a standard basis of comparison. To date, there are no consistently used assessments of competency or fitness to stand trial. Two known assessments of competency or fitness include the Competence Assessment for Standing Trial for Defendants with Mental Retardation (CAST-MR) (Everington & Dunn, 1995; Everington & Luckasson, 1992) or the Fitness Interview Test – Revised (FIT-R) (Roesch, Zapf, & Eaves, 2006). Some scholars have expressed concern that these tools should not act as a replacement for clinical judgement (e.g., Federoff, Griffiths, Marini, & Richards, 2000), while other researchers have suggested that regardless of whether a standardized assessment or clinical judgement is used, many individuals with IDD do not receive an adequate assessment of competency or fitness given that forensic professional may have limited experience with IDD (Griffiths et al., 2002). Finally, it is unknown whether persons with IDD are held to a higher standard of knowledge regarding the criminal justice system because they are more likely to be assessed for knowledge.

Historically, if a person could not be made fit or competent to stand trial (either due to mental illness or IDD), they could be held indefinitely in a forensic inpatient setting. However, recognizing that confinement in an inpatient setting violated individual rights to freedom, many countries have developed mechanisms to ensure that the individual's rights and freedoms are protected. In the United States, an individual may be released to the community once the time that is equivalent to the sentence has been served, or they may be involuntarily committed to a psychiatric hospital for further treatment (Baroff et al., 2004). In Canada, the Supreme Court of Canada held in *R. v. Demers* (2004) that it was unconstitutional to hold a person in a hospital if they are found permanently unfit. Therefore, many provinces have established mechanisms to ensure the rights of the persons with IDD and other conditions rendering them permanently unfit are protected. For example, in Ontario, individuals that are not found fit to stand trial may receive a conditional discharge that enables the individual to live in the community with specific conditions set out by the Review Board (e.g., live at approved address, maintain psychiatric treatment) (Ontario Review Board, 2011).

### *Determining Criminal Responsibility*

Similar to fitness to stand trial, historically it was assumed that persons with IDD could not appreciate right from wrong or the consequences of their actions and therefore were not to be held responsible for their actions (Baroff et al., 2004; Fitch, 1992). While competency or fitness to stand trial identifies the individual's ability to participate in court proceedings, criminal responsibility looks at whether the person is capable of understanding the nature and quality of the criminal act for which they have been charged (Baroff et al., 2004; Griffiths et al., 2002). Research has demonstrated that most people with IDD are considered criminally responsible for their actions. For example, Petrella (1992) found that 90% of individuals diagnosed with mild intellectual disability and 66% of individuals with a moderate intellectual disability were found criminally responsible for their actions. Jones (2007) suggested that this may account for why there is a higher number of incarcerated persons with mild and borderline IQs and higher detection of persons with IDD (and subsequently greater prevalence of IDD) in forensic inpatient settings.

Previously, individuals (including persons with IDD) who were found not criminally responsible would have been detained indefinitely in a psychiatric facility for public protection. In more recent years, several countries have enacted laws and legislation to protect persons from being detained for longer than the time they would have served had they been incarcerated. For example, the U.S. Supreme Court ruled that a person "committed only on the basis of incompetence could not be held more than 'a reasonable period of time' during which efforts to achieve competency would be pursued" (Baroff et al., 2004, p. 40), whereas the Ontario Review Board in Canada makes provisions for an absolute discharge when the individual is found to no longer be a significant threat to public safety (Ontario Review Board, 2011). When determining whether an individual constitutes a significant threat to the public, the Ontario Review Board will include an assessment of community supports (i.e., social service agency and family) that may contribute to reducing the threat that the individual might pose (Ontario Review Board, 2011). If an individual with IDD is found criminally responsible, it is important to note that the presence of an intellectual or developmental disability can be entered as a mitigating factor during sentencing which may result in a lesser sentence (Baroff et al., 2004). Furthermore, the individual may also be released to the community if there is appropriate community support to assist them (e.g., appropriate residential support, clinical treatment).

Finally, although there may be only a few countries that capital punishment remains a sentencing option for persons with IDD, forensic assessments may still be used to establish whether a person with IDD should be executed. Until the landmark case, *Atkins v. Virginia* (2002), capital punishment of persons with IDD was still an allowable sentence in the United States. In *Atkins v. Virginia* (2002), the US Supreme Court ruled that it was unconstitutional under the eighth amendment (regarding cruel and unusual punishment) to execute a person if they met the criteria for an intellectual disability – that is, they had a low IQ score (i.e., 70 or below), lacked adaptive functioning skills, and there is evidence of the onset of both low IQ and the lack of adaptive skills before the age 18. In 2014, *Hall v. Florida* (2014) further reinforced the importance of looking at adaptive functioning in addition to IQ. In this case, Hall had an IQ of 71 and the court ruled that hard determinations of IQ did not take into account factors such as margins of error in calculating IQ or impairments in adaptive functioning.

## Intellectual and Developmental Disabilities and Risk Assessments

The purpose of most forensic assessments is to establish risk, that is, to predict which individuals are at risk of committing future offenses. These assessments may be used by forensic clinicians to develop effective treatments and interventions to address risk factors and for public protection (Lindsay, Hastings, & Beech, 2011; Lindsay et al., 2009). It is important to note that not all individuals with IDD referred to a forensic unit will receive a risk assessment. Risk assessments may fall into one of two categories – static and dynamic risk variables. While static risk variables are unlikely to change (e.g., offense history), dynamic risk variables are often offense related and responsive to environmental changes (e.g., antisocial attitudes, staff complacency) (Lindsay et al., 2009).

Risk assessments may also include a variety of assessments including actuarial assessments and structured clinical judgment. Research has indicated that clinical judgment alone produces results only slight better than chance (Hanson & Thornton, 1999). As a result, several risk assessments based on reliable predictors of an offense have been developed to increase the accuracy of risk assessment (Hanson & Thornton, 1999). Though these tools were not initially designed to be used with individuals with IDD, a growing body of evidence indicates that these measures can be used effectively with individuals with IDD. Furthermore, some researchers and clinicians have been dissatisfied with the reductive nature of actuarial measures; therefore, assessments that promote structured clinical judgement have been developed that provide a happy medium between clinical judgment and actuarial assessments (Lindsay et al., 2009).

Several researchers have conducted comparative studies of various actuarial measures with persons with IDD and found that these measures can predict risk in persons with IDD with the same consistency as when used with patients without IDD (Gray, Fitzgerald, Taylor, MacCulloch, & Snowden, 2007; Lindsay et al., 2009; Lindsay et al., 2008). For example, Gray and colleagues (2007) compared the predictive efficacy of the Violent Risk Appraisal Guide (VRAG) (Quinsey, Harris, Rice, & Cormier, 2006), the Psychopathy Checklist – Screening Version (PCL-SV) (Hart, Cox, & Hare, 1995), and the HCR-20 Violence Risk Assessment (Webster, Douglas, Eaves, & Hart, 1997) in persons with IDD. They found that these measures were able to predict the risk of violent recidivism and general offending behavior over a 5-year period. In addition, Lindsay and colleagues (2008) compared the predictive validity on the VRAG (Quinsey et al., 2006), HCR-20 (Webster et al., 1997), and the STATIC-99 (Hanson & Thonston, 1999) for male offenders with IDD forensic settings. Similar to Gray and colleagues (2007), they found that the VRAG and HCR-20 had both discriminative and predictive validity for both general and violent reoffending. On the other hand, there is a body of literature that is highly critical of risk assessments in general, calling into question their highly subjective, rather than objective and empirical, nature and false dichotomies of risk and need. Hannah-Moffat (2004), for example, has written extensively about the fluid nature of inmate *needs* (i.e., violence, suicide) being interpreted as *risks*, particularly in the context of female offenders (Hannah-Moffat 2004). Another study pointed to professionals' reliance on assessments as defensible decisions found in pre-sentence reports for youth, for example (Hannah-Moffat & Maurotto 2003).

Risk assessments of sexual offending behavior may also include a phallometric assessment. Phallometric assessment measures physical arousal in the genitals using a penile plethysmograph. Several researchers have questioned the validity of using this method with persons with IDD given the rates of false responses observed in persons with IDD (Laws, 2002; Marshall & Fernandez, 2000; Tudway & Darmoody, 2005). Tudway and Darmoody (2005) suggested that caution be used when considering whether a phallometric assessment should be used and when interpreting the result of a phallometric assessment. They identified that many social influences (e.g., history of restrictive environments and denial of intimate relationships) may also play a significant role in the results produced. In addition, Lindsay and colleagues (2009) identified that there may be a referral bias that has influenced the few studies conducted regarding persons with IDD and phallometric assessment. That is, caregivers are more likely to be sensitive and responsive to indication that an individual is interested in children and youth than individuals interested in adults. In turn, this may create conditions in which a person responds with arousal to sexualized images and differential preferences but does not indicate that the individual will engage in a sexual offense.

## Intellectual and Developmental Disabilities and Forensic Treatments

Some specialized forensic inpatient treatment programs have been developed to address the needs of persons with IDD in forensic inpatient settings (e.g., Alexander et al., 2010); however, for the most part, most jurisdictions do not have specialized units or staff to support and address the needs of persons with IDD in forensic inpatient settings. As a result of this shortcoming, the effectiveness of treatments and interventions for persons with IDD may be limited. This in turn may contribute to the beliefs that persons with IDD are difficult to care for (Lin et al., 2017; Morrissey et al., 2017; Woodbury-Smith et al., 2018).

Adding to the complexity of treatment, considerable research has identified that persons with IDD have high rates of physical aggression while residing in forensic inpatient settings (Hogue et al., 2007; Tenneij, Didden, Stolker, & Koot, 2009). For example, Hogue and colleagues (2007) examined the frequency of externalizing behaviors of persons with IDD in a forensic inpatient setting. They found that persons with IDD engaged in more physical aggression than individuals without IDD. This creates complications for staff, including increased risks of burnout. Dennis and Leach (2007) identified that staff supporting persons with IDD in secure settings had a lower sense of personal accomplishment, higher emotional fatigue, and higher depersonalization – all of which put them at risk of stress and exhaustion. This risk may increase depending on the frequency and intensity of aggressive behavior observed and the amount of training on intellectual and developmental disabilities they received.

As identified by Griffiths and colleagues (2002), the first step in treatment for individuals with IDD in forensic inpatient settings is a complete assessment. This assessment should be different than the one that was conducted while the person was court-involved, which was focused on assessing risk or competency or fitness to stand trial. A good starting point for any forensic professional is a biopsychosocial assessment that determines the biological, psychological, and social factors that contributed to the behavior (see table 1) and ensures that the selected treatment goals match the behaviors and environmental conditions that contributed to the offence happening. As Day (2008) suggested, an offense committed by a person with IDD "occurs in the context of under-socialization, poor internal controls, and faulty social learning compounded by educational underachievement, lack of social and occupational skills, and poor self-concept" (p. 361). Similarly, Hingsburger, Griffiths, and Quinsey (1991) coined the term *counterfeit deviance* to describe the behaviours that appeared to be paraphilic in persons with IDD but that upon proper assessment of the environmental conditions of persons with IDD (e.g., oppressive attitudes towards sexual relationships between persons with IDD) revealed an alternative hypotheses for sexualized behavior.

**Table 1. Sample biopsychosocial factors that may contribute to criminal offenses and that need to be assessed and incorporated into forensic inpatient treatment.**

| Biological | Psychological | Social |
|---|---|---|
| Polypharmacology | History of trauma and abuse | Quality of supervision |
| Substance abuse and addiction | Offense-specific cognitive distortions | Lack of meaningful activities during the day |
| Drug side effects (e.g., orgasmic dysfunction) | Relapse prevention and coping skills | Family and caregiver competency and training |
| Medical illnesses (e.g., sexual transmitted infections, physical pain) | Socio-sexual knowledge and interpersonal skills | Poor access to resources (e.g., poverty) |
| Phenotypic behavior associated with genetic disorders | Executive functioning deficits (e.g., time management) | Access to privacy in the home |

Several forensic treatment programs have been developed for persons with IDD; however, most treatment programs have been researched in community settings. It is possible that these treatment programs could work in a forensic inpatient setting; however, special consideration would have to be given to generalization (i.e., helping the individual with IDD apply the learned skills once they returned to the community). Most treatments follow the *risk-needs-responsivity* model proposed by Bonta and Andrews (2007). The risk-needs-responsivity model emphasizes that treatments for offenders need to match the offender's risk level (risk); target criminogenic needs (needs); and match the offender's style of learning (responsivity) (Andrews, Bonta, & Wormith, 2011).

Several models of treatment have been examined for persons with IDD including applied behavior analysis, cognitive behavior therapy, and psychoeducational training. In addition, treatment has addressed a range of behaviors including anger management (e.g., Taylor, Novaco, Gillmer, & Thorne, 2002; Travis & Sturmey, 2013), cognitive distortions related to offending (Lindsay et al., 2009), and sexual offending (e.g., Singh et al., 2011), and also on teaching new skills (e.g., Burns & Lampraki, 2016). Though there have been several studies regarding several different treatments for persons with IDD, no consistent treatment package has been developed.

Finally, a promising treatment for persons with IDD in a forensic inpatient setting is dialectical behavior therapy (DBT). Dialectical behavior therapy was developed for persons with borderline personality disorder (Linehan, 1993); however, it is increasingly being used with a variety of groups, including persons with IDD. DBT is an intensive intervention that combines individual therapy with group skills training and *in situ* coaching for skills use (Linehan, 1993). The skills training program focuses on teaching participants skills in four core areas: mindfulness, distress tolerance, emotional regulation, and interpersonal skills (Linehan, 1993). Several studies have examined the use of DBT as a treatment for persons with IDD and forensic involvement. For example, Sakdalan, Shaw, and Collier (2010) examined the use of an adapted DBT skills group for persons with IDD and forensic involvement. They found that participants demonstrated improvements in measures of dynamic risk, coping skills, and general functioning. While these results in combination with other research conducted on the use of DBT with persons with IDD in both forensic inpatient units and other hospital settings are encouraging, more research is needed to validate this treatment modality. Several researchers (e.g., Taylor & Morrissey, 2012) identified that more research is required to determine the most effective modifications to the program to make it accessible to persons with IDD.

## Conclusions

To date, more research is required to completely understand persons with IDD in the forensic inpatient system. While there has been some research regarding the prevalence and other characteristics of persons with IDD, there is still far too little known about these individuals. Research has indicated that persons with IDD are capable of being competent or fit to stand trial, and capable of appreciating the nature of their actions at the time of the offense; however, more consideration needs to be given as to why persons with IDD are considerably overrepresented in forensic inpatient systems. At this time, there does not appear to be any research indicating the number of persons with IDD who are referred to a forensic inpatient unit for a fitness or competency assessment. Furthermore, given that research indicates that persons with IDD are more likely to remain within a forensic inpatient setting, it may be imperative to find more community-based forensic treatment programs that provide the required support and supervision required to address the risk that forensic professionals perceive in their assessments.

It is also important to understand the rationale for why persons with IDD are being referred and getting caught in the forensic inpatient system. Several scholars (e.g., Jones, 2007) have questioned whether persons with IDD can be effectively supported within the criminal justice system and have recommended diversion from the criminal justice system to more appropriate outcomes than incarceration when possible; however, both professionals and academics need to ask whether transfer to the forensic inpatient system represents an effective alternative to incarceration. Research has indicated that persons with IDD spend more time in forensic inpatient settings than individuals without an IDD, and diversion to the forensic mental health system risks reinforcing both criminal justice system and psychiatric professional's pathologizing the behaviors observed in persons with intellectual and developmental disability. As

Hingsburger and colleagues (1991) identified when describing counterfeit deviance, there may be several variables contributing to the offense of a person with an IDD that, when addressed properly, may reduce the risk of future offenses or increase the success of the individual within the community that may be outside of the scope of practice for a forensic inpatient setting.

Several actuarial risk assessments have demonstrated discriminative and predictive validity for persons with IDD; however, researchers have identified that risk assessments often include a combination of both actuarial and clinic judgement. This indicates the importance of forensic professionals being trained regarding the care and support of persons with IDD (Lin et al., 2017). As Woodbury-Smith and colleagues (2018) identified, one of the many challenges of addressing the need of persons with IDD who come into contact with the criminal justice system, and subsequently the forensic inpatient system is the limited number of specialists able to support persons with IDD in forensic treatment.

Finally, more research is needed regarding how to effectively treat persons with IDD who have come to the attention of the forensic inpatient system. Several studies suggested that persons with IDD are not housed in a setting that offers more support than what they need. As some researchers identified, this may reflect the lack of appropriate community placements. As suggested by Thomas and colleagues (2004), more community-based programs for persons with IDD are needed to ensure they are better able to access appropriate treatment in the community and not be confined beyond what would be experienced if they were detained in a detention center.

## References

Alexander, R. T., Green, F. N., O'Mahony, B., Gunaratna, I. J., Gangadharan, S. K., & Hoare, S. (2010). Personality disorders in offenders with intellectual disability: A comparison of clinical, forensic and outcome variables and implications for service provision. *Journal of Intellectual Disability Research, 54*(7), 650-658.

American Association on Intellectual and Developmental Disabilities (AAIDD). (2018). *Frequently asked questions on intellectual disability.* Retrieved from: https://aaidd.org/intellectual-disability/definition/faqs-on-intellectual-disability#.WvUattMvwcg

American Psychiatric Association. (2013). *Diagnostic and statistical manual of mental disorders* (5th ed.). Arlington, VA: Author.

Andrews, D. A., Bonta, J., & Wormith, J. S. (2011). The risk-need-responsivity (RNR) model: Does adding the good lives model contribute to effective crime prevention? *Criminal Justice and Behavior, 38*(7), 735-755.

Atkins v. Virginia. (2002). 536 U.S. 304, 122 S. Ct. 2242, 153 L. Ed. 2d 335.

Baroff, G. S., Gunn, M., & Hayes, S. (2004). Legal issues. In W. L. Lindsay, J. L. Taylor, & P. Sturmey (Eds.), *Offenders with Developmental Disabilities* (pp. 37 – 65). Hoboken, NJ: John Wiley & Sons, Ltd.

Bettridge, S., & Barbaree, H. (2008). *The forensic mental health system in Ontario: An information guide.* Retrieved from: https://www.camh.ca/-/media/files/guides-and-publications/forensic-guide-en.pdf

Bonta, J., & Andrews, D. A. (2007, June). Risk-need-responsivity model for offender assessment and rehabilitation. Retrieved from: http://www.courtinnovation.org/

sites/default/files/documents/RNRModelForOffenderAssessmentAndRehabilitation.pdf

Burns, J., & Lampraki, A. (2016). Coping with stress: The experiences of service-users with intellectual disabilities in forensic services. *Journal of Intellectual Disabilities and Offending Behaviour, 7*(2), 75-83.

Butwell, M., Jamieson, E., Leese, M., & Taylor, P. (2000). Trends in special (high-security) hospitals: 2: Residency and discharge episodes, 1986–1995. *The British Journal of Psychiatry, 176*(3), 260-265.

Craig, L. A., Stringer, I., & Hutchinson, R. B. (2017). Assessing mental capacity and fitness to plead in offenders with intellectual disabilities: Implications for practice. In K. D. Browne, A. R. Beech, L. A. Craig, & S. Chou (Eds.), *Assessments in forensic practice: A handbook* (pp. 172 – 197). Hoboken, NJ: Wiley Publishing.

Day, K. (2008). Treatment and care of mentally retarded offenders. In a. Do En & K. Day, *Treating mental illness and behavior disorder in children and adults with mental retardation* (pp. 359-390). Washington, DC: American Psychiatric Association Publishing.

Dennis, A. M., & Leach, C. (2007). Expressed emotion and burnout: The experience of staff caring for men with learning disability and psychosis in a medium secure setting. *Journal of Psychiatric and Mental Health Nursing, 14*(3), 267-276.

Everington, C., & Dunn, C. (1995). A second validation study of the Competence Assessment for Standing Trial for Defendants with Mental Retardation (CAST-MR). *Criminal Justice and Behavior, 22*(1), 44-59.

Everington, C. T., & Luckasson, R. (1992). Competence assessment for standing trial for defendants with mental retardation. *Worthington, OH: IDS.*

Fedoroff, J. P., Griffiths, D., Marini, Z., & Richards, D. (2000). One of our clients has been arrested for sexual assault: Now what?—The interplay between developmental and legal delay. In *Bridging the Gap—Proceedings 17th Annual NADD Conference. Kingston* (pp. 153-160).

Fitch, W. L. (1992). Mental retardation and criminal responsibility. In R. W. Conley, R. Luckasson, & G. N. Bouthilet (Eds.) *The criminal justice system and mental retardation* (pp. 121 – 136). Baltimore, MD: Paul H. Brookes.

Glaser, W., & Florio, D. (2004). Beyond specialist programmes: A study of the needs of offenders with intellectual disability requiring psychiatric attention. *Journal of Intellectual Disability Research, 48*(6), 591-602.

Gralton, E., James, A., & Crocombe, J. (2000). The diagnosis of schizophrenia in the borderline learning-disabled forensic population: Six case-reports. *The Journal of Forensic Psychiatry, 11*(1), 185-197.

Gray, N. S., Fitzgerald, S., Taylor, J., MacCulloch, M. J., & Snowden, R. J. (2007). Predicting future reconviction in offenders with intellectual disabilities: The predictive efficacy of VRAG, PCL-SV, and the HCR-20. *Psychological Assessment, 19*(4), 474-479.

Griffiths, D. M., Taillon-Wasmund, P., & Smith, D. (2002). Offenders who have a developmentally disability. In D. M. Griffiths, C. Stavrakaki, & J. Summers (Eds.), *Dual diagnosis: An introduction to the mental health needs of persons with developmental disabilities* (pp. 387 – 418). Sudbury, Canada: Habilitative Mental Health Resource Network.

*Hall v. Florida.* (2014). 134 S. Ct. 1986, 2004 & n.5.

Hannah-Moffat, K. (2004). Gendering risks at what cost: Negotiations of gender and risk in canadian women's prisons. *Feminism & Psychology. 14*(2), 243- 249.

Hannah-Moffat, K., & Maurutto, P. (2003). *Youth risk-need assessment: An overview of issues and practices.* Ottawa, Canada: Department of Justice Canada.

Hanson, R. K., & Thornton, D. (1999). *Static 99: Improving actuarial risk assessments for sex offenders* (Vol. 2). Ottawa, Ontario: Solicitor General Canada.

Hart, S. D., Cox, D. N., & Hare, R. D. (1995). *Hare psychopathy checklist: Screening version (PCL: SV).* Multi-Heath Systems.

Heerema, M. (2005). An introduction to the mental health court movement and its status in Canada. *Criminal Law Quarterly, 50*(3), 255–282.

Hingsburger, D., Griffiths, D., & Quinsey, V. (1991). Detecting counterfeit deviance: Differentiating sexual deviance from sexual inappropriateness. *The Habilitative Mental Healthcare Newsletter, 10*(9), 51-54.

Hogue, T. E., Mooney, P., Morrissey, C., Steptoe, L., Johnston, S., Lindsay, W. R., & Taylor, J. (2007). Emotional and behavioural problems in offenders with intellectual disability: Comparative data from three forensic services. *Journal of Intellectual Disability Research, 51*(10), 778-785.

James, D. V., Duffield, G., Blizard, R., & Hamilton, L. W. (2001). Fitness to plead. A prospective study of the inter-relationships between expert opinion, legal criteria and specific symptomatology. *Psychological Medicine, 31*(1), 139-150.

Jones, J. (2007). Persons with intellectual disabilities in the criminal justice system: review of issues. *International Journal of Offender Therapy and Comparative Criminology, 51*(6), 723-733.

Laws, D. R. (2002). Penile plethysmography: Will we ever get it right? In T. Ward, D. R. Laws, & S. H. Hudson (Eds.), *Theories and controversial issues in sexual deviance* (pp. 82-102). Thousand Oaks, CA: Sage.

Lin, E., Barbaree, H., Selick, A., Ham, E., Wilton, A. S., & Lunsky, Y. (2017). Intellectual and developmental disabilities and Ontario's forensic impatient system: A population-based cohort study. *Psychology, Crime, & Law, 23,* 914 – 926.

Lindsay, W., & Ansari, D. (2019). The challenges of managing offenders with intellectual and developmental disabilities through secure and community service pathways. *The Wiley International Handbook of Correctional Psychology* (pp. 159-168). Hoboken, NJ: Wiley Publishing.

Lindsay, W. R., Hastings, R. P., & Beech, A. R. (2011). Forensic research in offenders with intellectual & developmental disabilities 1: Prevalence and risk assessment. *Psychology, Crime, & Law, 17,* 3-7.

Lindsay, W. R., Hogue, T. E., Taylor, J. L., Steptoe, L., Mooney, P., O'Brien, G., ... & Smith, A. H. (2008). Risk assessment in offenders with intellectual disability: A comparison across three levels of security. *International Journal of Offender Therapy and Comparative Criminology, 52*(1), 90-111.

Lindsay, W., Holland, A., Taylor, J., Michie, A., Bambrick, M., O'Brien, G.,...Wheller, J. (2009). Diagnostic information and adversity in childhood for offenders with learning disabilities referred to and accepted into forensic services. *Advances in Mental Health and Learning Disabilities, 3*(4), 19-24.

Lindsay, W. R., van Logten, A., Didden, R., Steptoe, L., Taylor, J. & Hogue, T. E. (2017). The validity of two diagnostic systems for personality disorder in people with intellectual disabilities: A short report. *Journal of Intellectual Disabilities and Offending Behavior, 8*(3). pp. 104-110.

Linehan, M. (1993). *Skills training manual for treating borderline personality disorder* (Vol. 29). New York, NY: Guilford Press.

Lunsky, Y., Gracey, C., Koegl, C., Bradley, E., Durbin, J., & Raina, P. (2011). The clinical profile and service needs of psychiatric inpatients with intellectual disabilities and forensic involvement. *Psychology, Crime, & Law, 17*, 9-23.

Männynsalo, L., Putkonen, H., Lindberg, N., & Kotilainen, I. (2009). Forensic psychiatric perspective on criminality associated with intellectual disability: A nationwide register-based study. *Journal of Intellectual Disability Research, 53*(3), 279-288.

Marshall, W. L., & Fernandez, Y. M. (2000). Phallometric testing with sexual offenders: Limits to its value. *Clinical Psychology Review, 20*, 807-822.

Maulik, P. K., Mascarenhas, M. N., Mathers, C. D., Dua, T., & Saxena, S. (2011). Prevalence of intellectual disability: A meta-analysis of population-based studies. *Research in Developmental Disabilities, 32*(2), 419–436.

Morrissey, C., Langdon, P., Beach, N., Chester, V., Ferriter, M., Lindsay, W., ... & Alexander, R. (2017). A systematic review and synthesis of outcome domains for use within forensic services for people with intellectual disabilities. *BJPsych Open, 3*(1), 41-56.

Murphy, G. (2015). *People with learning disabilities and offending behaviours: Prevalence, treatment, risk assessment and services.* Retrieved from: https://www.kent.ac.uk/tizard/resources/forensicldservices.pdf

Ontario Review Board. (2011, February 25). *About us.* Retrieved from: http://www.orb.on.ca/scripts/en/about.asp

Palucka, A. M., Raina, P., Liu, S. K., & Lunsky, Y. (2012). The clinical profiles of forensic inpatients with intellectual disabilities in a specialized unit. *Journal of Learning Disabilities and Offending Behaviour, 3*(4), 219-227.

Parekh, R. (2018). *What is mental illness?* Retrieved from: https://www.psychiatry.org/patients-families/what-is-mental-illness

Petrella, R. C. (1992). Defendants with mental retardation in the forensic services system. In R. W. Conley, R. Luckasson, & G. N. Bouthilet (Eds.) *The criminal justice system and mental retardation* (pp. 79 – 96). Baltimore, MD: Paul H. Brookes.

Puri, B.K., Lekh S.K., Treasaden I.A. (2000). A comparison of patients admitted to two medium secure units, one for those of normal intelligence and one for those with learning disability. *International Journal of Clinical Practice, 54*(5), 300-305.

Quinsey, V. L., Harris, G. T., Rice, M. E., & Cormier, C. A. (2006). *The law and public policy. Violent offenders: Appraising and managing risk (2nd ed.).* Washington, DC, US: American Psychological Association.

*R. v. Demers.* (2004). 2 S.C.R. 489, 2004 SCC 46

Raina, P., & Lunsky, Y. (2010). A comparison study of adults with intellectual disability and psychiatric disorder with and without forensic involvement. *Research in Developmental Disabilities, 31*(1), 218-223.

Reed, S., Russell, A., Xenitidis, K., & Murphy, D.G.M. (2004). People with learning disabilities in a low secure in-patient unit: Comparison of offenders and non-offenders. *British Journal of Psychiatry, 185*, 499-504.

Roesch, R., Zapf, P.A., & Eaves, D. (2006). *FIT-R: Fitness Interview Test-Revised. A structured interview for assessing competency to sand trial.* Sarasota, FL, US: Professional Resource Press/Professional Resource Exchange.

Sakdalan, J. A., & Egan, V. (2014). Fitness to stand trial in New Zealand: Different factors associated with fitness to stand trial between mentally disordered and intellectually disabled defendants in the New Zealand criminal justice system. *Psychiatry, Psychology and Law, 21*(5), 658-668.

Sakdalan, J. A., Shaw, J., & Collier, V. (2010). Staying in the here-and-now: A pilot study on the use of dialectical behaviour therapy group skills training for forensic clients with intellectual disability. *Journal of Intellectual Disability Research, 54*(6), 568-572.

Singh, N. N., Lancioni, G. E., Winton, A. S., Singh, A. N., Adkins, A. D., & Singh, J. (2011). Can adult offenders with intellectual disabilities use mindfulness-based procedures to control their deviant sexual arousal?. *Psychology, Crime & Law, 17*(2), 165-179.

Stinson, J. D., & Robbins, S. B. (2014). Characteristics of people with intellectual disabilities in a secure US forensic hospital. *Journal of Mental Health Research in Intellectual Disabilities, 7*(4), 337-358.

Taylor, J., & Morrissey, C. (2012). Integrating treatment for offenders with an intellectual disability and personality disorder. *The British Journal of Forensic Practice, 14*(4), 302-315.

Taylor, J. L., Novaco, R. W., Gillmer, B., & Thorne, I. (2002). Cognitive–behavioural treatment of anger intensity among offenders with intellectual disabilities. *Journal of Applied Research in Intellectual Disabilities, 15*(2), 151-165.

Tenneij, N. H., Didden, R., Stolker, J. J., & Koot, H. M. (2009). Markers for aggression in inpatient treatment facilities for adults with mild to borderline intellectual disability. *Research in Developmental Disabilities, 30*(6), 1248-1257.

Thomas, S. D., Dolan, M., Johnston, S., Middleton, H., Harty, M. A., Carlisle, J., ... & Jones, P. (2004). Defining the needs of patients with intellectual disabilities in the high security psychiatric hospitals in England. *Journal of Intellectual Disability Research, 48*(6), 603-610.

Travis, R.W., & Sturmey, P. (2013). Using behavioural skills training to treat aggression in adults with mild intellectual disability in a forensic setting. *Journal of Applied Research in Intellectual Disabilities, 26*(5), 481-488.

Tudway, J. A., & Darmoody, M. (2005). Clinical assessment of adult sexual offenders with learning disabilities. *Journal of Sexual Aggression, 11*(3), 277-288.

Walker, N., & McCabe, S. (1973). *New solutions and new problems.* Edinburgh, United Kingstom: Edinburgh University Press.

Webster, C. D., Douglas, K. S., Eaves, D., & Hart, S. D. (1997). *HCR-20: Assessing risk for violence (version 2).* Burnaby, BC: Mental Health, Law, and Policy Institute, Simon Fraser University.

Woodbury-Smith, M., Furimsky, I., & Chaimowitz, G. (2018). Point prevalence of adults with intellectual developmental disorder in forensic psychiatric inpatient services inOntario, Canada. *International Journal of Risk and Recovery, 1*(1), 4 – 11.

World Health Organization. (2018). *International statistical classification of diseases and related health problems* (11th Revision). Retrieved from https://icd.who.int/browse11/l-m/en

*Chapter 5*

# Bridging the Gap in the Criminal Justice System for Persons with Intellectual Disabilities: A Model Program

*Mark Pathak, John Clarke & Stephanie Ioannou*

### Introduction

Throughout the world, people with an intellectual disability present challenges to legal jurisdictions. The readiness of the criminal justice system (CJS) to deal with both criminal acts committed against, and by, people with an intellectual disability is an important subject at a time when concerns regarding crime and disorder, the justice system, and social inclusion feature prominently in governments' agendas. Often people with intellectual disabilities, who come into contact with the criminal justice system, fall through the cracks of service because the unique needs of this population are not often understood well enough to provide appropriate supports and accommodations for them to have an equitable opportunity to ensure justice is served.

In the province of Ontario, Canada, some non-profit organizations offer court diversion programs for individual's with mental health challenges and intellectual disability who have committed a crime. These programs aim to steer these individuals away from the criminal justice system and into treatment within the mental health system (Canadian Mental Health Association, 2018; Cota, 2018). However, if an individual is not able to access these programs (i.e waitlists, severity of crimes) or is ineligible because they are a witness or victim, we are not aware of any structured programs that provide appropriate supports and accomodations once individuals with intellectual disabilities have made contact with the criminal justice system. This chapter reflects the experiences with one such program in the United Kingdom, including how issues with the current system were identified and brought to the forefront, and, consequently, how the program was developed and applied in practice. Although this is a slightly different theme from other chapters in the book, it can certainly be compared to Chapter 3 on court accommodations.

In this chapter, we will review the background of the Liverpool Model of Witness Support and Preparation (the Liverpool Program), a model situated within the English and Welsh Criminal Justice System. We will demonstrate, by sharing recommended practice, that it is possible to make the criminal justice system accessible and responsive to people with an intellectual disability and the ways in which this can be achieved by describing the program's development.

## Background

In 1996, when the Liverpool Program first began its work on a large-scale joint police and social services criminal investigation, there was very little information about the disadvantageous treatment of people with an intellectual disability. The research that was available suggested that:
1. Crimes are committed but never reported:
    - Do not consider the alleged action as a crime.
    - Tell a figure of authority who then takes it no further.
2. Once at the Police station, **Police Officers** said:
    - Only 35% have had any training about intellectual disability (Only 26% of these thought it was any good).
    - 71% said the training they had received was not helpful.
3. To prosecute or not to prosecute:
    - Every year there are 1400 cases of sexual abuse against people with an intellectual disability
    - Of 248 cases, only 63 were investigated, 2 went to court (less than 1%), with only 1 conviction (0.4%)
    - Crown Prosecution Service relies on the police to assess a person's abilities.
4. **Barristers (Crowns)** said:
    - 96% did not receive initial training on intellectual disability and only 8% had received such training since qualifying at the bar.
    - 90% saw the benefits of court preparation prior to trial.
    - 76% thought individuals with intellectual disabilities could be reliable witnesses.

In 1997, Andrew Saunders highlighted some of the problems faced by people with an intellectual disability when giving evidence; these included "memory: recalling information, particularly detail, can often be difficult for people with learning disabilities[1]" (p.7). Later he noted, "another problem is that of language. Some witnesses with learning disabilities have good memories of events, but have difficulty putting these into words. Similarly, some witnesses with learning disabilities have difficulty in understanding what they are being asked" (Saunders, 1997, p. 7). His research noted that very few of the witnesses had "effective pre-trial preparation" and that the "most successful pre-trial preparation took place when the particular weakness/concern of the victim-witness was identified and acted upon" (Saunders, 1997, p. 50).

When introducing a bill that later resulted in the *Youth Justice and Criminal Evidence Act* (1999) in England and Wales, Lord Williams of Mostyn (Great Britain Parliament, House of Lords, 1998) stated to the House of Lords that:

---

[1]Learning disability is the term used in the United Kingdom to describe individuals with intellectual or developmental disabilities.

> Too many cases involving the most vulnerable victims have been abandoned, or not even begun, because the victim cannot adequately give his side of the story ... the system has been focused too much on the criminal trials and not sufficiently on the needs and decent requirements of witnesses as complainants.

Later, the *Youth Justice and Criminal Evidence Act* (1999) introduced special measures that were potentially available to vulnerable witnesses in the UK. These special measures included the use of screens to shield the witness from the view of the defendant (s.23), giving evidence to the court from a separate room by a live-link (s.24), clearing the court and giving evidence in private (in sexual cases and cases involving possible intimidation) (s.25), having the judge and both barristers remove their wigs and gowns (s.26), provision of evidence in chief to be video-recorded and played in court (evidence in chief) (s.27), allowing video-recorded cross-examination (where evidence in chief is so recorded) (s.28), providing examination by barristers and judges through an intermediary (available to young/incapacitated and vulnerable witnesses [as defined by s. 16]) (s.29), and providing aids to communication given to witness (available only to vulnerable witnesses (as defined by S. 16)) (s.30). Furthermore, sections 34 to 38 of the special measures provisions for vulnerable and intimidated witnesses protects witnesses in certain cases from cross-examination by the accused in person, section 41 restricts the evidence and questions about the complainant's sexual behavior, and section 46 restricts the reporting by the media of information likely to lead to the identification of certain adult witnesses in criminal proceedings. (Ministry of Justice, 2011b).

Following adoption of *The Youth Justice and Criminal Evidence Act* (1999), a framework for implementation was developed, including a timetable and a series of comprehensive guidance documents. These documents included practice guidance for child witnesses, pre-trial therapy, training for persons in the criminal justice system regarding recognizing capability for vulnerable or intimidated witnesses, and guidance for achieving best evidence in criminal proceedings. The premise of this recognition was that:

> Early identification of the individual abilities as well as disabilities of each vulnerable adult is important in order to guide subsequent planning. An exclusive emphasis upon disability ignores the strengths and positive abilities that a vulnerable individual possesses. Vulnerable witnesses may have had social experiences that could have implications for the investigation and any subsequent court proceedings. For example, if the vulnerable adult has spent a long time in an institutional environment, they may have learned to be compliant or acquiescent. However, such characteristics are not universal and can be ameliorated through appropriate preparation and the use of Special Measures." (Ministry of Justice, 2011b, p. 5)

Furthermore, in order to establish best practice, several recommendations were made that were aimed primarily at police officers that focused on identifying learning disabilities: planning and conducting interviews with vulnerable and intimidated witnesses, which centred around issues of acquiescence and compliance; as well as advice on witness support and preparation including issues of accommodation.

Lastly, the *Vulnerable Witnesses: A Police Service Guide* (Ministry of Justice, 2011a) was the first tool to provide police with a series of prompts to help them identify vulnerable witnesses at the interview stage. This guide draws police officers' attention to common misconceptions (e.g., that people often confuse the terms *mental illness/health* and *intellectual disability/learning disability*) in addition to an appendix of common (medical) conditions which could affect a person's communication. Whilst intended only as a guide, these prompts remind police officers that the features making a witness vulnerable will be particular to that individual and that potential witnesses may have more than one area of vulnerability.

It is with these foundational documents and expectations in place that the Liverpool Model of Witness Support and Preparation emerged.

## Our Starting Point – The Liverpool Model of Witness Support and Preparation

This chapter is based on actual experiences – we are not offering educated guesses or pious hopes; it's not hypothetical or speculative, but concrete. We will offer a model of service that has been repeatedly employed to assist some vulnerable victims of serious crimes to give evidence to the best of their ability. The following recommendations are based on our experience with 71 witnesses in 51 trials (including retrials) that involved 45 prosecutions and 39 convictions. In all 51 trials, special measures were provided to assist the courts; the first 18 the special measures were using judicial discretion.

The power of this model is that it has allowed the development of a tri-partite protocol between the Crown Prosecution Services, Police and Liverpool City Council Investigation Support Unit, that has resulted in 3 acquittals, 2 accepted pleas, and one finding of guilty but of a lesser charge in 6 trials for persons with intellectual disabilities who were defendants.

## Preparation of Witnesses with an Intellectual Disability

In our experience, the police and *Crown Court Witness Support Services* took the view that adequate witness preparation simply requires a single visit to a court and a 30-minute talk with the Crown Court Witness Support Service about what may happen once they enter the courtroom. While this may have worked well for witnesses who do not have an intellectual disability, it tended to disadvantage individuals with intellectual disabilities because it presented too much new information, in too short a time, and in a way that was not suited to their learning styles. Changing the status quo – by focusing on thorough witness preparation - created shifts in perception and expectation, including those of the police and Crown Court Witness Support Service. Ultimately, all services developed an understanding of the learning capabilities of each individual witness, in each individual trial. They learned that people with intellectual disabilities are not a homogenous group, that they are as individual as you and I. Therefore, all parties have realized that the preparation process with one witness will be different from that with another.

Preparation work has two distinct elements: preparing the witness and preparing the court and its personnel. It will be revealed that these two areas overlap and reinforce each other. On the whole, witness preparation covers a range of information, understanding, and skills that a witness needs to absorb. While much of the process may be common to every witness, some unique processes will occur for each individual witness. On the one hand, some distinct pieces of work will occur to reflect the individual's personality and learning style; while on the other hand, pieces of work will appear because of processes within the criminal justice system. For example, the trial planning process may introduce the need for previously unconsidered pieces of work such as psychiatric and/or psychological assessments on behalf of the prosecution or defense, or re-interviewing by the investigating police officer.

Clearly an understanding of the purpose, process, and nature of the criminal justice system is needed by a witness with learning disabilities. When preparing the witness, the preparer may need to consider questions such as: "how much information do others need to know?" "what do people need to understand and learn?" and "when do they need to learn it?" While all witnesses are different, our practice has been shaped by the following "Rules of Thumb."

## Our 5 Rules of Thumb.

### 1. Individuals with an Intellectual Disability Need to Know What to Expect in Court and What Is Going to Happen to Them

A witness feels reassured if their support needs and any special measures are identified early on in the preparation process. For example, witnesses have checked out that one of us will be allowed to sit next to them in court as they are giving their evidence or that the court personnel will know that they cannot read.

### 2. Individuals with an Intellectual Disability Learn Best When They Need to

Preparation gathers pace when the proceedings have reached the committal stage of proceedings. This means that the case will go to Crown Court for trial. At this stage, any learning should focus on the fact that the person will soon be going to Crown Court. Furthermore, events are becoming real as opposed to hypothetical and should be talked as such (i.e., time scales).

### 3. Individuals with an Intellectual Disability Learn Best When They Are Taught in the Place Where the Knowledge Will Be Used

Only so much information can be given in the abstract, e.g. "when the Barrister (Crown) stands in front of you," "remember to talk to the judge/jury when you answer questions." Maps and plastic models may prove helpful with other witnesses in orientating them in the courtroom, but we have learned that for some of the witnesses we have prepared, this information is best understood "in reality." As they walk around the courtroom, stand in the witness box, see where the barristers, judge, and judge/jury sit, the experience is concrete, and the learning is therefore relevant.

### 4. Witnesses with an Intellectual Disability Absorb and internalize Information Best When It Is Offered and Taught by Credible Professionals.

Traditionally, intellectual disability services have tried to do everything themselves instead of getting other, more appropriate people involved – so residential workers, not financial advisors, have offered advice about financial management; or day staff, not career advisors, offer advice about daytime occupation. The list is endless. In all our trial work we give priority to the witness meeting with the different personnel involved with the trial, so that the roles associated with the people concerned are made clear to the witness. For example, witnesses know they have to take an oath, so the most appropriate person to demonstrate this part of the trial in England and Wales is the Court Usher. We encourage the Usher to let the witness practice saying the oath frequently. The gains from this practice include helping the Court Usher understand some of the needs of the witness, such as understanding how quickly or slowly to administer the oath. This increases the likelihood that this stage of the process will be familiar and straightforward when this is done "on the day of," and both the Usher and witness are prepared in the wider sense.

### 5. Witnesses with an Intellectual Disability Have Lives Alongside and Beyond Their Court Preparation and Appearance in Court

A witness's forthcoming court appearance can take over their lives. So, we have tried to ensure that services and careers continue to support the service user in their daily lives and routines. Life outside of the preparation process and after any trial has to be recognized, promoted and valued, as it is to this that the witness will return when the trial is over.

These five "rules of thumb" contain some important lessons for those involved in preparation work. Although various books, videos, and replica courtrooms have been produced to aid witnesses with intellectual disabilities prepare for court, in our experience, it is only when, the witnesses enter "their" courtroom does everything seem to make sense.

## The Eleven Stages of Witness Support, Preparation, and Court Report Work

### Stage One - Early Post Referral Information

This stage involves obtaining some basic information from the witness about their lifestyle such as their family background and who provides their primary support, what services they have received in the past, and current and anticipated services.

A lot of the background information may not come from the client but from the referring agency. In some rare instances, very little information has been provided by the referring agency and we have had to depend on the witness for some pieces of information. This has also been the case when the referral has been made by the family of the witness.

At this stage, it is also vitally important that our partner agencies know about the referral. Depending on whom the referrer is, we check, and record, that the police investigating officer, the Crown Prosecution caseworker and lawyer, and, if allocated, the witness's local authority social worker or health authority named health care worker all know of our involvement. It is not unusual for such personnel never to have heard of us or indeed the service we offer. In the days following a referral, it is not unusual for us to meet up with staff from the different agencies to explain or remind them of our role.

### Stage Two – Setting the Scene for Our Work.

The focus of stage two is on establishing a relationship with the witness. On most occasions this has been when we first meet the witness. If this has been the case, then a brief explanation of the work is given to the witness (in front of their main carer if appropriate). Included in this stage is making clear the boundaries of the preparation work, i.e. it will not include any discussion of the evidence – that is for the judge/judge/jury to hear and not the preparer. However, it may include areas such as any residual feeling left from the police investigation or contact, for example, "was I right to tell the police?" and "no-one has really told me what will happen next."

It is important at this stage that some ground rules about how to maintain a normal life outside the preparation are established with the witness and other significant people in their lives. Maintaining a normal life by doing their everyday things will have a major influence on how they cope with the demands of being a witness and how successfully they continue their life after the trial.

Issues of safety may also need to be discussed here. It may also be that the impact of the alleged crime is such that the witness may benefit from counselling to deal with this. It has been possible for witnesses to receive cognitive counselling, without jeopardizing their evidence or indeed the fairness of the trial.

The preparer must consider carefully where the bulk of their one-to-one work with the witness will occur. Generally, the work will be undertaken in a fairly quiet and private setting, interspersed with the occasional more social setting such as in a coffee bar or a walk around a park. It should be noted that generally, one-to-one work has never been done in the witness's home.

At the end of this meeting we also ask if there are any immediate questions from the witness or carer involving our work or indeed about the whole process of engaging with the criminal justice process. It is not unusual for the response of "I'll answer that in a few weeks" to be given.

It is not uncommon for non-local authority or community health services to confuse other disabilities with an intellectual disability. If the person meets the criteria for receiving our service (i.e. they have an intellectual disability and will meet the criteria of s.16 of the *Youth Justice and Criminal Evidence Act* (YEAR) (that they have a severe impairment of social functioning) then the work begins.

## *Stage Three – How the Person Got to Be Referred to Us*

We begin this stage by reminding individuals how they arrived at their present position. Witnesses may be asked to recall police interviews and any other meetings about the complaint which they may have attended *without* telling us their evidence. Defendants are asked their memories of any interviews and meetings with their legal representatives. Again, the evidence is not discussed. We track events and meetings up to and including their meeting with us. The witness is reminded that the aim of all the contacts they have had with the police, any court personnel, and even ourself is based on the fact that they are going to be a witness in court and give evidence.

This stage also takes account of the witness's early preconceptions about going to court and who they will meet in the courtroom. Discussions about having to give their evidence in court, feeling scared in the courtroom, and what to do about worried relatives and paid professionals need to be acknowledged and dealt with at an appropriate point in the process.

## Stage Four – Baseline Assessment of Understanding and Knowledge

During this stage the preparer should assess the witness's early understanding of the trial process. Topics include exploring the process of a trial and the witness's part in it. More precise details about the roles of courtroom personnel, how long the appearance in court is likely to last, and some early acknowledgement of what may be included in the court report will take place towards the end of this stage. Typically, witness's knowledge of court proceedings has been gleaned from television programs and cinema films. Witnesses often have an expectation of American style courtroom behaviors and expect that their experience in court to be far more dramatic then it may eventually be.

Sometimes at this stage witnesses have begun to tell other people about our involvement and the work we have started. Because of this and the possible disclosure of evidence to other people, witnesses have to be reminded that they should not discuss their evidence with anyone else.

## Stage Five – Correcting Expectations

Of all the stages we describe, it is this stage which we spend the longest in. Only once the preparer is fully satisfied that they understand what the witness thinks to expect in the courtroom can this stage begin. Stage five involves correcting their understanding of the personnel's jobs and roles as well as focusing on some of the witness's expectations of courtroom behavior.

Whilst usually being satisfied with our explanation of what will happen in court, on a few rare occasions some witnesses have taken strength from the drawing up of a different set of rules – "court rules."

Typically, these involve politeness in court, being patient in court, asking for help, or taking turns when talking. While many of these "rules" have been common to each of our witnesses, some unusual ones have been discussed. One witness found great strength from the rule of safety—"no one will hit you;" whereas, another witness found reassurance from a rule about being comfortable—"you can go to the toilet whenever you want to." Finally, another witness had feared arguments between the two barristers – and took comfort in the fact the judge's "rules" do not allow barristers to argue with each other.

Before we move onto the next stage, some extra observations about the work involved at these early stages can be made. In addition to verbal discussions, a lot of the learning and correcting can be reinforced using various visual aids and verbal exercises that are tailored to suit an individual's learning style. Often such sessions are repeated when necessary and eventually can be referred back to when necessary—"do you remember when we talked about asking for a break?"

All of our witnesses have also met the preparer's line manager during these early meetings, so witnesses have a clear understanding that the preparer is not working alone and is accountable to a "boss." In our experience, this has been an important piece of information for all witnesses and should never be ignored. It is an opportunity to give a human face to our process, to ensure that the witness has met an individual they can complain to if they are unhappy with anything done or said, and to be reassured that any such complaint will be taken seriously and dealt with. It also sets the pattern for the witness's introduction to all the other players in the criminal justice system, whose roles and responsibilities they will have to understand. The "boss" becomes a name and a person, "the barrister" later becomes a name and a person, and so on for everybody they will eventually meet.

It is also important to note that during these early stages all contact is non-courtroom. In the interest of effective preparation, we would advise preparers not to rush to visit the courtroom setting, meet the court staff, or practice taking the oath at this stage. Witnesses, carers, and some professionals may wish to jump to these points immediately. The preparer should carefully and methodically work through each stage and focus their work on "building up" the witness's understanding and experience slowly.

### *Stage Six – Early Introductory Visits to the Crown Court Building.*

Stage six includes early general visits to the court building. Usually this does not involve going inside courtrooms and certainly does not include observing actual trials in progress. General introductions to The Crown Court Witness Support Service staff occur with references made to having a "proper chat" later on.

Visits to the Crown Court building usually begin very informally before gradually becoming more focused on the personnel and courtroom procedure. Visits to the court building can start off with an apparently impromptu but really planned detour making a two-minute visit on the pretext of dropping off a letter or delivering a message. This is simply to get the witness across the threshold of an imposing, intimidating, and official building. Wandering around the whole building is very helpful in eliminating fears about the size of the building, by making it more familiar and understanding its layout (e.g. where the lifts, restaurants, and restrooms are).

### *Stage Seven – Establishing Links with Court-Based Personnel and Reinforcing the Messages from Stage Five*

While the previous stages require mainly verbal and illustrative approaches (e.g. standing a certain distance from the witness and saying, "the judge will be this close to you"), this stage involves the first physical experience of some information presented in stage five (i.e., showing the person the building where those people we have talked about work).

Stage seven establishes visits to Witness Support Services and a repetition of the explanation already offered in stage five of the roles of courtroom personnel and their respective jobs but this time by the Crown Court Witness Services (of Liverpool Crown Court).

In many ways, this stage is a "real" example of understanding our rule of thumb number four. Some messages are best delivered and reinforced by people who are seen to be part of the criminal justice process (i.e., they are the first living part of the trial process that a witness may encounter).

For the preparation to be experienced by the witness as steady, controlled, and natural, a great deal of work behind the scenes is essential. For example, for the witness to practice saying the oath with the usher in an empty courtroom a good deal of planning, negotiation, and some "script writing" may be required. Usually discussion takes place between the preparer and other court staff prior to a visit. On most occasions, the preparer plans how the visit will happen and what will be said. For example, when preparing one witness who was particularly distressed at the thought of appearing in court, the court usher was told that a series of three visits would be needed regarding his role in court. Such a series of visits were made easier by asking the Crown Court Witness Preparation Service to contact the usher and advise him how and why we planned the series of visits. The first was to accidentally bump into the usher while having a cup of tea in the cafeteria. He joined us briefly and discussed general matters before casually being introduced to the witness as the usher for their trial. He was primed to invite the witness to his court when we were ready to visit "his" courtroom (stage eight). In stage eight, the usher was then able to offer the appropriate support.

Knowing various personnel by their first names has proved crucial for witnesses with intellectual disabilities as the trial date approaches. As a way of maintaining focus, we have found it very helpful, while on an informal visit to the witness's home, to say to the individual, "Paul, the court clerk, says hello. Do you remember him?" What this does is to gently remind the witness that they will be going to court and that people are waiting there to help and support them.

Ultimately, the preparer will need to use the court visits to allow the witness to concentrate on a single focused learning objective. For example, we may identify the purpose of one visit as addressing "telling the truth;": if the witness does not know the answer to a particular question, they should say so and not guess at an answer. Often witnesses may be asked a question about the preparer's personal life that they would not know the answer to. The preparer identifies the best person to convey this particular message and briefs this person about the witness and suggest ways in which they may talk to the witness in a way that the witness will grasp. We frequently involved the Crown Court Witness Support Service Co-ordinator in this task.

After each visit the witness may need a lot of reminders about the important learning point. Once again, reminding the witness about particular things said by different court staff has helped them to recall facts when we have repeated the words of others in a non-court building setting. We have found it helpful to encourage the witness to be actively and creatively involved in the solutions to problems – rather than being the source of them. For instance, during a series of visits to the court building one particular witness would always sit in the meeting room with their head down when they talked. "The problem" we all worked on was not seen as a fault of the witness per se, but instead we approached it as it being a difficulty for the judge/jury. We suggested to the witness that they could help the judge/jury to do their job by raising their head when talking in the courtroom, so they could be heard. This worked; the witness gave their evidence clearly and audibly with their head up. During the preparation of another witness, a lot of time was spent encouraging a very softly spoken witness to raise the volume of their voice so the judge/jury would be able to hear their evidence. Ultimately, we realized that what was a problem for the court, audibility in this case, was being turned into a problem for the witness (i.e. volume). The solution was simple: To apply to the court for an amplification device for use during the trial.

We are surprised by the things witnesses report having gained strength from. Many of these have involved artifacts that have enabled the witness to feel supported by "the system" in that it was given to them by someone involved in "the system." In one trial, the manager of the local Crown Court Witness service gave the witness a semi-precious stone. On every subsequent visit to the court, even if just for a cup of tea in the restaurant with the preparer, this stone was carried. In addition, the witness held it as she gave her evidence. By far the most powerful artifact has been a copy of the oath written in large letters. Witnesses have carried this around in handbags and pockets and often produced it to signal that they knew the trial date was approaching. Another witness set up a "court file" that contained only a copy of the oath and a newspaper cutting about the manager of the Crown Court Witness Service. He brought this file to every one-to-one meeting he had with his preparer. In many ways, having something tangible from the court seemed to focus the witness mentally on the preparation work. If someone other than the preparer offers this artifact it reasserts our service principle that "we are working in a system with other people who want to help you."

## Stage Eight – Visiting the Courtroom and Taking the Oath

Stage eight involves two separate pieces of work occurring simultaneously:

i) Visits to the actual building cover tasks such as visiting the actual courtroom in which the witness will have to give their evidence, relating to the usher in that setting, and dealing with any new anxieties it may produce.

ii) The preparer and witness will rehearse the witness taking the stand and the oath and discuss how the witness feels so far. While the preparer should by now have a clearer assessment of what, if any, new skills the witness may need to develop, such as dealing with being confused and upset while giving evidence. There may still be some problems which only become apparent at this stage.

One person cannot adequately cover all the information that a potential witness requires, but one person should guide the process of delivering the information to ensure accuracy, pace, and reinforcement. There are some "messages" and pieces of vital information which are heard better when delivered by other people. For example, whenever issues of safety have been raised, we have tried to get the investigating police officer to talk to the witness. In addition, the court usher is the best person to assert the importance of telling the truth and to reassure the individual that it is fine to get upset in the courtroom, because of their association with the oath and the courtroom. Furthermore, if questions are asked about the oath later in the preparation process, we can respond "remember what Phil, the usher, said?" While this is occasionally enough to calm some of the witness's nerves and to remind them of what they have learnt, it may also signal the need for further visits and meetings with key court personnel to reinforce the message.

One particular witness we worked with seemed to get stuck at this point. We knew the witness would be distressed, and she was simply encouraged to "let it all out." During the second visit to her courtroom she became upset again. When this happened, the usher stepped in and talked about it being all right to get upset in court. On the third visit, the usher was able to get the witness to focus on saying the oath. By this stage the usher also demonstrated some understanding of the witness's needs and level of understanding.

Visits to the court room also allowed for some other unusual pieces of preparation work to be done according to the needs of the client. For example, the wearing of "court appearance clothes" by all for one of the final visits allowed for the individual to feel familiar. In most cases the penultimate visit to the vulnerable person was arranged as an impromptu activity. "You know what? I'm fed up of going to the court building and talking about court. Do you fancy a cup of tea in the local park instead?"

## *Stage Nine – Visits to Actual Trials*

Stage nine involves visits to actual trials in "their" courtroom, with "their" usher and in front of "their" judge.

These observation visits show *in situ* what being in court and giving evidence may be like – that a witness gets upset and is reassured, or a witness misunderstands a question and has to have it repeated. Our witnesses often compare their expectations of themselves giving evidence (particularly taking the oath) with what they see in front of them and will reflect on this, occasionally making comments such as "he said the oath too quickly" or "she didn't look at the judge/jury." Both preparer and witness regularly leave the observed court with a list of relevant comments or questions created by the experience of being in the courtroom. All of this confirms how well the witness has understood and assimilated the preparation process and if there are any parts of the preparation process that still need re-visiting.

A few days before the trial begins, all the planning work should have been done and a final relaxed pre-trial visit is made, with absolutely no task-agenda planned. This is quite simply a way of saying, with the witness, "we're ready."

## *Stage Ten – The Trial*

This is the day that all the work has been geared towards ensuring the witness is fully prepared. By now we would have many hours of preparation and some hours in court with barristers trying to get things ready for the actual trial day. Yet problems still arise. There may be delays on the day that were not foreseen at previous pre-trial reviews. The non-availability of a judge/jury, legal arguments, newly produced evidence that needs to be submitted. There is one other area that needs to be commented on – the emotions of the carers and family members. In our experience, they seem to be more nervous than the witnesses on the day of giving evidence.

Most witnesses have been scared about cross-examination but have seemed to manage well. Furthermore, they have worked to understand that once we walk into the courtroom, we are not allowed to say anything. They have also been told in advance that we are not allowed to discuss any part of the evidence and that we are only allowed to remind them of the procedures. In addition, we have also discussed beforehand that during any breaks, when alone, we are not allowed to answer the question from them of "am I doing okay?"

Breaks in evidence giving or cross-examination when we are alone with the witnesses are also interesting. Most witnesses have preferred to go home immediately after they have given their evidence. One witness however, who was the victim of a rather vicious rape, after giving his evidence was invited by the judge to remain in the courtroom. This individual sat next to the preparer listening to the testimony of the victimizer and muttered, "that's not true, that's not right." Sadly, the witness was not present later when the defendant was sentenced to nine years in jail. In most cases, few have wanted to know what the defendant said in their evidence; however, all have wanted to know the outcome of the trial. In the cases when there has been a conviction, all witnesses have been relieved; however, all have felt the sentence handed down by the court has been too lenient. In those few cases involving defendants, when there has been an acquittal, individuals with intellectual disabilities have been quite optimistic. While one witness told us "there was not enough evidence to prove it was them," another said, quite remarkably, "when you go to court you do not get what you want, you get the law."

## *Stage Eleven – Closure Work*

From the moment our work with a witness starts, we acknowledge that the day will come when we no longer see each other. Yet there are definite things that need to be covered in order for us to end the work.

Because of their poor literacy skills, none of our witnesses have been able to apply for compensation from *The Criminal Injuries Compensation Board* on their own. In some cases, carers or staff have offered to fill in the form on their behalf; other clients have not wanted their supporters to fill in the form as it means they would have to divulge fuller details of the incident, and, therefore, they wanted the Court Support Program to fill the form in. Occasionally, this event is also a symbolic act that has signified the end of our contact. For other individuals who were abused while in services run by agencies, we have recommended a number of legal firms who are experienced in offering advice about the possibilities of pursuing civil action.

In addition, there are other important visits that need to happen. We always go back to the Witness Services in the Crown Court to say "goodbye." We always walk up to the courtroom and say "goodbye" to it. As we walk away from the court building, we always turn around, look back at the huge building, and say "goodbye."

The whole process of saying goodbye is, in our opinion, vital to help people move on and put the reason why they needed to attend court into some form of perspective. Throughout the preparation process we stress the need for people to maintain their lifestyles. Witnesses are encouraged to keep attending their day centers, their evening clubs, and their trips out with support workers in order to reduce the impact of their involvement in the criminal justice system as much as is possible. Witnesses have found it quite easy to maintain their normal program of activities. We know that once our involvement with them ceases, it is to this lifestyle they return. In our opinion, being a witness in a trial should not be too interruptive or a life changing experience.

One rewarding part of the "closure" stage of work for us is when we reminisce with witnesses about how much people have changed through the process. We often remind them of how quiet and timid they may have been during our first meeting, how they may have been initially too scared to even walk into the Crown Court building, and how perhaps they could not say the oath because they were too nervous.

Despite all the preparation work involved in the eleven stages described previously, witnesses report a variety of emotions during the preparation work. They may get upset, angry, confused, or alarmed. Early in the whole process, time is invested developing awareness and understanding of how individual witnesses react to being nervous, frustrated or bewildered. No two witnesses have had the same needs or have absorbed information in a uniform manner. Even with the eleven stages of preparation, there have been some areas of work that we are never able to fully deal with. For example, concerns about being nervous or the fear of getting upset have often remained throughout all stages and during the trial. We consider it important to share with witnesses the ways we ourselves show our nervousness or anxiety. For example, Mark asks a witness if they have noted his stutter and then points it out every time it happens which seems to allow the topic of being nervous to be discussed. It gives the opportunity for him to enquire about the witness's feelings (e.g., "I've noticed that your leg is bouncing. Does that mean you are as nervous as me?"). There have been times when a witness has asked Mark if nerves were causing him to stutter. They went on to remind him that he had nothing to worry about and that it was okay to be nervous. This demonstrates how useful it is to acknowledge when and how such emotions occur and how they can be recognized and then dealt with.

By now the preparer should have a very clear idea of what pieces of information should be included in the final version of The Court Report (see below). The report is a summary of all the preparation work done and, as such, will reflect the skills, abilities, anxieties, foibles, and disabilities of the witness as they *now* are – at the end of the preparation process. This is because one aspect of the court report is to identify personal styles and characteristics, their meaning to the individual, and ways to encourage the witness to give off their best.

At closure, every person we have worked with has said the same thing – that they would have no hesitation about making a complaint in the future and would be willing to give evidence in court again if they needed to – but only with our support.

## The Court Report

The purpose of the court report must accord with our overall purpose in offering a support and preparation service to vulnerable individuals. This is, individuals with intellectual disabilities should be enabled to speak with their own voice and be heard. To that end, the specific purpose of the court report is to secure a fair trial by advising the court what to expect, identifying and explaining the need for any "Additional Measures to Assist" including "Special Measures" as under the *Youth Justice and Criminal Evidence Act* (1999; in England and Wales), removing or reducing obstacles to giving best evidence, and offering to judges and barristers clear advice and instructions on what they should do to help the person give best evidence.

Essentially every report will be different because vulnerable witnesses and defendants differ from each other. One strength of the court report is its ability to challenge the homogeneous approach which mental age at least in part, endorses. For one witness, it would be easy to regard them as a 7-year-old child, but it is worth bearing in mind that an adult with the mental age equivalency of 7-years-old may travel alone into the city center in the evening to attend a social function. However, they may also need a support worker to help them buy groceries (because they have a poor understanding of money) and successfully keep and care for a pet such as tropical fish. Furthermore, given that no one in court will have a mental age equivalency above that of a young adult, how helpful is this metric in determining any adult's competence? The report is an outline of the individual needs as a witness – specifically and uniquely. It is therefore not a social history, nor a clinical assessment tool. It deals only with those matters relevant to this witness's likely behavior and performance when participating in the criminal justice process.

There are definite links between the preparation process and the process of drafting a report. Sometimes as the preparation process is carried out, the preparer may identify a problem for the witness, which might need to be dealt with as an issue in the report. In our experience, the recognition of a possible problem early on has allowed us the opportunity and time to help the witness develop the skills to overcome that particular problem in some cases, so that it no longer requires much attention when the final draft of the report is completed.

The court report is only as good as the preparation process itself. There have been occasions in which important stakeholders in the process, (e.g., the CPS) have thought that all that was needed to get the person with an intellectual disability into court was a court report. It is not a magic wand; the court report is quite simply the tip of the iceberg of support and preparation work. After some of the informality of the preparation process, writing the report reminds both the witness/defendant and preparer that the trial is in fact a very serious affair. An understanding by all parties involved in the criminal justice system of how witness preparation and court preparation dovetail into production of the report is essential.

## The Court Report Matrix

The 12 sub-headings of the Court Report Matrix (see figure 1) are the result of the many changes in emphasis when preparing court reports. Our first court report arose because we were in a meeting with a barrister, and it was important to the team that the barrister understood how the witness would present when they gave their evidence. Each subsequent court report has been a development on its predecessor; and the number of sub-headings has slowly increased from an initial five, fairly global sub-headings, to the twelve more specific ones we have today. We consider that our current list of 12 sub-headings are presented in the sequence most suited to the criminal justice system. Yet we are mindful, that the form and content of a court report should continue to develop and change if it is to be flexible enough to reflect the individuality of the witness's it is meant to report.

**Figure 1. The 12 sub-headings found in the court report matrix. In Canada, special measures are referred to as "Testimonial Aids."**

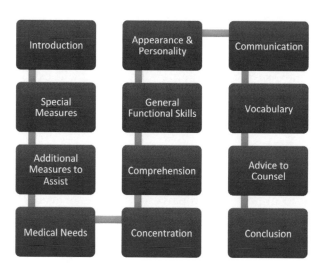

The court report is designed to provide a witness or defendant with intellectual disabilities the opportunity to speak for themselves and be heard. Advice to counsel is broken into two parts relating to when asking questions and when receiving a response:

i) *When asking (the witness's name) questions* – Does Counsel need to establish a rapport with the witness or can questioning begin immediately? Does Counsel need to explain the process of questioning i.e. taking turns. Does Counsel need to give permission to the witness to use certain words? Are there any non-verbal behaviors Counsel should avoid? (e.g., looking down at papers while the witness answers). If Counsel should wish to interrupt the witness's answer, how should this be done to avoid either silencing the person completely or provoking an irritable outburst?

ii) *When (the witness's name) answers* – How can the witness indicate that a particular question has not been understood given that, in our experience, witnesses are extremely reluctant to say, "I don't understand?" Can the witness say they disagree with an assumption made by Counsel? Are they able to say "I don't know" or will they avoid this in order not to appear foolish? Does the witness have a particular cognitive process or behavior pattern they go through in order to be able to give their answer?

In one case, we noted in the court report that it would be more appropriate to ask the individual questions based on events rather than dates and ages and then gave some examples. In the trial, the witness stated that the offences occurred in the middle of the night. At this point the judge intervened and asked the witness what *middle of the night* meant. After careful questioning, the judge was able to establish that the witness meant just after the second showing of the "big news" on BBC1 (UK TV media channel). In this case middle of the night meant 9.00 p.m. and not much later.

While many of the sub-headings have appeared in all of our reports, no two reports have been the same. Each witness has had different specific needs and the selection of sub-headings in our reports have reflected this. For each witness, there has usually been one sub-heading of greater significance than others and which particular sub-heading this is varies from witness to witness.

In sum, the focus of the court report is about identifying the barriers for the witness to give their best evidence and to devise strategies for removing or reducing them. These barriers may need to be removed by the individual or by the court. For example, in one case we were preparing, someone who sometimes used phrases such as "do you know what I mean?" and "you know, all that business" when replying to questions. If the barrister had indicated "yes," even non-verbally, after any of these phrases, this witness would simply have stopped talking. As far as this witness was concerned, if someone in court indicated that they understood what s/he meant to say then there was no need to say anything else.

## Who Does the Court Report?

The unique contribution to work with vulnerable witnesses, which our approach can make, is in the area of change. Social work intervention is about change, social workers are commonly referred to in professional parlance as "change agents," and social work practice is about promoting and adapting to change, both systemic and individual (Ginwright & James, 2002). Therefore, the role of the social worker in preparing the court report is not that of expert witness within a narrow range of expertise, but one of helping the witness to cope with a new and daunting experience by using a range of resources, while at the same time encouraging the criminal justice process to adapt to the needs of the witness in the interests of justice and as part of the promotion of citizenship rights. We regard the witness as a witness and not as a clinical specimen to be categorised by psychological tests of I.Q. or mental age. The court needs to know specifically and in detail how to deal with individuals with intellectual disabilities as a witness: their ability, potential, and shortcomings in that particular context. This will determine the relevance or otherwise of the information the court receives.

## What Is the Process of Preparing a Court Report?

The process of preparing a report is rooted in the belief that people with intellectual disabilities can learn new skills and become more competent at using the skills they already possess.

During the preparation process we explain to the witness that a report will be submitted to the court, and we explain its use. In our experience, once this has been shared with the witness, they are keen to take part – "does the judge know I cannot read or write?" or "they do know I get my numbers mixed up, don't they?" It is important that the witness knows what is going into the report and that they know who will see it. We are confident that every piece of information we have put into a report has been agreed upon by the witness.

Preparing a report takes a lot of time. We make notes throughout the preparation process which forms the basis of the court report, and it can be broken down into a series of clear stages. We have found it helpful to ask ourselves whenever we are with the potential witness, "is this relevant to being a witness?" or "is this likely to occur in court?" and "does the court need to know this?" If the answer to these is yes, then the information has been put into the report. Therefore, information about a witness's concern about a forthcoming holiday has been omitted, but information about the same witness's mother being ill in hospital has been included because this had an impact on them, as a witness.

Direct conversation and observation are equally valuable when working with people. It is important that the person acting as the preparer never stops listening to and talking with the potential witness. Sometimes when we have been supporting and preparing someone with learning disabilities they have, in the early stages of preparation, said that they felt okay about a particular topic under discussion, but their non-verbal communication has indicated clearly that they were confused and uncomfortable. Clearly when this happens, time has been spent on this, clarifying what is causing confusion. It is important that before the preparer moves on to the next topic of discussion or explanation the witness understands, to some extent, what was discussed or explained in the current discussion or explanation.

What Information Goes into a Court Report?

Generally, the court reports attempt to answer some of the questions we believe that Counsel would have regarding an individual's credibility as a witness. Such questions revolve around the issues of competence, reliability, and the ability of the witness, when appearing in court, to repeat their previously given testimony. Table 1 presents an example of information included in a court report.

## Table 1. Court Report Matrix and Examples

| | |
|---|---|
| **Introduction** - This section offers some basic information about the witness. It always describes how the witness lives - what they do during their day, the level of support they have, and their daily living skills and needs. It always states that the witness has an intellectual disability. | Anna has an intellectual disability and considerable attendant emotional needs. Anna dislikes the label "intellectual disability" and all matters connected with it. She prefers to use the term "having special needs" to describe herself and wishes others to do likewise. |
| **Special Measures** – These measures are detailed in Sections 23-30 of the Youth Justice and Criminal Evidence Act 1999. This section of the report details why the request is being made and explains how a particular measure would assist the witness to give "Best Evidence." | Anna has a fixed belief that if she sees the accused he will be able to enter her home and hurt her. Because of her concrete cognitive processes, she cannot be reassured in this regard. If she sees the accused, she is likely to be quite distressed and possibly unable to give her evidence in a way that does justice to herself. I recommend, therefore, that screens be provided to assist this vulnerable witness. |
| **Additional Measures to Assist** - This section deals with the need for any other additional forms of assistance, which the court could offer, to achieve Best Evidence without in any way compromising the defendant's right to a fair trial. | Preparer should sit next to Anna when she is giving her evidence. The use of some form of amplification system in the court would be of great assistance to her. A lot of time and energy has been devoted over the years in trying to increase the volume of her voice, but it remains exceptionally quiet. Not making an issue of this but simply providing amplification will greatly improve her confidence. |
| **Medical needs** – This section describes any medical needs which may affect the witness's ability to give evidence. | Anna has severe pre-menstrual tension and is going through menopause. When suffering from PMT she gets angry, calls people names, is irritable, and generally refuses to do anything. However, the period of pre-menstrual tension should have finished by the time she is due in court, and she regularly takes Oil of Primrose to help her. |
| **Appearance and Personality** – This section considers aspects of the witness's appearance or personality which may impinge on them giving their evidence. For example, do they get embarrassed? How do they show embarrassment? What should be done to minimise this? | Anna may keep her head down when talking and will need to be reminded to keep her head up and talk to the judge/jury. She may cough on a repeated basis. She tends to use this when she is uncomfortable in her environment. If she should start to cough, one should check out initially if she needs any water and then politely ignore it. She is a very respectful person and responds very well to respect shown to her |
| **General functional skills** – This section describes the witness's everyday living skills. Can they read and write? Can they count? Do they have a good grasp of time – including weeks, months and years? Can they use public transportation or manage their own money? This section is particularly important because it addresses some of the concerns which have in the past been crudely scooped up in the simple concept of Mental Age. | Anna finds the interconnection between years and numbers confusing. She can put things in a temporal context by relating them to concrete experiences of significance to her. |
| **Comprehension** – This examines how the witness understands what is happening to them and their part in it. How well do they understand what is going on around them? How well do they understand questions? What question form or question content is going to present problems for the witness? | Anna interprets or understands words which have a similar structure as meaning the same. For example, "a compliment" may be interpreted as "a complaint" and hence her reaction to and use of some words may be surprising to others. Her understanding of issues is without ambiguity, regardless of circumstance. It is either yes or no, with no maybes. There are some simple words which in combinations may confuse her, for example, not-guilty. |

| | |
|---|---|
| **Concentration** – This section addresses a number of issues around concentration – general ability, span, distractibility, refocusing. How long can the witness concentrate? Can they apply this concentration when required? What factors affect their ability to concentrate? If the witness needs a short break, will they be able to say so themselves or will someone else have to look out for indicators or signs of this? | *Anna cannot recognize when she loses her concentration. When she loses concentration or becomes confused she will lean her head to one side, drop her lower jaw a fraction, and gaze through you - as if saying with her eyes "what are you saying." A further indication of reduced concentration involves Anna in rubbing her eye, fidgeting, stroking her forearms (cuts and scars), or smoothing her fringe.* |
| **Communication** - This section looks at how and how well the witness can communicate. Are any physical aids required? Is their style of communication particularly slow, slurred, staccato, or monosyllabic? Do they have any particular non-verbal behaviors which are used in place of verbal responses or to expand or illustrate verbal responses? | *Anna will be very embarrassed about using sexual words and may blush and giggle nervously when asked to talk about intimate matters. Simply acknowledge that she is embarrassed and continue with the line of questioning. Having used the words a few times, her confidence should return.* |
| **Vocabulary** – This section examines how well the witness uses words to communicate. Are there any particular phrases or sayings they use which have particular significance for them? How well does the witness cope with using words essential to the trial? For example, sexual words? | *Certain phrases have significance for Anna and she may object to their use. She prefers the expression "of an age" to "adult." Should she object, an alternative expression should be sought.* |
| **Advice to Counsel** - This section offers advice to Counsel on how best to approach the particular vulnerable person. It advises how to reduce and avoid such difficulties or how best to confront them. It offers clues and cues for Counsel's greater understanding of this particular witness or defendant and suggests how the clues and cues can be used to enable them to give best evidence. | ***When asking questions:*** *When people use professional jargon, Anna will be unable to follow it. She has a strong desire to appear to understand what is going on around her. She finds it difficult to say that she cannot understand what is being said or being asked of her. She would rather give an inappropriate response than nothing. If this happens then simply asking her "do you understand"? will allow her to say no and questions can then be re-phrased.* <br> ***When answering questions:*** *If Anna feels uneasy with the subject matter she may well say "I'll tell you later" as a way of closing the issue down. If this should happen gently reminding her that it is safe to reply should be of assistance.* |
| **Conclusion** | *Include a brief summary of all key points in the report* |

## Addendums to the Report

While the aforementioned sub-heading forms the basis of the court report, there can be other sub-headings included which are specific to the particular witness. For one witness who had profound hearing loss we introduced (within *Medical Needs*) a section on *"Guidance Related to his Hearing"*.

Actual Liverpool Crown Court report examples:

- *Paul's hearing aid amplifies all sound indiscriminately to the same volume. Therefore, a door opening will be heard as loudly as a cough and as loudly as the voice of the person speaking to him.*
- *Some sounds distract Paul more than others. By far the most distracting sound to him is papers being shuffled.*

When the finished report is submitted to the trial judge and both sets of counsel, we always present the information using a series of "bullet points:" single focused pieces of information, which are precise and punchy.

Colleagues from other agencies in the criminal justice process have sometimes seemed to fear that we were wanting to change and challenge the whole process of attending court and giving evidence. We remain clear in our aspirations. We were not "Tilting at Windmills." We want the system to recognise and accommodate witnesses with intellectual disabilities and other forms of disability, without compromising a defendant's rights, so that what takes place is, in fact, a fair trial.

## The Liverpool Program Influenced a Shift in Paradigm

Not only did this program make huge steps in how people with intellectual disabilities were treated in practice within the criminal justice system, but it also represents a major shift in paradigm in how we are approaching persons with intellectual disabilities in the justice system. The creation of this program got people thinking and recognizing that there is in fact a problem and that there are ways to address the problem. It shone light on an issue that was previously accepted 'as the way it is' and was attributed to a person's intellectual disability rather than the greater systemic issues in failing to support and accommodate. It pushed the bar from 'we've always done it this way' to 'how we need to do it better.' One way that the Liverpool program influenced not only a shift in paradigm but in practice was through the application of this program on an international level through a pilot project in Ontario, Canada.

Application to Other Jurisdictions: Ontario, Canada Pilot Introduction of the Liverpool Program

In 2011, the Central East Networks of Specialized Care (CENSC) in Ontario Canada released their annual report and it indicated that:

1) 251 of CENSC clients were at risk of having an interaction with the criminal justice system

2) 24 of CENSC clients had been referred by either the police or the justice system

3) 136 of CENSC clients required legal assistance

4) 372 people were referred to the CENSC and 40% of the referrals required justice support

The data from the CENSC was clear: the individuals who were referred to their service required specialized support when they had interactions with the criminal justice system. When support services were reviewed in the region it became evident that we did not have the level of expertise that was available in the UK program. It was also evident that the court system itself was not equipped to support people who have been diagnosed with an intellectual disability and who required legal support. For these reasons, a pilot project using the UK model was started (Marinos, Griffiths, Fergus, Stromski, & Rondeau, 2014).

The Ontario pilot project made one adjustment to the overall program – it incorporated applied behavior analysis (ABA) in conjunction with a biopsychosocial approach to understanding offending behavior. Applied behavior analysis is a scientific approach to understanding the function of behavior and then using scientifically proven techniques to help increase socially acceptable behaviors. Cooper, Heron, and Heward (2007) described applied behavior analysis as a "…scientific approach for discovering environmental variables that reliably influence socially significant behaviour and for developing a technology of behavior change that takes practical advantage of those discoveries" (p. 3). The biopsychosocial model is defined as a "case formulation approach that includes consideration of the possible effects of multiple biomedical and psychological factors on the occurrence and reoccurrence of challenging behaviours." (Griffiths, Stavrakaki & Summers, 2002, p. 606). By incorporating these approaches, we not only establish a better understanding of the function of the behavior and how we may increase a socially significant behavior, we also understand the complete person and how their experiences and circumstances shape who they are.

To illustrate how these approaches can be applied in a courtroom setting, let's look at how a person who has been diagnosed with an intellectual disability may be better understood before they enter the court process. This individual has been known to hit their head aggressively to the point that they will bleed. It is important to understand the function (or why) they are hitting their head. Our ABA approach would lead us to understand that this person hits their head to escape stressful or unwanted situations. An evidence-based intervention would be used to help teach the person socially acceptable behaviors when faced with stressful or unwanted situations. The biopsychosocial model would then allow us to understand the person's medical, psychological, and environmental history, which would give us better insight on what approach to teach and when and where to teach it. In our example, it turns out that the person was involved in violent situations when the police were present. This is valuable information to know since it informs our decision to teach our intervention with police present before the person enters the courtroom. This is because the person may have been taught how to successfully handle the stress of the courtroom, but they would also need additional training to know how to use their techniques in the presence of the police. We would have missed this, and the behaviors would have returned in the courtroom, and we would have not known why.

Due to funding issues the Ontario Pilot was put on hold. It should be noted that in the early stages of the pilot we found some of the same barriers as the UK project. We found that some justice system staff did not think people who have been diagnosed with an intellectual disability could be credible witnesses. We also found that people with intellectual disabilities were afraid to participate in the court process. Finally, we found the court process itself was still not completely ready to handle the elements required to ensure a quality testimony from a person who had been diagnosed with an intellectual disability.

This should not be seen as a project that did not in fact have merit. During the time of the pilot we were able to discover an appetite for what the program was trying to accomplish. There was uptake from support staff, there was enthusiasm within the Networks of Specialized Care, and finally there was support from Legal Aid Ontario. The province of Ontario continues to work to ensure equity within its processes, and this pilot certainly began to help shape some potential changes for those who have been diagnosed with an intellectual disability.

## Conclusion

The beginning of this chapter outlined experiences in the UK court system that helped to identify problems with how persons with intellectual disabilities were treated in the criminal justice system. Consequently, this led to the creation of the Liverpool program. It was identified that adequate court preparation is more than a 30-minute talk with the Crown Court Witness Support Service; therefore, we outlined five rules of thumb for preparing witnesses and defendants. Next, we provided detailed information on the eleven stages of witness support and preparation, which identify key pieces of information that should be included in the court report. The five key points to remember for the court report are: (i) it is the individual witness who shapes the report, not vice versa, (ii) the purpose of the report is to change or affect the criminal justice system, with a particular reference to the assumptions held, (iii) the report, when drafted, is a distillation of the support and preparation process, not an end to itself, (iv) the best person to produce the court report is the person who does the preparation work, and (v) the process is dynamic and the report is a 'living' piece of work that develops as the person responds to being a witness/defendant.

The Liverpool program described in this chapter reflects experiences implementing a program designed to support and accommodate individuals with intellectual disabilities in the criminal justice system. The development of this program represents an important shift in paradigm for how we approach persons with intellectual disabilities within the criminal justice system: persons with intellectual disabilities have unique needs and lived experiences that need to be recognized and supported to ensure they have fair and equitable opportunities for justice.

## References

Canadian Mental Health Association. (2018). *Justice services*. Retrieved from https://ontario.cmha.ca/documents/justice-services/

Central East Networks of Specialized Care (CENSC). (2011). *Annual Report*. Toronto, ON: Central East Networks of Specialized Care.

Cooper, J. O., Heron, T. E., & Heward, W. L. (2007). *Applied behavior analysis* (2nd ed.). Upper Saddle River, NJ: Pearson Education Inc.

Cota. (2018). *Mental health court support*. Retrieved from http://www.cotainspires.ca/content.php?doc=657

Ginwright, S., & James, T. (2002). From assets to agents of change: Social justice, organizing, and youth development. *New directions for youth development, 2002*(96), 27-46

Great Britain Parliament, House of Lords, (1998). *The parliamentary debates (Hansard): House of Lords official report*. London: H.M. Stationery Office.

Griffiths, D., Stavrakaki, C., & Summers, J. (Eds.) (2002). *Dual diagnosis: An introduction to the mental health needs of persons with developmental disabilities*. Sudbury, ON: Habilitative Mental Health Resource Network.

Marinos, V., Griffiths, D., Fergus, C., Stromski, S., & Rondeau, K. (2014). Victims and witnesses with intellectual disability in the criminal justice system. *Criminal Justice Quarterly*. 517-30.

Ministry of Justice. (2011a, March). *Vulnerable and intimidated witnesses: A police service guide*. Retrieved from: https://so-fi.org/wp-content/uploads/vulnerable-intimidated-witnesses.pdf

Ministry of Justice. (2011b, March). *Achieving best evidence in criminal proceedings: Guidance on interviewing victims and witnesses, and guidance on using special measures*. Retrieved from: https://www.cps.gov.uk/sites/default/files/documents/legal_guidance/best_evidence_in_criminal_proceedings.pdf

Royal Society for Mental Handicapped Children and Adults (1997). *Barriers to justice: A MENCAP study into how the criminal justice system treats people with learning disabilities.* London, UK: Royal Society for Mentally Handicapped Children and Adults.

Saunders, A. (1997). *Victims with learning disabilities: Negotiating the criminal justice system* (Occasional Paper 17). Oxford, UK: Centre for Criminology Research, Oxford University.

*Youth Justice and Criminal Evidence Act*, c. 23 (1999).

# Part III:

## Supporting Individuals with IDD Who Have Offended in the Community

*Chapter 6*

# The Dignity of Risk and Culture of Care: Community Risk Assessment and Management for Offenders with Intellectual Disabilities

*Jessica Jones, Rebekah Ranger & Paul Fedoroff*

## Introduction

As individuals with intellectual disabilities (ID) are given more choices and opportunities to become autonomous citizens within their own communities, they are also exposed to new experiences and sometimes risky situations that may exploit their vulnerabilities. With this move to social inclusion, a new ethical dilemma has been identified regarding the dignity of risk for persons with ID. Perske (1972) proposed the term *dignity of risk* to reflect the right of an individual with ID to take risks when engaging in life experiences and the right to fail in taking these.

The following chapter will review the above definition in the current context of the lives of individuals with ID, followed by a discussion of mainstream risk assessment and how it is applied to persons with ID. We then suggest that with valid and reliable risk assessment measures for this population a comprehensive picture of an individual's level of risk and mitigating factors can be identified. Further, it is proposed that the *culture of care* or tolerance of risk of the service system that supports the individual will also influence the level of autonomy and consequences imposed in the management of the offender with ID. Thus, it is argued that community risk assessment and management for individuals with ID can be improved with a balanced framework that accounts for not only an accurate measure of risk for the person with ID and their caregiver environment but also addresses the care philosophy and risk threshold of the supporting agency. This culture of care can directly influence an individual's risk of recidivism based on an agency's principles of supporting autonomy and their perceived responsibility in mitigating risk.

## Dignity of Risk for Persons with ID

The balance of allowing an individual with ID to make autonomous choices comes with the acknowledgement of possible consequences, good and bad, as well as recognition of the freedom to make poor decisions. This is because autonomy includes the right to be wrong. The decision to advocate for autonomy is generally made with the presumption that an individual is their own decision maker and has the capacity to make informed choices when given the appropriate information. In cases of individuals with ID, the added challenge of intellectual capacity issues, and the associated need to find an alternative decision maker (e.g. next of kin), that can act in *the best interest* of the individual, further complicates the picture of self-determination and individual rights.

Given that an individual with ID is presumed competent to make their own decisions, the question remains as to how much should caregivers and agencies intervene in these decisions. Presuming the individual with ID is able to understand the nature, seriousness, and consequences of their actions, to what degree should caregivers and agencies that support an individual with ID mitigate the risk imposed while allowing for respect and dignity of the person themselves? Ideally, caregivers can assist individuals with ID to appraise the risk and benefits of their planned decisions and actions. Thus, for offenders with ID, issues of capacity and competence concerning decision-making cannot be presumed. By the nature of having an intellectual disability, it is highly likely that at some time in their life, individuals with ID will receive external support or supervision in the decisions that they make.

Herein lies the premise of Perske's *dignity of risk* and the contemporary challenge of risk assessment and management of supporting individuals with ID in the community. He argues that in denying individuals with ID exposure to appropriate and reasonable risks commensurate with their functioning, there is an increased risk of a deleterious effect on their dignity, personal development, and perspectives by others (Perske, 1972).

In most jurisdictions, legislation and social policies outline the requirement for support agencies to optimize an individual's well-being and quality of life while protecting their right to make autonomous decisions. This responsibility includes the right to make mistakes and receive the consequences without bias, including individuals with ID who are exhibiting high-risk behaviors and require external guidance by caregivers and staff in managing the risks incurred. Put simply, the overarching dichotomy attempts to balance how much to protect individuals from the consequences of their high-risk behaviors and how much to protect their autonomy and allow them to learn from the consequences.

## Prevalence of Offenders with ID

Following the closure of institutions for individuals with disabilities, the prevalence of offenders with ID in the community has been a common query by policy makers and researchers alike. Previous literature has revealed a wide prevalence, ranging from 0.5 – 10%, depending on the definitions used, settings studied, and the methodologies utilized (Fazel, Xenitidis, & Powell, 2008; Jones, 2007; Lindsay, Hastings, Griffiths & Hayes, 2007; Noble & Conley, 1992; Petersilia, 2000). Researchers have argued that prevalence studies are highly influenced by the environment in which they take place (Day, 1994; Hogue et al., 2006). Earlier work has highlighted that methodology has a direct impact on prevalence rates as studies either utilized case reviews or prospective methods, both of which can influence the reliability and validity of information (MacEachron, 1979; Mason & Murphy, 2002; McCord, McCord & Zola, 1959; Walker & McCabe, 1973).

Research definitions and terminology have had a significant impact on studies. Many studies include participants with "low average" intelligence (i.e., IQ score of 80 – 90; Farrington et al., 2006; Lindsay, Hastings & Beail, 2013), which is a group that is well represented in the criminal justice system, but which is diagnostically different from offenders with ID (Hayes & McIlwain, 1988; Holland, 1991; Murphy, Harrold, Carey & Mulrooney, 2000). Other studies have questioned whether there is a true overrepresentation of offenders with ID in legal settings (Crocker, Cote, Toupin & St.-Onge, 2007) due to the inclusion of participants with "borderline intellectual functioning" (i.e., IQ score of 70 – 75; Fedoroff, Richards, Ranger, & Curry, 2015; Gray, Fitzgerald, Taylor, MacCulloch & Snowden, 2007; Jones, 2007; Lindsay et al., 2013). Recent research has moved away from prevalence studies, to focus on the importance of understanding the pathways that offenders with ID take within and around the criminal-justice system and the unique factors that pre-determine their outcomes (Carson et al., 2010; Lindsay et al., 2010).

With the dual aims of optimizing community integration and minimizing the risk of offending for individuals with ID, the field of risk assessment applied to this population has grown significantly in the last two decades. Risk assessment research involving people without ID has contributed to the understanding of the predictive validity of specific variables related to both violent and sexual recidivism. These variables have included historical, childhood, offense-related, and clinical diagnostic factors (Camilleri & Quinsey, 2011; Hanson & Harris 2001; Harris, Rice, & Quinsey, 1993; Quinsey, Harris, Rice, & Cormier, 1998; Webster, Eaves, Douglas & Wintrup, 1995).

**Mainstream Risk Assessment**

In the field of forensic mental health, the risk assessment path is relatively clear. The risk of behavior is defined, the factors influencing the risk are identified, and the individual is informed of the potential consequences of their behavior. The legal consequences can range from social marginalization to custodial confinement dependent on the seriousness of the offense and legal precedent.

Risk assessments can be classified in two overarching categories: actuarial measures and structured professional judgment. Actuarial risk measures are broadly used since accuracy and reliability can be calculated (Hanson, 1998), and they have been shown to be more exact than risk assessments based purely on clinical judgment alone (Hanson & Bussière, 1998). Hence, clinicians tend to over-estimate the risk of the individual since the risk of over-estimation to themselves is less than the risk of under-estimation (e.g., it is less risky to admit a person who says they are suicidal to an inpatient unit than to send that person home, even though from an actuarial perspective, most people who say they are suicidal do not act on their stated wish). Actuarial risk measures can be further divided by the type of variable. For example, there are *static factors*, which are based on historical data and cannot change (e.g. age of first offense); and *stable factors*, which can vary within the individual but are more constant over time (e.g. criminogenic attitudes) (Hanson & Bussière, 1998).

Although these two categories of factors have been found to be empirically reliable in estimating the future risk of recidivism, current researchers are still questioning the validity and objective nature of actuarial assessments (Hannah-Moffat & Shaw, 2001; Hannah-Moffat & Maurutto, 2003).

Furthermore, these factors do not consider the dynamic variables that have been shown to have an equitable effect on risk of recidivism. The two types of dynamic factors are *stable dynamic factors*, which include clinical and psychometric variables that change gradually (e.g. a pattern of alcohol abuse) and *acute dynamic factors*, which include relapse prevention and maintenance variables that can change quickly (e.g. acute emotional problems) (Hanson & Harris, 2000).

In general, static factors contribute to a prediction or probability of long-term recidivism, while dynamic factors can be targeted in treatment and supervision levels, which in turn will affect recidivism. Dynamic factors are also more sensitive to the individual's specific needs, such that targeting the individual's needs within the context of risk provides for a better long-term outcome (Hannah-Moffat & Maurutto, 2003). Regardless of the theoretical debate about how mutually exclusive and independently predictive various risk variables are, there is a growing consensus about the validity and usefulness of a convergent approach to risk assessment. Both approaches are considered in order to provide a better appraisal of an individual's risk of re-offending and to identify which factors should be targeted in therapy and in other interventions (Beech & Ward, 2004; Boer, 2006; Fedoroff et al., 2015; Mann, Hanson & Thornton, 2010; Singh, Grann & Fazel, 2011). Thus, a convergent approach not only ascertains the baseline of recidivism but also identifies priorities for a risk management plan.

## Risk Assessment for Persons with ID

Over the past decade, important developments have been made by researchers to straddle approaches used for offenders with and without ID (Blacker, Beech, Wilcox & Boer, 2011; Boer, McVilly & Lambrick, 2007; Boer, Tough & Haaven, 2004; Lindsay et al., 2008). Studies have shown that general risk assessment measures, both for violence and sexual offending, can be applied with relative validity to offenders with ID, although generally with less predictive accuracy than for offenders without ID (Camilleri & Quinsey, 2011; Fedoroff, et al., 2015; Fitzgerald, Gray, Taylor, & Showda, 2011; Gray et al., 2007; Lindsay et al., 2008; Lofthouse et al., 2013; Quinsey, Book, & Skilling, 2004; Tough, 2001; Wilcox, Beech, Markall & Blacker, 2009). Comparison and cohort studies have included the Violent Risk Appraisal Guide (Quinsey et al., 1998), HCR-20 (Webster et al., 1995), the Static-99, Static-99R and Static 2002R (Babchishin, Hanson &, Helmus 2012; Hanson & Thornton, 1999), the Rapid Risk Assessment of Sex Offense Recidivism (Hanson, 1997), the Sexual Violence Risk – 20 (Boer, Hart, Kropp, & Webster, 1997), and the Sex Offender Risk Appraisal Guide (Quinsey et al., 1998).

However, the degree of accuracy of these instruments in samples of offenders with ID has been questioned by a number of researchers (Boer et al. 2004; Gray et al, 2007; Lindsay et al, 2008). Overlapping actuarial risk appraisal variables include core familial instability, childhood behavior problems, and anti-social attitudes. Other studies have explored the relative impact of individual dynamic variables within samples of offenders with ID that account for their unique environmental situations (i.e. congregate living and supervised residences) (Blacker, Beech, Wilcox & Boer, 2011; Boer et al. 2007; Lofthouse et al., 2013; Raina, Arenovich, Jones & Lunsky, 2013; Wilcox, 2004).

Some studies have explored the idea that although there is overlap in recidivism risk factors between individuals with and without ID (Gray et al., 2007; Lindsay & Beail, 2004), there is evidence to support specific risk factors within samples of offenders with ID (Blacker et al, 2011; Boer et al. 2004; Lindsay et al., 2008; Lofthouse et al., 2013). Such studies highlight the incidence and low base rates of certain variables within the ID population that inevitably differ from the common risk factors within offender populations without ID (Boer et al. 2007; Lambrick, 2003; Lindsay et al. 2013; Wilcox, 2004, Wilcox et al., 2009). For example, marital status, childhood residence, school behavioral problems, and chronic unemployment will weigh heavily for individuals with ID due to their sheltered upbringing and susceptibility to poor coping and limited problem-solving skills, an artifact of their impaired intelligence irrespective of criminal or anti-social risk factors. Hence, based on mainstream actuarial risk factors, people with ID are in danger of being viewed as inherently at higher risk for future offending. Furthermore, some researchers have proposed that dynamic risk variables in persons with ID may be equally predictive as underlying static risk factors (Lindsay et al., 2004; Lofthouse et al., 2013, Lofthouse, Lindsay, Totsika, Hastings, & Richards, 2014; Steptoe, Lindsay, Murphy, &Young, 2008).

It has been the original work of some forensic and ID researchers (Boer et al., 2007; Lindsay et al., 2004) who have expanded the convergent model of risk assessment with the innovative measures of the Assessment of Risk and Manageability for Individuals who Offend Sexually [ARMILLIDO-S] (Boer et al., 2004), the Dynamic Risk Assessment and Management System [DRAMS] (Lindsay et al. 2004), and the Current Risk of Violence [CuRV] (Lofthouse et al., 2014). Their work accounts for the unique context that offenders with ID exist due to the inevitable impact of the environment and caregiver influence on risk. A person with ID, regardless of level of intellectual or functional impairment, will likely have some external support, either continuously or intermittently, throughout childhood and well into adulthood. Indeed, in some jurisdictions financial and residential support is dependent on having a formal support agency or worker to assist with the range of services. Supports can range from disability pensions for the semi-independent individual to scheduled activities for individuals requiring daily supervision in group homes. These supports clearly will have an influence on the person's behavior, autonomy, risk level, and propensity to high-risk behavior.

For offenders with ID, Boer and his colleagues (2007) argued that the level of risk imposed by an individual with ID should be understood in the context of the environment and current circumstances. Thus, an offender's risk level may not change but the risk provided by the environment can. Further, offenders with the same level of predictive risk may be in different environments that significantly increase or decrease their risk manageability. In the ARMILLIDO-S (Boer et al., 2004), environmental staff-related factors that are assessed include both dynamic stable variables (e.g., communication amongst staff and attitudes of staff), and dynamic acute variables (e.g., daily supervision levels and behavioral monitoring by staff). As seen in

Figure 1, his risk assessment model also includes offender specific variables that are unique to individuals with ID including dynamic stable factors (e.g., ability to tell time or dependence on others) as well as dynamic acute factors (e.g., compliance with behavior support plan and day program). Recent studies have shown comparative accuracy for these ID specific risk assessment tools when matched to mainstream measures such as the STATIC-99 or the VRAG (Blacker et al., 2011; Fedoroff et al., 2015; Lofthouse et al., 2013). Further dynamic assessments such as the DRAMS and CuRV are also promising tools that are aimed at addressing the need for staff-friendly assessments of risk and, in particular, predicting aggression in clinical environments for individuals with ID (Lofthouse et al., 2014; Steptoe et al., 2008).

**Figure 1: Risk Assessment for Persons with intellectual disabilities**

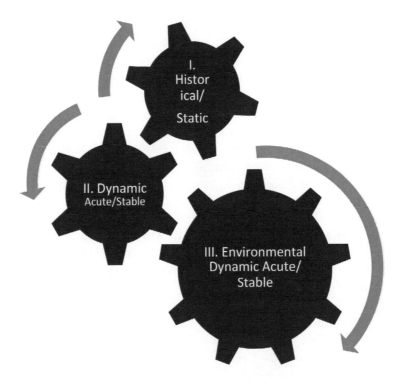

## Community Risk Management for Persons with ID

The differences in caregiver response to offending behaviors between individuals with or without ID are salient when examining their daily functional environment. For example, an individual with ID who has a longstanding history of challenging and aggressive behaviors may require intermittent hospitalizations while living in the community supported by a developmental service agency. It is likely the aggressive behavior is viewed from diverse perspectives dependent on the system the individual is cared within (e.g., in an inpatient ward or in a community group home). Accordingly, the caregiver perspectives will be influenced by each of their respective experiences and thresholds for tolerating high-risk behavior. Inevitably, the diversity and range of care philosophies from normalization (Wolfensberger, Nirje, Olshansky, Perske & Roos, 1972) and social role valorization (Wolfensberger, 1983) to supporting segregation for individuals with ID can directly influence the interpretation of risk levels and what constitutes risky or 'offending' behavior beyond clear criminal code infractions.

Environmental and vocational supports for individuals with ID provided in the developmental service sector are multiple but vary from a range of meaningful occupations and living situations to the subtleties of staffing models and supervision styles. The current focus on community inclusion has allowed for innovative housing opportunities, leaving behind the history of institutions built during a time of asylums and the belief in the importance of institutionalization. The philosophical goals of facilitating autonomy and independence have fostered caregiver models of semi-independent living, host families, and specialized homes in the community. The latter models of support have developed with the aim of maximizing self-care and normalizing the field through person-centered planning and access to generic services within education, employment, and recreation.

However, all the models described above require the individual with ID to accept at least some external support and accommodation despite underlying attempts to respect the rights of the individual and their dignity to choose their lifestyle and level of autonomy. The impact of staff and agency support, therefore, cannot be underestimated in the field of risk assessment as it applies to individuals with ID. Static and dynamic variables that are associated with reoffending in the general population are inevitably influenced by the proximity and reliability of the caregivers that surround an individual with ID from the time they require supports as a young child to adulthood and beyond.

Researchers have highlighted that a staff's value systems, attitudes, and attributions will significantly affect how they interact with and respond to the person with ID and their potential high-risk behaviors (Dilworth, Phillips & Rose, 2010; Hastings, Reed & Watts, 1997; Jones, Ouellette-Kuntz, Vilela & Brown, 2008; Mills & Rose, 2011; Rose, 2011; Watts, Reed & Hastings, 1998). Thus, how a staff member experiences and then interprets an individual's challenging behavior will directly influence whether it is viewed as 'criminal' behavior requiring a legal response. From a wider lens, caregiver agencies that either have a "normalization" approach with expectations of the individual similar to the general population or a "protective" approach with expectations of entitled accommodations will substantially influence decisions at every level concerning that person's life. How the agency responds to problematic behaviors may be determined by how highly they value the principle of supporting autonomy and their perceived responsibility to mitigate risk.

Community agencies that advocate for social integration are well intentioned but may inadvertently foster the misguided principle that normalization equates to treating and perceiving people with ID "just like you or me." This flawed principle can influence how caregivers, agency philosophies, and the criminal justice system approach their responsibilities to this population. An unintended consequence of this approach is that the person's risk of re-offense may increase due to a mismatch between overestimation by caregivers and actual ability of the person with ID to perform at the expected level. Anecdotally, it is not uncommon for community agency staff to encourage a legal response for an individual's behavior "so they learn consequences to their actions." However, when sent to hospital for assessment, inpatient staff comments such as "individuals with ID don't belong in the forensic mental health system" are not uncommon. Thus, risk assessment measures that are reliable and validated specifically for people with ID may increase caregivers' abilities to set realistic expectations and appropriate responses based on an individual's accurate risk level within the context of their environmental demands.

## Risk Assessment of the *Culture of Care* in the ID System

Alongside the emerging research into the validity of risk assessments for this population, it is suggested that in addition to the inclusion of immediate environmental variables (e.g., staffing factors), that the domain of an individual's wider support system or 'culture of care' needs to be accounted for. Clinicians and caregivers in the field are well aware that risk management is disproportionally different in a community group home setting as compared to a hospital unit despite the same behavior profile.

In a large-scale study examining pathways of offenders of ID across the UK forensic system, researchers found that referrals to secure services for offenders with ID was influenced not only by the level of IQ and severity of index offene but also by the system from which they were referred. They found that community care teams tended to refer within levels of service, such that offenders living in the community tended to remain in community services. However, referrals from residential or specialty homes tended to result in transfers to secure detainment units (Carson et al., 2010; Lindsay et al., 2008, 2010, 2013; Wheeler et al., 2009). Thus, risk levels for offenders with ID are influenced and somewhat dictated by the surrounding system of the individual and their particular philosophy of care. Hence, an offender with ID and their relative *perceived* risk will be highly influenced by the culture of care within services whose respective approaches span the continuum of normalization.

It is therefore proposed that the overarching philosophies and related policies of community agencies may be viewed along a continuum of risk tolerance or risk threshold. Accordingly, some support agencies may be predominantly risk averse in their approaches, while others may be focused on minimizing risk, and some may promote active risk management (e.g. supervised exposure). Therefore, the difference is that an individual with ID who exhibits the same challenging behavior such as impulsive aggression, may be secluded or isolated in a group home, or be supported by staff that may intentionally avoid certain environments in the community in one agency. In contrast, another agency may actively manage risk in the community by allowing the individual with ID to be exposed to risky situations with supervised support to address vulnerabilities and practice relapse prevention plans.

This ethical dilemma involving risk and the culture of care is especially important to the groups of offenders with ID and dual diagnosis (i.e., persons with ID and psychiatric diagnosis). The latter is more so, given the recent movement away from institutional confinement to approaches of community integration and management for individuals who may lack capacity. For example, the implementation of mental health courts and community diversion strategies within the criminal justice system have created novel and complex opportunities for community agencies in their ability to offer support to a variety of offenders. Thus, current risk assessment approaches for offenders with ID need to address not only the conventional actuarial and dynamic risk an offender with ID represents but also their environmental or situational risk given their surrounding service system and the staff that are deemed responsible for them.

It is argued that the legal pathway of the offender with ID is sometimes set even before contact with the police and criminal justice system. This is due to pre-existing presumptions about the role and responsibilities of the person's support system, irrespective of the individual's actual risk level. Therefore, the need for reliable and appropriate risk assessment measures specifically designed for individuals with ID are essential and necessary in order to contextually identify risk profiles. Furthermore, accurate risk profiles can then facilitate treatment plans that allow for increased autonomy and freedom while accounting for measured risk by the individual, immediate caregivers, and surrounding culture of care (see Figure 2).

## Figure 2: Risk Assessment and Management Framework in ID

In this regard, establishing a validated risk assessment and management framework for offenders with ID is an outcome that is not substantially different from Perske's argument almost half a decade ago about the challenge of ensuring the dignity of risk for individuals with ID. Many professionals and researchers alike worry that mainstream risk assessment instruments can stigmatize a person with ID by labelling them as "high-risk." However, comprehensive assessment techniques that include structured clinical judgment and the recognition of dynamic risk factors mean that the former label of "high-risk" may become a label of "low-risk." Accordingly, a risk paradigm that includes both a convergent risk approach and accounts for the caregiver culture of care may permit greater levels of autonomy and higher levels of safety both to the individual with ID and the community and, therefore, safeguarding Perske's dignity of risk.

# References

Babchishin, K., Hanson K., & Helmus, L. (2012). Communicating risk for sex offenders: Risk ratios for Static-2002R. *Sexual Offender Treatment, 7*(2), 1 – 12.

Beech, A., & Ward, T. (2004). The integration of etiology and risk in sexual offenders: A theoretical framework. *Aggression and Violent Behaviour, 10*, 31-63.

Blacker, J., Beech, A., Wilcox, D., & Boer, D. (2011). The assessment of dynamic risk and recidivism in a sample of special needs offenders. *Psychology, Crime & Law, 17* (1), 75-92.

Boer, D. (2006). Sex offender risk strategies: Is there a convergence of opinion yet? *Sexual Offender Treatment, 1*, 1-4.

Boer, D. P., Hart, S. D., Kropp, P. R., & Webster, C. D. (1997). *Manual for the Sexual Violence Risk – 20: Professional guidelines for assessing risk of sexual violence.* Vancouver, B.C.: The Mental Health, Law, and Policy Institute.

Boer, D., McVilly, K. & Lambrick, F. (2007). Contextualizing risk in the assessment of intellectually disabled individuals. *Sexual Offender Treatment, 2*(2), 1-4.

Boer, D. P., Tough, S., & Haaven, J. (2004). Assessment of risk manageability of developmentally disabled sex offenders. *Journal of Applied Research in Intellectual Disabilities, 17*, 275-284.

Camilleri, J. A., & Quinsey, V. L. (2011). Appraising the risk of sexual and violent recidivism among intellectually disabled offenders. *Psychology, Crime & Law, 17*(1), 59-74.

Carson, D., Lindsay, W., O'Brien, G., Holland, A., Taylor, J., Wheeler, J., …. Johnston, S. (2010). Referrals into services for offenders with intellectual disabilities: Variables predicting community or secure provision. *Criminal Behaviour and Mental Health, 20*, 39-50.

Crocker, A. J., Cote, G., Toupin, J., & St-Onge, B. (2007). Rate and characteristics of men with an intellectual disability in pre-trial detention. *Journal of Intellectual & Developmental Disability, 32*, 143-152.

Day, K. (1994) Male mentally handicapped sex offenders. *British Journal of Psychiatry, 165*, 630-639.

Dilworth, J., Phillips, N., & Rose, J. (2010). Factors relating to staff attributions of control over challenging behaviour. *Journal of Applied Research in Intellectual Disabilities, 24*(1), 29-38.

Farrington D., Coid, J., Harnett, L., Jolliffe, D., Soteriou, N., Turner, R., & West, D. (2006). *Criminal careers up to age 50 and life success up to age 48: New findings from the Cambridge study in delinquent development* (Report No. 299). London, UK: Home Office Research, Development and Statistics Directorate.

Fazel, S., Xenitidis, K., & Powell, J. (2008). The prevalence of intellectual disabilities among 12.000 prisoners: A systematic review. *International Journal of Law and Psychiatry, 31*, 369-373.

Fedoroff, P., Richards, D., Ranger, R., & Curry, S. (2015). The predictive validity of common risk assessment tools in men with intellectual disabilities and problematic sexual behaviours. *Research in Developmental Disabilities, 57*, 29-38.

Fitzgerald, S., Gray, N., Taylor, J., & Snowdon, R. (2011). Risk factors for recidivism in offenders with intellectual disabilities. *Psychology, Crime and Law, 17*, 43-58.

Gray, N. S., Fitzgerald, S., Taylor, J., MacCulloch, M. J., & Snowden, R. J. (2007). Predicting future reconviction in offenders with intellectual disabilities: The predictive efficacy of VRAG, PCL-SV and the HCR-20. *Psychological Assessment, 19*, 474 - 479.

Hannah-Moffat, K., & Maurutto, P. (2003). *Youth risk/need assessment: An overview of issues and practices.* Ottawa, Ontario: Department of Justice Canada.

Hannah-Moffat, K., & Shaw, M. (2001). *Taking risks: Incorporating gender and culture into the classification and assessment of federally sentenced women in Canada.* Ottawa, Ontario: Status of Women Canada.

Hanson, R. K. (1997). *The development of a brief actuarial risk scale for sexual offence recidivism* (User Report 97-04) Ottawa, Canada: Department of the Solicitor General of Canada.

Hanson, R. K. (1998). What do we know about sex offender risk assessment? *Psychology, Public Policy, and Law, 4*(1-2), 50 - 72.

Hanson, R. K., & Brussiere, M. T. (1998). Predicting relapse: A meta-analysis of sexual offender recidivism studies. *Journal of Consulting and Clinical Psychology, 66*, 344-362.

Hanson, R. K., & Harris, A. (2000). *The Sex Offender Need Assessment Rating (SONAR): A method for measuring change in risk levels 2000-1.* Ottawa, Canada: Department of the Solicitor General of Canada.

Hanson, R. K., & Harris, A. (2001). A structured approach to evaluating change among sexual offenders. *Sexual Abuse: A Journal of Research and Treatment, 13(2)*, 105-122

Hanson, R. K., & Thornton, D. (1999). *Static 99: Improving actuarial risk assessments for sex offenders (Vol. 2).* Ottawa, Canada: Solicitor General Canada.

Harris, G. T., Rice, M. E., & Quinsey, V. L. (1993). Violent recidivism of mentally disordered offenders: The development of a statistical prediction instrument. *Criminal Justice and Behavior, 20*, 315-335.

Hastings, R., Reed, T., & Watts, M. (1997). Community staff casual attributions about challenging behaviours in people with intellectual disabilities. *Journal of Applied Research in Intellectual Disabilities, 10*(3), 238-249.

Hayes, S., & McIlwain, D. (1988). *The prevalence of intellectual disability in the New South Wales prison population - An empirical study.* Canberra, Australia: Report to the Criminology Research Council.

Hogue, T. E., Steptoe, L., Taylor, J. L., Lindsay, W. R., Mooney, P., Pinkney, L., & O'Brien, G. (2006). A comparison of offenders with intellectual disability across three levels of security. *Criminal Behaviour & Mental Health, 16*, 13-28.

Holland, A. (1991). Challenging and offending behaviour by adults with developmental disorders. *Journal of Intellectual and Developmental Disability, 17*, 119-126.

Jones, J. (2007) Persons with intellectual disabilities in the criminal justice system: Review of issues. *International Journal of Offender Therapy and Comparative Criminology, 51*(6), 723-33.

Jones, J., Ouellette Kuntz, H., Vilela, T., & Brown, H. (2008). Attitudes of community developmental services agency staff toward issues of inclusion for individuals with intellectual disabilities. *Journal of Policy and Practice in Intellectual Disabilities, 5*(4), 219-226.

Lambrick, F. (2003). Issues surrounding the risk assessment of sexual offenders with an intellectual disability. *Psychiatry, Psychology & Law, 10*, 353-358.

Lindsay, W. R., & Beail, N. (2004). Risk assessment: Actuarial prediction and clinical judgement of offending incidents and behaviour for intellectual disability services. *Journal of Applied Research in Intellectual Disabilities, 17,* 229-234.

Lindsay, W., Hastings, R., & Beail, N. (2013). Why do some people with intellectual disability engage in offending behavior and what can we do about it? Editorial. *Journal of Applied Research in Intellectual Disabilities, 26,* 351-356.

Lindsay, W. R., Hastings, R. P., Griffiths, D. M., & Hayes, S. C. (2007). Trends and challenges in forensic research on offenders with intellectual disability. *Journal of Intellectual & Developmental Disability, 32,* 55-61.

Lindsay, W. R., Hogue, T., Taylor, J. L., Steptoe, L., Mooney, P., Johnston, S., & Smith, A. H. W. (2008). Risk assessment in offenders with intellectual disabilities: A comparison across three levels of security. *International Journal of Offender Therapy & Comparative Criminology, 52,* 90-111.

Lindsay W. R., O'Brien, G., Carson, D., Holland, A. J., Taylor, J. T., Wheeler, J, R.,... Johnston, S. (2010). Pathways into services for offenders with intellectual disability: Childhood experiences, diagnostic information and offence variables. *Criminal Justice and Behaviour, 37*(6), 678-694.

Lofthouse, R., Lindsay, W., Totsika, V., Hastings, R. & Richards, D. (2014) Dynamic risk and violence in individuals with intellectual disability: Tool development and initial validation. *Journal of Forensic Psychiatry & Psychology, 25,* 288-306.

Lofthouse, R., Totsika, V., Hastings, R., Lindsay, W., Hogue, T. & Taylor, J. (2013). How do static and dynamic risk factors work together to predict violent behavior amongst offenders with an intellectual disability? *Journal of Intellectual Disability Research, 58*(2), 125-133.

MacEachron, A. E. (1979). Mentally retarded offenders: prevalence and characteristics. *American Journal of Mental Deficiency, 84,* 165-176.

Mann, R., Hanson, R. & Thornton, D. (2010). Assessing risk for sexual recidivism: Some proposals on the nature of psychologically meaningful risk factors. *Sexual Abuse: A Journal of Research and Treatment, 22,* 172-190.

Mason, J., & Murphy, G. (2002). Intellectual disability amongst people on probation: Prevalence and outcome. *Journal of Intellectual Disability Research, 46,* 230-238.

McCord W., McCord J. & Zola, I.K.(1959). *Origins of crime: A new evaluation of the Cambridge-Somerville Youth Study.* Columbia Press. New York.

Mills, S., & Rose, J. (2011). The relationship between challenging behavior, burnout and cognitive variables in staff working with people who have intellectual disabilities. *Journal of Intellectual Disability Research, 55*(9), 844-857.

Murphy, M., Harrold, M., Carey, S., & Mulrooney, M. (2000). *A survey of the level of learning disability among the prison population in Ireland.* Dublin, Ireland: Department of Justice, Equality and Law Reform.

Noble, J. H., & Conley, R. W. (1992). Toward an epidemiology of relevant attributes. In R. W. Conley, R. Luckasson, & G. Bouthilet (Eds.), *The criminal justice system and mental retardation* (pp. 17-54). Baltimore, MD: Brookes Publishing.

Perske, R. (1972). The dignity of risk and the mentally retarded. *Mental Retardation, 10*(1), 1-6.

Petersilia, J. (2000). *Doing Justice? The Criminal Justice System and Offenders with Developmental Disabilities.* Berkeley, CA: California Policy Research Center.

Quinsey, V. L., Book, A., & Skilling, T. A. (2004). A follow-up of deinstitutionalized men with intellectual disabilities and histories of antisocial behaviour. *Journal of Applied Research in Intellectual Disabilities, 17,* 243-254.

Quinsey, V., Harris, G., Rice, M., & Cormier, C. (1998) *Violent offenders: Appraising and managing risk.* Washington, DC: American Psychological Association.

Raina, P., Arenovich, T., Jones, J., & Lunsky, Y. (2013). Pathways into the criminal justice system for individuals with intellectual disabilities. *Journal of Applied Research in Intellectual Disabilities, 26,* 5, 404-409.

Rose, R. (2011). How do staff psychological factors influence outcomes for people with developmental and intellectual disability in residential services. *Current Opinion in Psychiatry, 24,* 5, 403-407.

Singh, F., Grann, M., & Fazel, S. (2011). A comparative study of violence risk assessment tools: A systematic review and meta-regression analysis of 68 studies involving 25,980 participants. *Clinical Psychology Review, 31,* 499-513.

Steptoe, L., Lindsay, W., Murphy, L., & Young, S. (2008). Construct validity, reliability and predictive validity of the Dynamic Risk Assessment and Management System (DRAMS) in offenders with intellectual disability. *Legal & Criminological Psychology, 13,* 309-321.

Tough, S. (2001) *Validation of two standardized assessments on a sample of adult males who are intellectually disabled with significant cognitive deficits* (Master's thesis). University of Toronto, Toronto, Canada.

Walker, N., & McCabe, S. (1973). *Crime and insanity in England.* Edinburgh, Scotland: Edinburgh University Press.

Watts, M., Reed, T., & Hastings, R. (1998). Staff strategies and explanations for intervening with challenging behaviours: A replication in a community sample. *Journal of Intellectual Disability Research, 41,* 258-263.

Webster, C. D., Eaves, D., Douglas, K. S., & Wintrup, A. (1995). *The HCR-20: The assessment of dangerousness and risk.* Vancouver, Canada: Simon Fraser University and British Colombia Forensic Psychiatric Services Commission.

Wheeler, J., Holland, A., Bambrick, M., Lindsay, W., Carson, D., Steptoe, L., …O'Brien, G. (2009). Community services and people with intellectual disabilities who engage in anti-social or offending behavior: Referral rates, characteristics and care pathways. *Journal of Forensic Psychiatry and Psychology, 20*(5), 717-740.

Wilcox D. (2004). Treatment of intellectual disabled individuals who have committed sexual offences: A review of the literature. *Journal of Sexual Aggression, 10,* 85-100.

Wilcox, D., Beech, A., Markall, H., & Blacker, J. (2009). Actuarial risk assessment and recidivism in a sample of UK intellectually disabled sexual offenders. *Journal of Sexual Aggression, 15,* 977-106.

Wolfensberger, W. (1983). Social role valorization: A proposed new term for the principle of normalization. *Mental Retardation, 21*(6), 234-239.

Wolfensberger, W., Nirje, B., Olshansky, S., Perske, R. & Roos, P. (1972). *The Principle of Normalization in Human Services.* Toronto, Canada: Institute of Mental Retardation.

*Chapter 7*

# Challenges in Community Support for Offenders with Intellectual Disabilities Who Have Offended

*Deborah Richards, Samantha Stromski & Dorothy M. Griffiths*

On Monday April 14th, 2008, the Toronto Star published a news article about Leroy Humphrey, a man with an intellectual disability who was arrested for an assault at his group home. The title read: "Stuck behind bars with no place to call home" (Crawford, 2008). Crawford reported that Leroy spent a number of weeks in jail while the community agencies in his life worked tirelessly to arrange new housing and a support plan for him. The challenge faced by the community agencies was the length of time it took to develop an adequate support plan, leaving Leroy vulnerable in jail where he was taunted and physically assaulted by the other inmates. Leroy highlighted a major challenge for those with intellectual disability who are in custody when he was quoted as saying, "at least I had a roof over my head" (final paragraph). This case brought to light the need for proper planning and problem solving for those with intellectual disability involved with the criminal justice system to address the lack of adequate housing and resources. The article went on to address these issues by suggesting that solutions should focus on increasing trained staff, housing, and programs for high-risk individuals with intellectual disabilities.

## Introduction

Since the early 1970s, institutionalization for persons with intellectual disabilities (ID) has been declining throughout North America (Griffiths, et al., 2016). As such, persons with ID who commit offenses are often remanded to care in a community agency rather than being placed in jail or prison believing that the "accused may cope poorly in prison, or because the accused is viewed as less reprehensible, and the principle of general or specific deterrence as not relevant" (Griffiths, Thomson, Ioannou, Hoath & Wilson, 2018, p27). In addition, offenders who have served time in jail will be returning to the community and will need supports.

Effectively supporting offenders in the community is one of the most challenging tasks facing community service providers. There are many factors to be considered and decisions to be made to ensure that offenders are not just placed in the community but supported in a manner that will reduce the probability of their re-offending and provide them with the supports and treatment needed to create a foundation for a future.

In this chapter, the authors provide nine key decision points that are critical to be explored when supporting offenders in the community. It is suggested that with the implementation of these outlined strategies, offenders' susceptibility to imminent incarcerations will be greatly reduced, and the likelihood of positive community presence and interactions for this vulnerable group can irreversibly lead to improved lives. In the sections that follow, each of these steps in the decision model will be explored more fully. The chapter reflects the experience of the authors within their practice within Ontario, Canada, although the principles are consistent with what is recommended practice in other jurisdictions both in Canada and internationally.

## Factor 1: Identification of Intellectual Disability and Mental Health Disorders

### a) Suspicion and Identification of Intellectual Disabilities

Jones (2007) reported that according to numerous studies the prevalence rates of individuals who have ID within the criminal justice system (CJS) widely range anywhere between 2% and 40%, depending on how ID is defined. Within the prison system there tends to be uncertainty regarding the actual percentages of this disadvantaged group due to a lack of identification of ID (Fazel, Xenitidis, & Powell, 2008).

Holland, Clare, and Mukhopadhyay (2002) stated that there are two distinct groups of people with cognitive delay who offend and find themselves within the criminal justice system: those *with* an ID diagnosis and those *without* an ID diagnosis. The individuals who have not been assessed or have fallen through the cracks prior to incarceration are more vulnerable since they are typically misunderstood and placed in the general population of offenders, which increases their risk of victimization. Worse yet, and the most concerning, is the failure of professionals in the criminal justice system to identify persons with ID when it comes to the vital matter of the death penalty in the USA (Beail, 2002).

The consensus is that succinct data regarding who has ID within the criminal justice system needs to be available to all sectors to understand this disadvantaged group while in custody and to ensure seamless releases (Rowley, 2013). Not only is a cognitive delay often misunderstood in the context of the criminal justice system, but there is also little known within this system about the required supports and resources should a person have been diagnosed with ID (Baldry, Clarence, Dowse, & Troller, 2013).

It is well documented that there are a number of challenges associated with the assessment and diagnosis of an ID within the criminal justice system (Fedoroff, Richards, Ranger & Curry, 2016). These individuals tend to lack adequate supports once they are released into the community because an ID often goes undetected with the criminal justice system. According to Rowley (2013), a mild cognitive impairment has a higher probability of going unidentified for those who display no obvious signs of a delay. This is due to inconsistencies in what constitutes a cognitive delay by justice professionals (Baldry et al., 2013). The methodologies employed in making a clinical diagnosis of ID are often inconsistent and based on varying criteria (Craig & Lindsay, 2010; Fedoroff et al., 2016).

In a review conducted by Beail (2002), it was reported that the Hayes Ability Screening Index (HASI; Hayes, 2002) provides an encouraging preliminary tool for early identification; as such its usefulness has been demonstrated within the criminal justice system in the US. When criminal justice staff suspect the possibility of an ID, the Hayes Ability Screening Index is a reliable means of identifying people which can then prompt the need for a referral for a more comprehensive psychological assessment.

Furthermore, recognition of disorders such as fetal alcohol spectrum disorder (FASD) and autism spectrum disorder (ASD), that often accompany the diagnosis of ID require more than assessing an intelligence quotient (IQ) score; and further assessment of communication, self-care, daily living, decision making, social and interpersonal interactions, vocational interests, and health and safety skills are essential. This is done through assessing adaptive and executive functioning, and it is important for understanding the level of assistance or specialized needs that a person requires. Furthermore, this type of assessment can aid professionals within the criminal justice system in determining the sentence that is suitable for the individual given his/her disability and the crime, in addition to the type of setting the individual receives while in or out of custody.

Even when it is known that the person has a previous diagnosis of ID, the initial involvement within the legal system does not necessarily allow for this type of information to be at the forefront during initial questioning at the police station, during the bail hearing, or within the correctional holding facility should the individual be placed into custody pre-trial. However, if a person is receiving supports from a developmental service agency, there is a greater likelihood that information pertaining to intellectual functioning will be available. Furthermore, a support staff may offer information and act as an extension of the person during police questioning as well. Having an initial link to an agency or advocate from the initial stages is invaluable in determining how the criminal justice system proceeds in terms of pre-trial, sentencing, and releases.

One of the dangers associated with the failure to detect a cognitive delay is the absence of appropriate supports, which will increase the likelihood of potential intersections with the criminal justice system. Rowley (2013) stated that individuals with ID are at a great disadvantage over those in the general population as they are less likely to know their rights, less able to make decisions around their defense, and at greater risk of victimization and re-offending due to the lack of supports. Identification and a clinically accurate diagnosis require that the specialized and unique needs of people with ID can be put into place before, during, and after incarceration (Sondenaa, Palmstierna, & Iversen, 2010).

For individuals with ID who are not connected to developmental services prior to becoming involved with the criminal justice system, it is usually by chance that someone within the legal system uses their "best guess" to determine whether or not an individual has an ID. Even if there is suspicion of the presence of an ID at some stage of the criminal justice system process, there remain the problems of knowing how to proceed, accessing adequate supports, and navigating the appropriate systems to attain suitable resources since professionals within the criminal justice system do not have expertise in this area. Their expertise is in the implementation of the law; therefore, they may need to carry out the law even when they recognize an exceptional individual need. If an exceptional individual need is suspected, the criminal justice system professional may only deem it relevant to the individual if it is so severe that it brings into question fitness to stand trial or criminal responsibility.

In Ontario, Canada, the Ontario Ministry of Community and Social Services funded an initiative to allow for the provision of supports to a person with ID who becomes involved in the legal system, as well as to act as a liaison for the legal professionals (Gauthier, 2014). When a person is suspected to have an ID, the police, correctional staff, or courts can request involvement from a Dual Diagnosis Justice Case Manager (DDJCM). The Dual Diagnosis Justice Case Managers are all affiliated with the Community Networks of Specialized Care and funded by the Ministry to advance the needs of persons who have a dual diagnosis in all areas of the province.[1] The Dual Diagnosis Justice Case Manager works specifically with individuals who have a diagnosis of ID or a suspicion of an ID. Furthermore, their role is twofold; the case manager provides advice and direction to the person in navigating the lengthy, and often confusing legal process and serves as a resource for the professionals in the criminal justice system for setting up assessment referrals to determine if there is an ID or a mental health need. If an ID is identified, the Dual Diagnosis Justice Case Manager can seek out information on it through past records or by making referrals to appropriate resources to gain a better understanding of the person regarding intellectual and adaptive functioning.

The development of the Dual Diagnosis Justice Case Manager position created a valuable resource for professionals in the criminal justice system, enabling the process to move forward for an individual with ID who has been charged. Without the involvement of the Dual Diagnosis Justice Case Manager and the appropriate diagnosis, the offender often remained in custody with nowhere to reside when released and no plan for effective services and supports, whereas the involvement of the Dual Diagnosis Justice Case Manager and the appropriate diagnosis for the individual can result in the development of a plan and connections that may change the trajectory of their life and potentially reduce recidivism following release. Let's explore the case of Jason below:

> Jason is a 19-year-old who was removed from his family because of sexual and physical abuse and severe neglect causing hospitalization at the age of two. He was placed into the care of the Children's Aid Society. He was labeled as a troubled child with severe behavior problems; however, no formal developmental assessments were conducted. He was incarcerated numerous times for assaultive behavior as a young offender, and professional reports stated that he had conduct disorder. At 15 years of age, his lawyer sexually assaulted him on the way to his group home from the courthouse. Jason continued with more incidents of criminal acts and was eventually placed into a secure setting for young offenders. At 18 years of age, he was discharged from custody and placed on youth probation into his adult years.

---

[1]See http://www.community-networks.ca/collaboration/dual-diagnosis-justice-case-managers/

But where would he go?

While he was in custody, the Dual Diagnosis Justice Case Manager became involved since there was suspicion of cognitive delays and fetal alcohol spectrum disorder (FASD). After a referral for psychometric testing, he was assessed and diagnosed with a mild intellectual disability. Further assessment also revealed that he met criteria for FASD along with a number of co-morbid conditions such as attention deficit hyperactivity disorder (ADHD) and a generalized anxiety disorder with further investigation of post-traumatic stress disorder (PTSD). Jason now qualified for supports from developmental services given his new diagnosis.

To summarize, identification of an ID is critical to obtaining appropriate care and interventions during the legal process (Sondenaa et al., 2010) and successful community reintegration depends on a formalized diagnosis of ID in order to put into place adequate supports and necessary funding specific to individual needs (Rowley, 2013; Young, van Dooren, Claudio, Cumming, & Lennox, 2016).

## *b) Suspicion and/or Identification of a Dual Diagnosis*

People with ID who are involved with the criminal justice system are more likely than those without an ID to have co-morbid psychiatric conditions (Dias, Ware, Kinner & Lennox, 2014; Young et al., 2016). Dias and colleagues (2014) found that 52.5% of prisoners in an Australian study who met criteria for ID had co-occurring mental health disorders, whereas Day (1994) and Lindsay (2002) both reported 32% of offenders had a psychiatric diagnosis or a major mental illness. In other words, at least one third of offenders with ID have a dual diagnosis of a psychiatric illness.

Haut and Brewster (2010) reported that individuals with ID may not be assessed for a mental health problem since it is assumed that the psychiatric and emotional indicators are an extension of the ID rather than the result of a mental illness. This has been described in the literature as *diagnostic overshadowing* (Reiss, Levitan & Szyszko, 1982). Rowley (2013) stated that there needs to be a clear understanding that an intellectual disability is distinct from a mental illness and that a dual diagnosis can result in further complications because of these complex needs.

Furthermore, Baldry and colleagues (2013) underlined the need to evaluate whether an individual has a mental health disorder and/or an ID. If a dual diagnosis is present, there may be multiple and compounding social disadvantages and increased vulnerability for harm. For example, the presence of a co-occurring mental illness significantly increases the likelihood of people with ID having histories of both victimization and offending. Thereby, Watson, Richards, Hayes, LeComte and Taua (2012) detailed the importance of identification of a co-morbid psychiatric condition thorough investigation and assessment to obtain an accurate diagnosis.

The recognition and presence of a definitive diagnosis can increase the network of available supports thus reducing the person's likely exposure to harm. Let's explore the case presented below:

Steve had a history of aggressive behavior throughout his early years and into his adult years. He was severely neglected and abused as a child and as a young adult.

He lived in an institution from 8 years of age until 20 years old before moving into a community residential facility. He continued to display aggressive behaviors, and his support staff believed that he might also have underlying mental health issues. He therefore had numerous visits to the psychiatric hospital over the course of a few years, and although sedative medications were often prescribed for him, he appeared to be getting worse. Medical staff said he was simply acting out and attention seeking; they placed him on several neuroleptic medications. He experienced severe side effects from these medications. As the side effects worsened, it became evident that he required medical expertise that understood individuals with complex needs and yet these experts seemed to be non-existent.

> During one admission to the psychiatric unit at the hospital, Steve struck a nurse with a coffee cup and was consequently charged with assault with a weapon. He was now facing the confusion of the criminal justice system. He was released on a recognizance order to appear in court. In the meantime, support staff sought out the professional services at a teaching hospital in Toronto, Canada. They were fortunate enough to have assistance from a neuro-psychiatrist who did a full assessment on Steve and had a keen interest in working with people with ID. This assessment included both a genetic and psychiatric assessment. It was determined that Steve had a rare genetic disorder called Coffin Lowry syndrome which is linked to severe mental health problems. This medical report was provided to the courts, and Steve was placed in the court diversion program where he had to follow the rules of the agency. The agency then began planning for Steve and was able to acquire appropriate treatment based on his mental health diagnosis while also considering the medical problems related to the genetic disorder. Steve's aggression greatly diminished after the appropriate treatment was put into place and the support team understood his complex needs.

As demonstrated in this example, it is not good enough to simply brush off an individual's behavior as attention seeking or acting out when they have an ID. It is necessary for a careful and thorough mental health assessments to be completed and this becomes even more evident when the person has been involved in the criminal justice system (Haut & Brewster, 2010). Fedoroff and Richards (2012) have developed a forensic clinic that sees patients who have a primary diagnosis of ID in addition to problematic sexual behaviors and other co-morbid conditions. They report that the success of this clinic has been the involvement of the multi-system interactions of the support network in the individual's life towards reintegration in one's community that promotes safety and autonomy.

### Factor 2: Lifestyle Planning

Riches, Parmenter, Wiese, and Stancliffe (2006) emphasized the importance of pre- and post-release planning and support. Placing appropriate supports before, during, and after incarceration is likely to reduce harm, improve outcomes, and increase success for community reintegration (Baldry et al., 2013). Buntinx and Schalock (2010) endorsed an approach of individuality and examination of each person in a case-by-case situation. Individualized planning should consider health and well-being, community participation, and personal abilities

Implementation of three key components that enhance community presence and participation can be implemented through a streamlined and systematic approach. First, it is important to understand the core components to quality of life measures that can increase social inclusion and decrease societal exclusion. By understanding the core values of quality of life, planners can begin to predict the factors that are currently impacting the individual's life. Secondly, improved quality of life is developed through a thorough biomedical, psychological, and socio-environmental assessment and treatment plan that encompasses the whole person. Lastly, using a person-centered planning process is, by definition, a way in which to establish methods of supporting people towards meeting their personal goals (Mansell & Beadle-Brown, 2004). Buntinx and Schalock (2010) suggested that there are clinical and service benefits from using an approach that combines medical, behavioral ,and social disciplines.

## a) Quality of Life

Quality of life identifies life both at its worst and at its best (Schalock, et al., 2002). For individuals involved with the criminal justice system, one can easily argue that they are experiencing life at its worst. The principles of quality of life suggest that the conditions of life are determined on an individual basis with both subjective (personal) and objective (unbiased) factors (Verdugo, Navas, Gomez and Schalock, 2012). Schalock and his colleagues (2002) also suggest that quality of life is achieved when there are individualized, meaningful life experiences, and the person has an interconnected life that they are enjoying. This is measured by key life conditions such as emotional well-being, interpersonal relations, material well-being, personal developmental, physical well-being, self-determination, social inclusion, and rights (Schalock, et al, 2002). Verdugo and his colleagues (2012) further suggest that quality of life measures could be examined and assessed by the level of independence, social participation, and well-being a person's experiences. For this to be successful, it is essential that people be treated with impartiality, feel empowered, and have experiences in life that are enjoyable regardless of their criminal history.

Verdugo and his colleagues (2012) also identified that having supports is not enough; there needs to be evidence of the four principles to promote quality of life standards. The first principle is relationships apply to all people, regardless of disability. The second is an individual's needs and wants are carried out through opportunities that are life enriching. Thirdly, both subjective (personal) and objective (unbiased) factors are considered. Finally, it is understood that the environment plays a key role in influencing behavior. While the development of this framework represents a move towards the augmentation of supports and evaluating personal outcomes, it is necessary to ensure that appropriate specialized assistance is present to implement (Buntinx & Schalock, 2010).

## b) Biomedical, Psychological, and Socio-Environmental (BPS)

Engel (1977) conceptualized the biopsychosocial model as an alternative model of medical care that considered biological factors (genetic, biochemical, etc.), psychological factors (mood, personality, behavior, etc.), and socio-environmental factors (cultural, familial, and socio-economical, etc.) to develop a plan of care. This model has since been incorporated in the care of individuals with ID with psychiatric diagnoses and mental health needs. Kaplan and Coogan (2005) outlined the importance of utilizing this model to better understand the whole person by gaining greater knowledge beyond the medical condition. The interwoven relationship in the biomedical, psychological, and socio-environmental model significantly influences the types of services and supports needed to create a seamless transition into the community and a treatment plan for offenders with ID.

## c) *Person-Centered Planning*

The key principles in person-centered planning are rights, independence, choice, and inclusion. Ward (2007) pointed out that person-centered planning is a way in which a person can achieve goals. Specifically, O'Brien's (1987) person-centered planning model for people with ID was designed to increase the individual's ability to make personal choices, to develop further abilities, to have respectful treatment, to ensure social roles, and to obtain relationships that promote growth. Mansell and Beadle-Brown (2004) developed a 3-point plan to guarantee that O'Brien's (1987) five themes are carried out by understanding and focusing on the individuals' desires and competencies rather than looking at what the person is unable to do. Planning, based on solution-focused thinking, can make a tangible difference as long as the premise is on personal growth, development, and empowerment (Mansell & Beadle-Brown 2004).

> Jim was arrested for possessing approximately 5000 computer images that involved child pornography. While in custody, he was referred to the Dual Diagnosis Justice Case Manager by the prison social worker since she had a suspicion that Jim had an intellectual disability. A referral was made to a developmental service agency that specializes in psychological and psychiatric clinical assessments. Once he was released on a Bail Recognizance Order, a psychological assessment was completed. The assessment confirmed a diagnosis of a mild intellectual disability. Additionally, he was also seen by a psychiatrist who diagnosed him with a generalized anxiety disorder and attention deficit hyperactivity disorder (ADHD), which led to genetic testing. This testing confirmed that Jim had a genetic syndrome, namely Fragile X. He continued to be followed by the psychiatrist and a clinical psychotherapist in a sexual behaviors clinic specializing in treatment of people with intellectual disabilities.
>
> Jim was sentenced to a 3-year probation order (out of custody sentence) for the possession of child pornography. His sentence also involved him being placed on the Sex Offender Registry, which required that he report to and be photographed by the local police department annually for 10 years. In addition, an Order of Prohibition was imposed that restricted Jim from attending public places where it could be reasonably expected to find people under the age of 16, in addition to no access to the internet for 10 years.

Jim continues to live at home with his father and brother, has secured supports from a local developmental agency to increase his life skills, and has received weekly therapy through a special needs funding secured by the probation and parole office. In addition, he attends a sex offender management group specific to people with intellectual disabilities. A person-centered plan (PCP) was completed with Jim and his support network including his father, brother, therapist, two support workers, his probation officer, and the police officer who manages him on the registry. Jim recognizes the need to have a network of supports that will guide and direct him towards making legal, healthy decisions for his future. The person-centered plan was a positive experience, and Jim was able to set a number of goals towards a future free of crime.

There are a number of presenting challenges when an individual with an ID is ready for release from prison or has been sentenced to a probation order. The concerns are usually centered on how to proceed with planning for a person in a way that will first and foremost keep the community safe. This can be achieved by ensuring that the person with ID has a life worth living and one that they can feel personal growth by means of setting and achieving goals.

Systems of supports that focus on bettering human functioning has been significantly researched over the past 30 years (Buntinx & Schalock, 2010). Creating individualized support plans that have an assessment and treatment strategy along with a person-centered plan enhances individuality and independence.

Achieving effective lifestyle planning may at times seem like a balancing act. However, it is important to keep in mind that each unit (biopsychosocial evaluation, person-centered planning and quality of life), although separate processes, all coalesce to establish the same result of ensuring that the individual is able to transition into having community presence, participating, and being free of further incarcerations. By interweaving these three approaches, the rates of success will only increase (Buntinx & Schalock, 2010). Baldry and her colleagues (2013) stated that the "establishment of such services in a comprehensive manner would enhance the capacity for non-custodial options, which in turn may reduce harms and enmeshment within the CJS..." (p. 229).

## Factor 3: Delegating a Point Person

When individuals with ID interact with the justice system as an accused, a new host of responsibilities and expectations emerge. This may include applying for legal aid, accessing a lawyer, attending court dates, and/or fulfilling the expectations of a probation officer. In addition to a new set of legal responsibilities, the individual is introduced to a new network of professionals that they may be required to interact with. This may include police officers, lawyers, and/or court support workers.

As offenders, individuals with ID continue to be faced with the challenge of navigating the health sector, developmental sector, and justice sector – often at the same time. This presents an added complexity when supporting this population, as there are many professionals responsible for providing a 'piece of the puzzle' to a person-centered approach of care. Each sector may be responsible for providing treatment or support to the individual in a specific area of their life. The following table

(Table 1) provides a comprehensive but not exhaustive list of important persons that may be involved in the support of an individual with ID:

## Table 1. Important persons involved in supporting individuals with intellectual disabilities

| Justice Professionals | Police Officers<br>Defense Lawyer<br>Crown Attorney /Prosecuting Attorney<br>Detention Centre Staff<br>Probation Officer<br>Court Support Workers |
|---|---|
| Health Professionals | General Physician<br>Psychiatrist |
| Social Service Sector Professionals | Behavior Therapist<br>Mental Health Worker<br>Case Manager<br>Developmental Support Worker<br>Social Worker<br>Speech and Language Pathologist<br>Occupational Therapist |
| Family Members | Mother/Father<br>Husband/Wife/Partner<br>Children<br>Siblings<br>Extended Family |

Delegating a single professional or a lead agency to bridge the gap between the social service sector, legal sector, health sector, and the individual accused can assist in providing a person-centered approach to treatment and support and streamlining community collaborations.

> Jean Pierre is a 34-year old man who lives at home with his parents. He has never received any formal supports other than when he attended school many years previous. He was diagnosed with a moderate ID at age 18 when he began receiving disability funding. His first language is French, and this is the main language spoken in his home. Most recently, Jean Pierre was charged with arson as he set a fire to the loft apartment over his parents' garage where he was residing at the time. He is currently in custody and his parents don't know where to turn. In a brief introduction, the social worker at the detention holding center observed that Jean Pierre was displaying behaviors that appeared to be in line with autism. She referred him to the Dual Diagnosis Justice Case Manager, who confirmed that he had an intellectual disability, after speaking to his parents. A referral was then made for Jean Pierre to receive further assessments to determine whether he had autism in addition to limitations around his cognition. The Dual Diagnosis Justice Case Manager, who was bilingual, was delegated as the "point person" because he was able to communicate with the parents and Jean Pierre in French and the service providers in English. This proved to be invaluable for everyone. He began developing a plan with Jean Pierre's

parents. Within two weeks Jean Pierre was released on a recognizance order for 24-hour, 1-1 supervision. His parents were his surety.

A risk assessment on fire-setting was completed through the courts prior to sentencing. It was determined that Jean Pierre was a moderate risk to reoffend and recommended that he receive psychiatric follow-up for anxiety and depression, group therapy with other individuals who have been involved with the law, and 1-1 supports. It was also advised that he received training for employment, increased community presence, and relationship training. The Dual Diagnosis Justice Case Manager coordinated the services during the time he was involved with the legal system, so that when it was time for sentencing he was set up with an agency who supported him in a home with another male who also had an ID and was French speaking. Staff were hired who were fluent in French as well. Eighteen months later, the court case was completed, and Jean Pierre received a sentence of 3-years probation with a number of conditions.

Difficulties can arise when there are multiple systems working with an individual who don't necessarily have the same mandate regarding care and support. For example, Griffiths, Taillon-Wasmund and Smith (2002) suggested that different systems may use varying language and have different ways of labeling the individual, resulting in conflicting approaches. This emphasizes the importance of having a designated lead agency or professional who is knowledgeable of all the service systems to assist the individual with an ID to navigate the numerous systems, as well as to bring together all support services in a holistic way.

The key responsibilities of the 'point person' includes:
1. Coordinating a range of services and supports
2. Following up on referrals and services the individual may be on waitlists for
3. Monitoring the implementation of the support plan
4. Keeping all professionals involved in the treatment and support plan informed of significant updates
5. Arranging case conferences/planning meetings when required.

## Factor 4: Bridging the Gap Between Various Service Systems: A Collaborative Approach

Once a lead agency or professional takes responsibility for ensuring the implementation and monitoring of the treatment plan, an increased focus can then be placed on coordinating the range of supports necessary. No single service can adequately provide a well-rounded support plan for individuals with intellectual disabilities independently; it requires partnerships and open communication between the various services involved (Dart, Gapen, & Morris, 2002). For a collaborative approach of support to be successful, all service systems must be willing to work together. This can include but is not limited to the individual, family members, doctors, psychiatrists, mental health workers, developmental support workers, case managers, behavior therapists, lawyers, probation officers, and social workers.

The Law Commission of Ontario (2012) outlined the challenge that individuals with intellectual disabilities sometimes encounter when accessing needed services and supports from various sectors in the province. They suggested:

> Laws, policies and programs often fail to take into account that an individual may, for example, be at one and the same time a mother, a person with a mental health disability, a person with a sensory disability and a job-seeker. Laws, programs and services will often deal with each of these attributes separately, so that although many supports may be available, the individual must cobble together a patchwork of services for themselves, none of which addresses the whole person or the particularity of the barriers she or he faces (p. 50).

This argument speaks not only to the challenges that can come with accessing accommodations and support, but the added complexity of agencies, programs and professionals working in silos. Services that support individuals with ID often provide support independently from one another. This can sometimes lead to not only gaps in service but possible duplication of service between agencies and programs. Providing effective support for offenders with ID requires a collaborative approach by professionals in the community.

> Jonathan was adopted at the age of 6, and the family immediately noticed that he had difficulty with anger outbursts especially towards their other two children. As well, his teacher said he had severe behavior challenges that were disruptive in his new classroom. He was assessed and diagnosed with Fetal Alcohol Syndrome Disorder (FASD) and ID at the age of 7 years. He continued on a path of aggression and ongoing school problems. By the age of 18 he was arrested for the fifth time for assault; the fifth assault involved the police officer that was arresting him. He would now be tried in adult court. His parents stated they could no longer be responsible for Jonathan as they were exhausted and had no resources to support his multiple needs.

> Jonathan remained in custody until his court case was settled as there wasn't anywhere for him to live that could provide adequate support. During this time, planning was occurring with multiple service agencies and professionals. After approximately 8 months, Jonathan was released into the care of an agency that supported individuals with ID. They had located a home for him to move into that had two other young adult males. Additionally, the government office of developmental disabilities made a decision to provide funding dollars for the agency in order to provide 1-1 supports 8 hours per day. This support was in addition to the existing staffing in the home.

> Although the plan above appears comprehensive, the staff in the agency had not been trained. For them to effectively support him, they required specialized training around strategies in working with people who have FASD, anger management approaches, and the criminal justice when it pertains to people with ID. The local clinical service agency took on the task of training.

They began training for 4 weeks prior to Jonathan's move and were able to train each staff. As well, the behavior consultant from the clinical service had been visiting Jonathan and his family over the past 4 months and had also developed a Behavior Support Plan. Staff received full training on the bio-psycho-social model. Upon release Jonathan was appointed a Probation Officer who was a specialist in ID. She became part of the team and was provided all of the necessary information to ensure Jonathan's success. As well, Jonathan was referred to a psychiatrist, specializing in FASD, who agreed to begin following him once he was released from custody.

Jonathan's family want to continue to be involved in their son's life but don't feel they can take him home right away. Because Jonathan just turned 18 and he had a developmental disability, the children's mental health clinic agreed to family therapy to promote family centeredness. Staff also got to know the family and welcomed them into Jonathan's new home.

One year later, Jonathan invited all of the important people in his life to his Lifestyle Plan. His probation officer was pleased with the progress he made in the year and noted that she was certain it was due to the collaborative approach with the services and support. Jonathan has not had one intersection with the law in the past year.

A consensus statement on FASD prepared by the Government of Alberta (2009) emphasized the importance of a collaborative approach to support. They noted that individuals with FASD interact with many sectors within the community, and it is paramount that professionals within the community and within the legal system work together to ensure that individuals with FASD are receiving comprehensive and optimal support in all areas of their lives (Government of Alberta, 2009). This was echoed by the Law Commission of Ontario (2012) who identified that for individuals to achieve substantive equality within the legal system there needs to be a collaborative relationship between community members, including justice professionals and community agency workers. This approach to support and treat can ensure that individuals with disabilities are able to access their legal rights in a meaningful way (Law Commission of Ontario, 2012).

## Factor 5: From Emergency to Stability

When an individual with an ID becomes involved with the criminal justice system there is a sense of urgency to arrange the necessary services and supports. At the time of release from custody, there is an immediate expectation that services such as housing will be available, but this can be a challenge since services in the developmental sector are not always readily available. Furthermore, individuals with ID have unique and complex needs that cannot always be supported through mainstream services such as homeless shelters. As such, it is important that professionals who are supporting this population are aware of these barriers and are able to collaborate with various sectors and community agencies in order to develop and create person-centered approaches to support.

In 2016, the Ombudsman released a report (Dube, 2016) that discussed the investigation into the support and services offered by the Ministry of Community and Social Services in Ontario for those with ID. This report included 60 recommendations to improve the accessibility of services of those with ID such as adequate housing and improving interactions with the justice system (Dube, 2016). The following recommendations from Dube's (2016) report addressed the issue of emergency housing for those in crisis:

*Recommendation 8:* The Ministry of Community and Social Services should ensure that there are adequate crisis beds throughout the province to serve the urgent needs of adults with developmental disabilities (p. 43).

*Recommendation 31:* The Ministry of Community and Social Services should take the lead and work with other ministry partners to develop a responsive and proactive system of residential supports to divert adults with developmental disabilities away from the criminal justice and correctional systems (p. 88).

*Recommendation 56:* The Ministry of Community and Social Services should review regional practices for using unfilled permanent residential vacancies with a view to encourage temporary use of such vacancies for urgent cases (p. 122).

These recommendations highlight the very real barriers that individuals with ID face, the importance of having adequate housing for those in crisis, as well as the importance of addressing unique needs. It is paramount to recognize the varying needs of this population because there is not a "one size fits all" model of service. This speaks to the increasing need of multidisciplinary support where services from all sectors work together in order to ensure they do not "fall through the cracks" when waiting for service that is geared specifically to what that individual wants and needs.

> Terry, a 35-year-old man with an ID, was recently released from a federal prison where he served his full 5-year sentence for child pornography. This would mean that he would not be involved with probation and parole and essentially would have no one who will be checking in with him. Since he was part of Children's Services and in foster care up until he was 18 years of age, he has no family or anyone he can count on to help him when he is released.
>
> Prior to his release, the social worker within the prison began corresponding with the team of developmental service professionals in the region where Terry would be residing. In addition, she contacted Circles of Support and Accountability (COSA)[2], a volunteer organization that promotes restorative

---

[2]Circle of Supports and Accountability (COSA) is a volunteer organization that originated in 1994 in Ontario, Canada as a result of a need that was identified for a man with an intellectual disability who had been incarcerated on a number of occasions for sex offenses related to minors. He was being released from prison knowing there was a high-risk of re-offense because he had no supports or services and past recidivism, leaving the prison in a quandary (Wilson, McWhinnie, Picheca, Prinzo, & Cortoni, 2007). It was, at this time, that a group of volunteers formed the COSA model. This premise of COSA is simple. It is community-based program that is made of trained staff and volunteers in the promotion of re-integration of sex offenders into the community by providing "support, advocacy, and a way to be meaningfully accountable in exchange for living safely in the community" (Wilson et al., 2007, p. 8). By implementing these strategies, community safety is enhanced. To date, COSA groups have organized throughout Canada, the United Kingdom, and parts of the United States.

justice for sex offender community reintegration. They agreed to be involved upon Terry's release. Consequently, Terry was greeted by the Circles of Support and Accountability group when he arrived in his hometown. They told him they had a place for him to stay on a temporary basis until housing was secured and that they would help him find adequate long-term housing.

The volunteers knew that Terry had a developmental disability and contacted the local Developmental Services Ontario (DSO) office to ensure he would be placed on the referral list for services. Services such as the local developmental services agencies, clinical services, and the sexual behaviors clinic received referrals. Terry's name immediately came up at an emergency meeting as he was prioritized as a high need for services. The case coordinator from Departmental Services Ontario took the lead and was able to secure some funding for supports after 8 weeks. An agency agreed to begin planning with Terry, and they immediately connected with Circles of Support and Accountability as they saw them as an integral component to their team. Terry was psychologically assessed by clinical services and immediately began social work services. He also received individual treatment from the sexual behaviors clinic for the problematic sexual behaviors. He was also placed in a sex offender group specific to individuals with cognitive delays. Terry was supported completely by COSA for the first 6 months until the lead agency was able to set him up in a group home with two other men who had similar difficulties. COSA stayed involved with Terry where he would attend weekly groups. He also connected well with one of the volunteers and saw him as a good support.

Extensive waitlists and limited appropriate services can pose an additional challenge for offenders with disabilities. Adequate housing, funding, and community resources are not often immediately available when the individual is released from custody. It is important that the individual along with their support team have an in depth understanding of not only what the individual *needs* but *wants* in terms of service provisions. This will ensure that services are not introduced to the individual that are not desired. The stability that comes along with adequate services takes time and must be phased into the individual's life as it becomes available. When an individual is initially released from custody, initial needed services can be introduced such as housing (e.g., crisis bed program, shelters, or staying with family or friends, etc.). In addition, connecting with probation, accessing mental health services, and meeting with a physician for medication are often required. As time progresses and waitlists shorten, other long-term services such as supportive independent living, behavior therapists, social work, and/or day programs will begin to become available. Through the process from emergency to stability it is important that the individual's core support team continues to work together to ensure that a person-centered treatment plan is effectively carried out and the individual does not become lost in the revolving door of the criminal justice system.

## Factor 6: Training for Professionals

### *a) Criminal Justice Professionals*

It has been identified that there is a lack of understanding by professionals within the legal system related to people with ID (Ford & Rose, 2010). The first point of contact for a person when there is an intersection with the law is the police, and yet the police receive little to no training in terms of identifying and understanding the complexities that can accompany a person with ID (Ford & Rose, 2010). Rowley (2013) stated that administrators should prioritize education and training for not only the police but also practitioners, the courts, and others working within the justice sector.

In a review of prisons and the overall awareness and knowledge of people with ID among prison personnel, it was found that there is a particular need for staff training among prison staff (Fazel et al., 2008). Additionally, Young and colleagues (2016) found that staff training designed to build the skills needed to best support prisoners with ID was welcomed by corrections staff. Staff training was seen as a solution to improving the interactions prison staff have with people with ID. Further training regarding the different services and resources that are available for this specialized group should also be provided to forensic teams and prison and correctional staff who have frequent encounters with people with ID (Green, Cook, Stewart, & Salmon, 2017; Young et al., 2016).

From in-custody habitation to the community reintegration phase, it is vital that probation officers who are assigned to an individual with ID are knowledgeable and prepared. While they may have a solid understanding of criminal offenses and how to work with people from mainstream society, there remain several differences that pose unique challenges when working with people who have an ID.

### *b) Developmental Service Professionals & Families*

Riches and his colleagues (2006) identified that developmental service professionals also lack the knowledge and skills needed when they are faced with supporting individuals who have intersected with criminal justice system. Training could have the advantage of shifting from crisis management because of involvement with the justice system to effective interventions and risk management (Riches et al., 2006).

McConkey and Ryan (2001) found that support staff were more confident with their decision making if they had received some form of a forensic-type training. Garrett (2006) spoke of the importance of integrating family and developmental service staff when providing community-based treatment with individuals who are facing legal problems. Understanding the risks of re-offending and factors surrounding that risk can prevent further involvement with the legal system.

> Shawn is an 18-year-old male with an ID who was accessing adult pornography and stumbled across child pornography. He lived with his parents, and when they discovered what he was doing, they told him he had to stop. After a month, he had not stopped this behavior, and his father called the police. They found hundreds of child pornography images on his computer, and he was consequently arrested. After spending 3 weeks in custody Shawn was granted bail.

His mother sought help and was referred to a forensic psychiatrist specializing in sexual disorders. The forensic psychiatrist queried whether there was an intellectual disability. His mother said that he always had attention problems and didn't do well in school settings. Therefore, the forensic psychiatrist introduced Shawn and his family to a clinician who specialized in problematic sexual behaviors and intellectual disabilities. The doctor and the clinician had a suspicion of autism spectrum disorder in addition to a developmental delay. An assessment revealed that he had an ID and was also being treated for an anxiety disorder and obsessive-compulsive disorder.

His lawyer used the disability related issues as his defense, and he was given a 2-year probation order with restrictions, such as no internet or Wi-Fi access. At this time, referrals were also made to local developmental agencies as he became too difficult for his parents to manage, and he was placed in a group home for people with autism. The staff of the home were trained in problematic sexual behaviors and how to implement treatment plans. After this training, they stated they felt more comfortable in providing the necessary safeguards around boundaries, personal space, outings, etc. In addition to the staff within the agency being trained, the probation officer also was in attendance. Having both staff from the agency and the probation officer trained aided in having consistent supports for Shawn.

Finally, training for all sectors in understanding other disciplines is important in building confidence and supporting individuals. Improving knowledge and awareness through training and professional development opportunities amongst all professionals and caregivers is important in reducing the likelihood of further complications with the law (Ford & Rose, 2010).

## Factor 7: Balancing Risks and Rights

The field of intellectual and developmental disabilities has in recent years adopted a rights-based focus for the provision of services. Some of the impetus for this lay in the emergent focus on self-determination and choice for persons with disabilities as echoed in United Nations Convention on the Rights of Persons with Disabilities (UN-CRPD) (United Nations, 2006).

While there has been increasing attention paid to addressing the human rights of persons with intellectual disabilities, there has been very little research or discussion regarding the rights of offenders (Ward, Gannon, & Birgden, 2007). However, when working with individuals who have offended and are living in the community perhaps on bail, by deferral from the criminal justice system, or after having served a sentence and now on parole, a community service provider is faced with the challenge to balance the agency belief in the rights of those it supports to self-determination against the agency obligation to protect the public and the individual from a re-offense.

Although risk management must take precedence – the agency has a duty to protect the individual and the community – there are many factors that must be integrated into the plan to ensure that managing risk does not unduly infringe on the rights of the individual. Without careful consideration, either end of the risk-rights spectrum can be detrimental. Often zealous agencies may overemphasize risk to protect both the individual and the reputation of the agency. However, other agencies who are philosophically driven by the desire to provide self-determination will emphasize rights as their guiding principles. The former may protect the agency but unduly restrict the rights of the individual; the latter may ensure the individual has their rights upheld but fail to ensure that their security needs or those of others are protected. Then there are agencies that are lax in their approach and protocols, and these agencies offer a greater threat to both rights and risk as there may be no consistent or underlying principles guiding their direction.

Ioannou (2013) conducted a study of three types of community services for offenders with ID. In this case, the offenders had committed sexual offenses. She compared typical group homes in which an offender was integrated with other persons with ID with treatment settings in the community where offenders were clustered for treatment services and transitional settings where an offender might go after treatment and before moving into a community group home. She found that the three settings differed greatly on the degree to which they emphasized rights compared to risk. The group home settings predominantly focused on the rights of the individual to make choices, the treatment home focused most on risks, and the transitional settings showed a greater balance in their discussion of rights and risks. This difference may reflect the relative risk that the various offenders in the different settings posed or their relative stage in the treatment and reintegration process. If this were so it would represent a responsible response to the risk-rights dilemma.

Ward, Gannon and Birgden (2007) have provided the most balanced perspective on this dilemma regarding the rights of sex offenders, a group who for many represent the greatest challenge to this balancing act. They suggested that:

> Human rights create a protective zone around persons…all human beings should be afforded human rights, including sex offenders, although some of the freedom rights of offenders may be legitimately curtailed by the State… offenders are both holders and violators of human rights is particularly significant when applying this construct to assessment and treatment… both the offender's rights, and those of others, should be acknowledged and incorporated into treatment…treatment can assist the offender to live a life that is both personally meaningful to him and offence free. Under this premise, neglecting the needs and rights of the offender could constitute a grave mistake, since he is likely to be less motivated to make meaningful long-term changes (p. 197).

Their argument goes further than just advocating for the rights of offenders. It implies that offenders need to be assessed for risk so that they are not unduly restricted, but it also further states that the movement to greater self-determination is based on the hope of rehabilitation as an outcome of treatment. Management is not treatment. Offenders require environments that will explore the reasons for the offense and work towards reducing risk for re-offending, not through punishment and restrictions, but by building resiliency within the individual that will promote a life in which the person is less likely to reoffend. Research has shown that contrary to what is typically assumed, punishment does not reduce reoffending (McGuire, 2002). Instead,

Ward, Gannon, and Birgden (2007) suggested that the treatment of offenders with dignity enhances the likelihood of treatment responsivity and compliance.

Four elements have been suggested as key to establishing environments to prevent re-offenses. (Griffiths et al., 2018). First, managing risks involves establishing environments that reduce the factors that could either not promote the reduction of the offending behaviors or that could inadvertently promote them, while at the same time infusing the environment with factors that promote that reduced offending behavior. Second, it requires selected and trained staff members who are familiar with the person's offense history and the strategies needed to ensure that the elements of effective intervention are in place both in the home and the community. Third, the environment must provide planned opportunities for learning and engagement. Finally, access to social relationships that promote social motivation to not offend is required.

The nature of the environment recommended provides a foundation to achieve what offender researchers have called the Good Lives Model (GLM) (Ward & Stewart, 2003). The Good Lives Model is a rehabilitation approach used in the treatment of sexual offenders that is based on the assumption that, "the best way to reduce risk is by helping offenders live more fulfilling lives" (Ward, Mann, & Gannon, 2007, p. 94). The premise is that offenders will have what Ioannou, Griffiths, Owen, Condillac, & Wilson (2014) have called a "life worth keeping."

> Nick is a 25-year-old man who has been diagnosed with ID and autism. He was arrested 2-years previous for sexual assault of a minor female and found guilty of one count. He was in custody for 8 weeks following his arrest, which was considered time served. He was also sentenced to 3 years of probation with conditions, in addition to being placed on the Sex Offender Registry.
>
> He is supported by a local Community Living agency where the staff working with Nick have received adequate and appropriate training on assessment and treatment for offenders. The agency has a rights-based model that is in place for each person supported. When the agency management and staff worked with the clinician who specialized in sex offender treatment, they advocated for Nick to ensure that the promotion of his rights were embedded into the plan. This was a balancing act as there was also an understanding that the safety of others had to be at the forefront of the plan.
>
> Nick's family wanted to have regular contact with him, but there was a problem with underage siblings in the home. Nick's parents were provided basic offender treatment training and given protocols to follow in the event that Nick refused to follow his supervision order in the presence of those under the age of 16 years. It was decided it would be in Nick's best interest to not have overnight visits since he was continuing to be treated for his impulsivity, and there was a fear that he may initiate non-supervised contact with one of his siblings. Staff were also made available during the day visits if there were any concerns and acted as back up for the parents.

During the next 3 years (probation order completion), it was decided that this was the critical point to ensure that the treatment plan slowly and gradually increased planned learning opportunities for Nick. He was supervised in his community, but there were times that staff would keep their distance from him with an "eyes on" strategy. These were planned events but acted as a catalyst to increase or decrease supervision in his treatment. In addition, the agency wanted to ensure the supervision was being decreased once he began learning the appropriate skills, as this level of supervision was a rights issue.

Lastly, staff slowly began supporting and encouraging friendships while making sure that appropriate boundaries were adhered to (e.g., not phoning a new friend ten times per day). In addition, Nick's person-centered plan identified that he eventually wanted a girlfriend. Two years into his probation order Nick met a girl who was 25-years-old and also supported by the agency. Nick began to have unsupervised time with his girlfriend. Relationship counselling was put into place for the two of them. Nick is also a member on an integrated ball hockey team and plays baseball in the summer with his new friends. His family and staff go along and cheer him on. He has plans to live in his own supported apartment in the future, and staff are encouraging this process as they want to promote his right to be independent.

Although Ward, Gannon, & Birgden (2007) noted the importance of respecting the rights of offenders in treatment and support settings, they further cautioned that "offenders also have obligations not to harm others (entitlements and duties are related concepts in human rights) and any treatment plan should include evidence that respect for other's rights is at the foremost of clinicians' minds, and risk management and reduction aspects of treatment have been included" (p. 204). The concept of Rights, Respect and Responsibility has been a fundamental principle in teaching persons with intellectual disabilities about their rights and their responsibility to also respect the rights of others (Griffiths, Owen, & Watson, 2011). The rights of an offender must be "balanced against the core interests and basic human rights of others and the safety of the community-at-large" (Ward, Gannon, & Brigden, 2007, p.197).

## Factor 8: The Transition from Jail to the Community

The transition from jail back into the community can pose an increased risk for recidivism. Individuals with ID who return to the community, when released from custody, may encounter challenges in finding housing and accessing basic necessities such as clothing and food. These challenges highlight the need for service providers to develop a comprehensive discharge plan that evaluates the individual's risk of re-offense.

The goal of every custody release plan is to make the transition as seamless as possible, and to address any factors that may inhibit this goal. Understanding the nature and severity of the individual's offense can have a positive impact in obtaining treatment, housing, and services.

Ward and Hudson (1998) developed a framework that focuses on gaining an understanding of an individual's sexual offending behavior. This framework has four 'pathways' that conceptualizes sexually deviant behavior Table 2 provides a brief summary of Ward and Hudson's (1998) pathways to offense:

## Table 2 Summary of Ward and Hudson's Pathways to Offense

| Avoidant-Passive | • Individuals lack the coping skills to self-regulate their urges to take part in sexually deviant behavior<br>• Individuals may deny they have sexually deviant urges or attempt to distract themselves |
|---|---|
| Avoidant-Active | • Individuals recognize their urges and actively use coping strategies to try to avoid and control sexual deviant behaviors |
| Approach-Automatic | • Over-learned behaviors<br>• Sexual offending based on impulse. There is often a lack of planning of the sexual offense, but it occurs when the situation is presented |
| Approach-Explicit | • Planned sexual offense<br>• The individual is able to self-regulate but actively chooses to take part in the sexual offense |

Keeling and Rose (2005) suggested that individuals with ID may more often be categorized in the Avoidant-Passive or Approach-Automatic pathway of offending. When considering the Avoidant-Passive pathway, Keeling and Rose (2005) argued that individuals with ID share similar characteristics, such as difficulties developing effective coping strategies to assist with avoiding sexually deviant behavior. Comparably, individuals with ID can be characterized as being impulsive or lacking insight, similar to that of individuals who take the Approach-Automatic pathway.

> Adam was recently released from custody, after he was found guilty of and doing time for exposing himself in the park near his home as well as at an outdoor summer event where there are children present. Three months prior to his release there were several case conferences to plan for his release. It was important that the transition into the community be as seamless as possible and included treatment components that were applicable to his offending behavior.

> After a comprehensive risk assessment was completed, it was decided that Adam would require full supervision especially during the first stages of treatment. The clinician designed his treatment plan around an approach-automatic framework since Adam was described as impulsive and thought to react without thinking about the consequences of his actions. This lack of insight accompanied with impulsive behavior had been an ongoing problem and was hypothesized to be the major factor around public exposure. It was this impulsivity that prompted full supervision in his treatment plan, to be monitored and evaluated on regular intervals. Adam is also seeing a psychiatrist on a regular basis to ensure he is receiving the most appropriate type of treatment for attention deficit hyperactive disorder (ADHD).

> After a year of full supervision, the clinician suggested that Adam be provided with the opportunity to walk to the variety store independently.

This was difficult for staff since they fear that Adam's impulsive actions could result in further exhibitionism and the likelihood of him being arrested again. An updated risk assessment was completed to provide further clarity on the current level of risk that Adam presented. It was determined that his level decreased to a low/moderate risk of re-offense. The fact that he was supervised 24 hours per day and was administered his medication was considered a protective factor and lowered his level of risk. It was also decided that staff would shadow Adam when he walked to the variety store. After 3 months, Adam did not exhibit any risky, or impulsive behaviors. Staff were more at ease with him going to short destinations without supervision but were not comfortable with him leaving his residence for extended periods of time. Adam was okay with this and his treatment strategies remained in place and were evaluated and adapted in regular intervals.

Applying this conceptual framework of offending behavior can assist clinicians in developing a person-centered and individually-tailored approach to treatment that takes into account the specific offense variables and the pathway to offending of an individual. For example, Ward and Hudson (1998) suggested that individuals who follow an Avoidant-Passive pathway may require a treatment plan that focuses on increasing skills regarding relationship building and problem solving whereas the treatment plan for an individual who falls in the Approach-Explicit pathway may require an entirely different approach. Offenders are not a heterogeneous group, and, as such, treatment and support plans cannot be generalized to this population as a whole. Comprehensive assessments to evaluate risk can be a first step in addressing the specific treatment needs of individuals. This way of thinking can assist in creating an effective treatment plan that considers individual difference and how it contributes to re-offending behavior.

## Factor 9: Ongoing Evaluation to Ensure Reduced Recidivism

The goals of assessing and evaluating risk is threefold. The first goal is to recognize and determine the level of risk that a person poses. The second provides important information on the development of treatment and management strategies. The final goal involves understanding what supervisory needs are required for the re-integration into the community (Fedoroff et al., 2016).

Risk assessment requires the use of accurate and valid instruments. Research over the past two decades has revealed a number of methods and approaches to examine the re-offense of individuals who have ID and problematic sexual behaviors, but little has been done regarding other types of crimes. Boer, Tough, and Haaven (2004) developed a risk assessment tool called the ARMIDILO-S that is specific to individuals with ID. It evaluates both static and dynamic variables that include environmental and societal factors, important in the identification of recidivism. Static variables include factors that cannot be changed, such as presence of an intellectual disability; whereas dynamic variables include factors that are potentially changeable such as anger management. This tool can be an important evaluative tool pre/post treatment since risk can change over time depending on the treatment effects and protective factors. Therefore, it is important to include ongoing evaluation and review when it comes to making decisions to adjust current practices (Russell & Darjee, 2012).

Offenders with ID are often lacking effective treatment options due to eligibility criteria for mainstream treatment programs (Jones, 2007). Access to comprehensive treatment for people with ID is challenging due to the limited available resources (Fedoroff & Richards, 2012; Jones, 2007). As a result, supporting agencies or probation officers are often left to develop treatment plans with various strategies to manage and treat the problem.

Developing a treatment plan for community re-integration is essential. Putting post-release supervision in the initial stages is needed to facilitate healthy coping strategies (Rowley, 2013). However, the degree of supervision and time frame for supervision needs to have an evaluative component. For example, once a person has consistently shown that s/he is able to manage the risk factors or vulnerabilities that led to an offense, then supervision can be changed accordingly. In order to avoid liability-related circumstances, well-meaning agencies have resorted to the use of lifelong supervision as a management strategy with no plan to build skills that would allow for a decrease of the level of supervision (Richards & Fedoroff, 2016). By evaluating progress, agencies can determine whether decreased supervision is a viable option and be confident with their decisions. Although some offenders will be able to earn reduced management strategies, some will require scaffold management or even extended management on an ongoing basis. Factors that lead to the latter condition are the individual's willingness to participate and cooperate in treatment, the individual's skill level, and the outcome of treatment of mental health needs.

Garrett (2006) suggests monthly reviews of treatment plans that consider amendments or adaptations and treatment effectiveness. Because of the stigma attached to criminal behavior and the impact this has on one's self-esteem, it is especially important that strategies to address success are built into treatment plans.

Balancing the individual's rights and freedoms while safeguarding the community by evaluating how to use the least restrictive practices is the primary consideration in an evaluation. This promotes positive lifestyle outcomes as we can see with the case of Jordan.

> Jordan is a 30-year-old man who was released from prison with a 3-year probation order. The order restricts him from having Wi-Fi or being in the company of anyone under the age of 16 without supervision by a person who understands his charges. He moved into a 24 hour supported group home with two other men. Staff were trained on problematic sexual behaviors and treatment program. Since Jordan also had a number of bouts of anger and aggression, part of his treatment included an anger management group and he was also provided a behavior support plan (BSP)[3]. The agency decided that Jordan would not be unsupervised.
>
> To determine risk, phallometric testing at a sexual behaviors clinic was administered for Jordan to verify his sexual interest in children. In addition, the ARMIDILO-S was conducted by a clinician specializing in ID and

---

[3] A Behavior Support Plan is based on an assessment process that typically involves a functional analysis and produces an action plan to reduce the challenging behavior through environmental changes and teaching of appropriate behaviors.

problematic sexual behaviors. Results indicated he rated moderate to high risk of re-offense. The protective factors were related to the 24-hour supervision and the current medications he was receiving for ADHD and an anxiety disorder. He was also treated for the diagnosis of sexual disorder (pedophilia).

There were a number of behavioral challenges during the following year regarding compliance issues, aggression, and pushing boundaries. Therefore, stress reduction strategies were implemented through a mindfulness-based treatment. The sexualized behaviors drastically decreased, and there were no recorded incidents of Jordan attempting to interact with children, contact anyone underage, etc. The agency had a process in place to provide clients an opportunity to put in complaints if they felt their rights were being infringed upon, and Jordan put a complaint stating he didn't want to always be supervised. This complaint was taken seriously, but also the agency had to be cognizant that they had a responsibility to keep the community safe.

Since the treatment program mainly focused on his pedophilic interests, it was decided that an evaluation was required. Therefore, the ARMIDILO-S was repeated as a post-evaluation. Jordan's risk was lowered to moderate range of re-offense. This was also based on the medication success regarding impulsivity and reduced sex drive. Given this new rating and knowing that there were just 2 years left on Jordan's probation order it was decided that he would be provided opportunities to be unsupervised for short visits to the local convenience store with the intention to increase the frequency and time of his unsupervised time. Data were collected to verify his success.

In addition to evaluating Jordan's sexual pre-occupations, there was a document review over the past year regarding incidents of aggression and anger outbursts. This revealed some improvement but not enough gains to warrant a change in the process. What was evident was his recognition of the problem. The therapist decided to use strategies incorporated from dialectical behavior therapy (DBT) to address the anger issue further as this was preventing him from moving towards increased independence. The agency also addressed the anger problem with the psychiatrist asking him to evaluate this issue. The doctor reviewed this and discussed new medication options with Jordan. He agreed to do a trial and see the doctor again in 6 weeks.

A person-centered plan update was also completed. Jordan invited his family, his co-worker, and his two main support staff in addition to his therapist to the meeting. He disclosed that he wanted to live in his own apartment once his probation order was fulfilled. As well, he wanted to work towards having an intimate relationship. Since Jordan set realistic goals for his future, staff were more convinced that the process they had in place was moving in the right direction. Sex offender treatment strategies that are geared towards increasing opportunities and changing his sexual thought patterns create a sense of hope for Jordan. The plan for the agency is to create a respectful, rights-based, person-centered blueprint that ensures Jordan gains more and more control over his life.

According to Russell and Darjee (2012), a common mistake occurs when too many restrictions are placed on an individual. They further suggested that good practice is to have an evaluation process in place that identifies the least degree of restriction that is likely to lead to positive strides for the person but also ensures protection of others.

## Conclusion

There is an overrepresentation of people who have intellectual disabilities and co-morbid psychiatric conditions within the criminal justice system (Baldry et al., 2013; Dias, et al., 2014; Young et al., 2016). People with ID are known to experience extreme difficulty when involved in the legal system. From the initial point of arrest to the final stages of planning reintegration into the community can prove to be extremely problematic if there are no supports in place.

Early planning that includes assessment and treatment options involving the collaboration of multisystem stakeholders is key to successful community reintegration. Collaborative partnerships that includes police, courts and prisons, and forensic mental health and developmental services are a necessary and purposeful step towards more appropriate responses when someone with ID and a mental health disorder comes into contact with the criminal justice system upon post release (Fazel et al., 2008; Riches et al., 2006). Formalized coordination of services involving the criminal justice system and developmental services prior to discharge can contribute to successful community reintegration and reduction of risk of further intersections with the law (Young et al., 2016).

While it is important to recognize that the majority of people with ID do not become entangled with the criminal justice system, it is equally important to understand that people with ID are subjected to multiple forms of social disadvantage, and their experiences may result in involvement with the criminal justice system. Vulnerability factors leading up to possible intersections with the law can include the etiology of the ID, social circumstances and poverty, and limitations in access to appropriate professional supports. A generally accepted conclusion is that people with ID who offend should not be incarcerated because of the increased risk of being victimized within the system (Jones, 2007). Early detection and recognition of an ID is the single most important factor towards ensuring appropriate supports are in place to decrease victimization within the criminal justice system (Fazel et al., 2008). Navigating the legal system is a challenge at best so having a diagnosis that allows for developmental services to become involved in the process will lessen the likelihood of lengthy in custody sentences.

Effective supports in the community depend on a number of factors. Transitional stages of change require a trusting relationship with the person who has an ID and their support system. Their lived experiences have often involved social exclusion, loss of basic rights, and marginalization. A human rights philosophy needs to be at the forefront when planning with this group with the assurance that these basic rights are upheld. Respect for one's right to a meaningful life that embraces the theoretical underpinning of autonomy should be supported in any type of treatment plan while promoting community safety. Community participation and full presence typically afforded to other members of society needs to be the basis of treatment for people with ID who are being reintegrated from a correctional setting. Obstacles towards this goal are often related to the lack of appropriate supports and expertise.

Individuals with ID are frequently dependent on others (family members or paid caregivers) to assist them in making healthy choices, and yet many are not connected to a support system that advocates for them. Training for those who are working closely with this group needs to be a priority as it is well documented that those who have increased knowledge and awareness are more likely to have a positive attitude and are comfortable with their judgement.

Over the past decades, there has been an increasing awareness of developmental disorders that has led to enhanced identification and specialized treatment of various disorders such as FASD and different genetic disorders. According to Rowley (2013), the lack of identification prevents the legal representatives and courts from responding appropriately. Given that people with ID are vulnerable to a number of factors including victimization and mental health disorders, it is important to have a range of services, both in the community and the criminal justice system, that is able to support the degree of challenges and complex needs that an offender with an ID will require (Rowley, 2013). Non-custodial alternatives that are tailored to the specific characteristics of people with ID should be strongly considered over incarceration. It is a responsibility amongst stakeholders, from all of the professions, to ensure that vulnerable members in our society are able to live safely in their communities. This requires effective working relationships that strive for the best outcome through appropriate supports. Community re-integration that includes full citizenship must be taken into consideration.

## References

Baldry, E., Clarence, M., Dowse, L. & Troller, J. (2013). Reducing vulnerability to harm in adults with cognitive disabilities in the Australian criminal justice system. *Journal of Policy and Practice in Intellectual Disabilities Volume, 10*(3), 222–229.

Beail, N. (2002). Constructive approaches to the assessment, treatment and management of offenders with intellectual disabilities. *Journal of Applied Research in Intellectual Disabilities, 15,* 179-182.

Boer, D., Tough, S., & Haaven, J. (2004). Assessment of risk manageability of intellectually disabled sex offenders. *Journal of Applied Research in Intellectual Disabilities, 17,* 275-283.

Buntinx, E. H. E., & Schalock, R. L. (2010). Models of disability, quality of life, and individualized supports: Implications for professional practice in intellectual disability. *Journal of Policy and Practice in Intellectual Disabilities, 7*(4), 283-294.

Craig, L. A., & Lindsay, W. (2010). Sexual offenders with intellectual disabilities: Characteristics and prevalence. In L. A. Craig, W. R. Lindsay, & K. D. Browne (Eds.), *As-

*sessment and treatment of sexual offenders with intellectual disabilities: A handbook* (pp. 13-36). West Sussex, UK: Wiley & Sons, Ltd.

Crawford, T. (2008, April 14). *Stuck behind bars, with no place to call home.* Toronto Star. Retrieved from: https://www.thestar.com/life/health_wellness/2008/04/14/stuck_behind_barswith_no_place_to_call_home.html

Dart, L., Gapen, W., & Morris, S. (2002). Building responsive service systems. In D. M. Griffiths, C. Stavrakaki, & J. Summers. (Eds.), *Dual diagnosis: An introduction to the mental health needs of persons with developmental disabilities* (pp. 282-323). Sudbury, ON: Habilitative Mental Health Resource Network.

Day, K. (1994). Mentally handicapped sex offenders. *The British Journal of Psychiatry, 165*(5), 630-635.

Dias, S., Ware, R. S., Kinner, S. A., & Lennox, N. G. (2014). Co-occurring mental disorder and intellectual disability in a large sample of Australian prisoners. *Australian & New Zealand Journal of Psychiatry, 47*(10), 938-944.

Dube, P. (2016). *Nowhere to turn: Investigation into the Ministry of Community and Social Services' response to situations of crisis involving adults with developmental disabilities.* Ombudsman Report. Retrieved from: https://www.ombudsman.on.ca/Files/sitemedia/Documents/NTT-Final-EN-w-cover.pdf

Engel, G. L. (1977). The need for a new medical model: A challenge for biomedicine. *Science, 19,* 129-136.

Fazel, S., Xenitidis, K., & Powell, J. (2008). The prevalence of intellectual disabilities among 12000 prisoners – A systematic review. *International Journal of Law and Psychiatry,* 31(4), 369-372. doi:10.1016/j.ijlp.2008.06.01.

Fedoroff, J. P. & Richards, D. (2012). Innovative approaches to ethical issues in the care of people with intellectual disabilities and potentially problematic sexual behaviours. *Journal of Ethics and Mental Health, 7,* 1-9.

Fedoroff, J. P., Richards, D., Ranger, R., & Currie, S. (2016). Factors related to sexual re-offense in men with intellectual disabilities and problematic sexual behaviour. *Research in Developmental Disabilities, 57, 29-38.*

Ford, H., & Rose, J. (2010). Improving service provision for intellectually disabled sexual offender. In L. A. Craig, W. R. Lindsay, & K. D. Browne (Eds.), *Assessment and treatment of sexual offenders with intellectual disabilities: A handbook* (pp. 343-364). West Sussex: Wiley & Sons, Ltd.

Garrett, H. (2006). Development of a community-based sex offender treatment programme for adult male clients with learning disability. *Journal of Sexual Aggression, 12*(10), 63-70.

Gauthier, S. (2014). Dual diagnosis justice issues information: Northeast human services and justice coordinating committee. Retrieved from: http://www.hsjcc.on.ca/dufferin-local-hsjcc/committee-business/regional-and-local-hsjcc/north-east-regional-hsjcc/our-work-north-east-regional-hsjcc/hsjcc-document-library-north-east-regional-hsjcc/220-dual-diagnosis-justice-information-booklet-2014-04/file on July 2nd, 2017).

Government of Alberta. (2009). Consensus statement on fetal alcohol spectrum disorder (FASD): Across the lifespan. *Institute of Health Economics Consensus Statements, 4,* 1-24.

Green, C. R., Cook, J. L., Steward, M., & Salmon, A. (2007). FASD and the criminal justice system. Canada FASD Research Network. Retrieved from: http://canfasd.ca/wp-content/uploads/sites/35/2016/05/FASD-and-Justice-Nov-16.pdf on May 30th, 2017.

Griffiths, D., Owen, F., Hamelin, J., Feldman, M., Condillac, R. A., & Frijters, J. (2016). History of institutionalization: General background. In D. M. Griffiths, F. Owen, & R. A. Condillac (Eds.), *A difficult dream: Ending institutionalization for persons with intellectual disabilities with complex needs* (pp. 7-16). Kingston, NY: NADD Press.

Griffiths, D. M., Owen, F., & Watson, S. (Eds.) (2011). *The rights agenda: An action plan to advance the rights of persons with intellectual disabilities.* Welland, ON: 3Rs Community University Research Alliance.

Griffiths, D., Taillon-Wasmund, P., & Smith, D. (2002). Offenders who have a developmental disability. In D. M. Griffiths, C. Stavrakaki, & J. Summers (Eds.), *Dual diagnosis: An introduction to the mental health needs of persons with developmental disabilities* (pp. 387-418). Sudbury, ON: Habilitative Mental Health Resource Network.

Griffiths, D., Thompson, K. Ioannou, S., Hoath, J., & Wilson, R. (2018). *Sex offending behavior of persons with an intellectual disability: A multi-component applied behavior analytic approach.* Kingston, NY: NADD Press..

Haut, F., & Brewster, E. (2010). Psychiatric illness, pervasive developmental disorders and risk. In L. A. Craig, W. R. Lindsay, & K. D. Browne (Eds.), *Assessment and treatment of sexual offenders with intellectual disabilities: A handbook* (pp. 89-110). West Sussex, UK: John Wiley & Sons, Ltd.

Hayes, S. C. (2002). Early intervention or early incarceration? Using a screening test for intellectual disability in the criminal justice system. *Journal of Applied Research in Intellectual Disability, 15,* 120-128.

Holland, T., Clare, I. C. H., & Mukhopadhyay, T. (2002). Prevalence of criminal offending by men with intellectual disabilities and the characteristics of offenders: Implication for research and service development. *Journal of Intellectual Disability Research, 46*(1), 6-20.

Ioannou, S. (2013). *Managing risk in a culture of rights: Providing support and treatment for sex offenders with intellectual disability in community-based settings.* Unpublished Master of Arts Thesis. Brock University, ON.

Ioannou, S., Griffiths, D., Owen, F., Condillac, R., & Wilson, R. J. (2014). *Managing risk in a culture of rights: Providing support and treatment in community-based settings for persons with intellectual disabilities who sexually offend.* ATSA Forum, 26(1), 1-11. Retrieved from: http://newsmanager.commpartners.com/atsa/issues/2014-02-11/4/.html

Jones, J. (2007). Persons with intellectual disabilities in the criminal justice system. *International Journal of Offender Therapy and Comparative Criminology, 651*(6), 723-733.

Kaplan, D. M., & Coogan, S. L. (2005). The next advancement in counselling: The bio-psycho-social model. In G. R. Walz, J. C. Bleuer, & R. K. Yep (Eds.), *Vistas: Compelling perspectives on counselling* (pp. 17-25). Alexandria, VA: American Counseling Association.

Keeling, J. A. & Rose, J. L. (2005). Relapse prevention with intellectually disabled sexual offenders. *Sexual Abuse: A Journal of Research and Treatment, 17*(4), 407-423.

Law Commission of Ontario (2012). *A framework for the law as it affects persons with disabilities: Advancing substantive equality for persons with disabilities through law, policy and practice.* Toronto: Author.

Lindsay, W. (2002). Research and literature on sex offenders with intellectual and developmental disabilities. *Journal of Intellectual Disability Research, 46*(1), 74-85.

Mansell, J. & Beadle-Brown, J. (2004) Person-centred planning or person-centred action? Policy and practice in intellectual disability services. *Journal of Applied Research in Intellectual Disabilities, 17*, 1-9.

McConkey, R., & Ryan, D. (2001). Experiences of staff in dealing with client sexuality in services for teenagers and adults with intellectual disability. *Journal of Intellectual Disability Research, 45*(1), 83-87.

McGuire, J. (2002). Integrating findings from research reviews. In J. McGuire (Ed.) *Offender rehabilitation and treatment: effective programmes and policies to reduce re-offending* (pp. 3–38). Chichester, UK: Wiley.

O'Brien, J. (1987). A guide to lifestyle planning: Using the activities catalogue to integrate services and national support systems. In B. Wilcox, & G. Bellamy (Eds.) *The activities catalogue: An alternative curriculum for youth and adults with severe disabilities* (pp. 175-189). Baltimore. MD: Brookes.

Reiss, S., Levitan, G. W., & Szyszko, J. (1982). Emotional disturbance and mental retardation: Diagnostic overshadowing. *American Journal of Mental Deficiency, 86*(6), 567-574.

Richards, D., & Fedoroff, J. P. (2016). Helping those with intellectual disabilities. In S. B. Levine, C. B. Risen, & S. E. Althof (Eds.), *Handbook of clinical sexuality for mental health professionals*, 2nd ed. (pp. 250-262). New York, NY: Brunner/Routledge.

Riches, C. V., Parmenter, T. V., Wiese, M, & Stancliffe, R. J. (2006). Intellectual disability and mental illness in the NSW criminal justice system. *International Journal of Law and Psychiatry, 29*, 386-396.

Rowley, M. (2013, June). The invisible client: People with cognitive impairments in the Northern Territory's Court of summary jurisdiction, Paper presented at the Criminal Lawyers Association of the Northern Territory 14th Biennial Conference, Bali. Retrieved from: https://www.humanrights.gov.au/sites/default/files/Sub40%20Appendix%20Central%20Australian%20Aboriginal%20Legal%20Aid%20Service%20Inc.pdf

Russell, K., & Darjee, R. (2012). Managing the risk posed by personality disordered sex offenders in the community: A model for providing structured clinical guidance to support criminal justice services. In L. Johnstone & C. Logan, (Eds.), *Managing clinical risk: A guide to effective practice* (pp. 217-232). London, UK: Willan Publishing.

Schalock, R., Brown, I., Brown, R., Cummins, R. A., Felce, D., & Parmenter, T. (2002). Conceptualization, measurement, and application of quality of life for persons with intellectual disabilities: Report of an international panel of experts. *Mental Retardation, 40*(6), 457-470.

Sondenaa, E., Palmstierna, T., & Iversen, V.C. (2010). A stepwise approach to identify intellectual disabilities in the criminal justice system. *The European Journal of Psychology Applied to Legal Context, 2*(2), 183-198.

United Nations (2006). *Convention on the Rights of Persons with Disabilities.* Retrieved from: http://www.un.org/disabilities/convention/conventionfull.shtml

Verdugo, M. A., Navas, P., Gomez, L. E., & Schalock, R. L. (2012). The concept of quality of life and its role in enhancing human rights in the field of intellectual disability. *Journal of Intellectual Disability Research, 56*(11), 1036-1045.

Ward, T. (2007). On a clear day you can see forever: Integrating value and skills in sex offender treatment. *Journal of Sexual Aggression, 13*(3), 187-201.

Ward, T., Gannon, T.A., & Birgden, A. (2007). Human rights and the treatment of sex offenders. *Sex Abuse, 19,* 195-216. doi: 10.1007/s11194-007-9053-4.

Ward, T., & Hudson, S. M. (1998). A model of the relapse process in sexual offenders. *Journal of Interpersonal Violence, 13*(6), 700-725.

Ward, T., Mann, R. E., & Gannon, T. A. (2007). The good lives model of offender rehabilitation: Clinical implications. *Aggression and Violent Behavior, 12,* 87-107.

Ward, T., & Stewart, C. A. (2003). The treatment of sex offenders: Risk management and good lives. *Professional Psychology: Research and Practice, 34,* 353–360.

Watson, S. L., Richards, D., Hayes, S., Lecomte, J., & Taua, C. (2012). The right to consent to treatment. In F. Owen, D. Griffiths, & S. Watson (Eds.), *The human rights agenda for persons with intellectual disabilities* (pp. 139-168). Kingston, NY: NADD Press.

Wilson, R., McWhinnie, A., Picheca, J. E., Prinzo, M., & Cortoni, F. (2007). Circles of support and accountability: Engaging community volunteers in the management of high-risk sex offenders. *The Howard Journal, 46*(1), pp. 1-15.

Young, J. T., van Dooren, K., Claudio, F., Cumming, C., & Lennox, N. (2016). Transition from prison for people with intellectual disability: A qualitative study of services professionals. *Trends & Issues in crime and criminal justice, Australian Institute of Criminology, 528,* 1-12.

# Part IV:

## Special Topics/Populations

*Chapter 8*

# Offenders with Autism Spectrum Disorder: A Case of Diminished Responsibility?

*Layla Hall & Jessica Jones*

## Introduction

Autism spectrum disorder (ASD) is a neurodevelopment disorder characterized by impairments in social communication, as well as restricted or stereotyped interests and behaviors (American Psychiatric Association (APA), 2013). Individuals with ASD often demonstrate intense adherence to very specific routines and interests (Bishop et al., 2013) and have also been shown to have difficulties with theory of mind (Baron-Cohen, 2011), moral reasoning (Shulman, Guberman, Shilling, & Bauminger, 2012), and use of social language or pragmatics (Eigsti, Marchena, Schuh, & Kelley, 2011). Additionally, individuals with ASD can experience impairments in executive functioning (Geurts, Vries, & van den Bergh, 2014), often struggle with emotional regulation (Laurent & Rubin, 2004), and have increased chances of being diagnosed with a co-morbid mental illness (Hofvander et al., 2009). This pattern of traits, which impact thinking, reasoning, and emotional judgment, presents complications in the context of criminal behavior and offending. As well, they represent important considerations regarding how these factors might be relevant when individuals with ASD offend and need to be accounted for when considering legal proceedings.

There is growing recognition that characteristics related to an underlying diagnosis of autism spectrum disorder should be taken into consideration in legal dispositions. Recently this has been highlighted by the case of Mr. Lauri Love, a British man diagnosed with autism spectrum disorder who was accused of allegedly hacking into computers of U.S. government agencies. In this case, it was deemed that Mr. Love should be tried in the UK and not be extradited to the United States due to an acknowledgment of his mental status. It was argued that mental health provisions within the U.S. prison system were not adequate to keep Mr. Love safe and that extradition would be oppressive given his mental conditions (Holden & Shirbon, 2018). This high court ruling emphasizes the critical need and legal importance of understanding how to appropriately and fairly address conditions such as ASD within the criminal justice system across jurisdictions in order to accommodate a just and equitable legal response.

In this chapter we argue that characteristics that are commonly associated with an ASD diagnosis could serve as mitigating factors that influence evaluations of criminal intent, criminal responsibility, and culpability among individuals with ASD who offend. Furthermore, with the recent reformulation of the diagnosis of ASD in DSM-5 (American Psychiatric Association, 2013), the spectrum of ASD and severity levels will inevitably have implications for the interpretation of criminal responsibility for this population. Notably, the ideas presented in this chapter will primarily focus on individuals with ASD who are less severely impaired cognitively and have a higher level of functioning (e.g., Asperger syndrome). Accordingly, these individuals are most commonly found fit to stand trial and do not necessarily meet criteria for the Not Criminally Responsible on Account of Mental Disorder (NCRMD) defense but who likely still present with mitigating factors that influence criminal intent and hold significance for decisions regarding sentencing and disposition. Later in the chapter, we will provide a brief discussion regarding the influence of the heterogeneity of ASD and symptom severity on criminal offending.

Concerns about the determination of criminal responsibility in persons with ASD have been discussed more recently throughout the literature (Cashin & Newman, 2009; Freckelton, 2013; Freckelton & List, 2009; Katz & Zemishlany, 2006; Mayes 2003; Mouridsen, 2012; Weiss, 2011). Although links between ASD traits and criminal responsibility have been theorized, no model or framework has been proposed to explain the mechanism by which such factors could facilitate diminished criminal responsibility or culpability. Cohen, Dickerson and Forbes (2014) emphasized that there is a need to evaluate criminal intent differently for persons with ASD, compared to other groups, due to specific impairments related to the disorder. Furthermore, they warn that failure to consider unique factors related to criminal responsibility in this population may lead to inaccurate judgments and inappropriate sentencing decisions. In light of these issues, the following chapter aims to integrate pertinent traits commonly associated with the ASD diagnosis with an established cognitive model of criminal offending in order to provide a comprehensive understanding of how an ASD diagnosis can influence criminal responsibility and culpability and in how the justice system can respond appropriately and fairly.

Specifically, we will argue that characteristics associated with ASD, including impairment in theory of mind, moral reasoning, and the social use of language, can distort one's ability to accurately appraise the nature and gravity of actions. Further, we will propose that characteristics such as difficulties with executive functioning, emotional and behavioral regulation, and circumscribed interests or repetitive behaviors can interfere with one's ability to accurately appraise and appreciate the consequences of a person's actions on themselves and others involved. Through the development of this model, this chapter will provide a valuable resource to criminal lawyers, prosecutors, expert witnesses, mental health professionals, and policy developers so that they might better understand specific impairments associated with ASD that potentially mitigate offending and thus make connections to arguments about intent in relation to criminal responsibility and culpability.

## Criminal Offending in Individuals with ASD

A number of studies have been conducted to investigate the prevalence of ASD within the criminal justice system (Enayati, Grann, Lubbe, & Fazel, 2008; Kumagami & Matsura, 2009; Robinson et al., 2012; Siponmaa, Kristiansson, Jonson, Nyden, & Gillberg, 2001; Soderstrom, Sjodin, Darlstedt, & Forsman. 2004), the rates of offending among individuals with ASD (Allen et al., 2008; Brookman-Frazee et al., 2009; Ghaziuddin, Tsai, & Ghaziuddin, 1991; Lindsay et al., 2014; Lundström et al., 2014; Mouridsen, Rich, Isager, & Nedergaard, 2008), and the types of offenses committed by individuals with ASD (Allen et al., 2008; Hare, Gould, Mills, & Wing, 1999; Kumagami & Matsuura, 2009; Mouridsen et al., 2008). Inevitably, variability in methodology and experimental design has resulted in a high degree of inconsistent results. Differences in findings among these studies may be attributed to salient factors such as the level of functioning and severity of ASD in the study samples, setting (e.g., psychiatric hospital versus prison), screening process for ASD diagnosis, comorbid conditions, sample size, participant age, and gender differences.

Regardless of the variability in approach and results, there is consistent support for the finding that ASD is somewhat over-represented within the criminal justice system, despite no elevation in rates of offending among individuals with ASD compared to the general population (Dein & Woodbury-Smith, 2010). King and Murphy (2014) conducted a recent systematic review of literature on these topics and reported prevalence rates within the criminal justice system above 1% across all studies. This indicates that the rate of ASD within the criminal justice system is likely slightly elevated in comparison to the total population of prevalence of ASD, which is currently estimated to be 1% (Lai, Lombardo, & Baron-Cohen, 2014). This same literature review found that individuals with ASD commit the same number or fewer offenses than matched controls and that the types of crimes committed by individuals with ASD tend not to differ from the types of crimes committed by individuals without ASD (King & Murphy, 2014). These findings appear to be true both when compared to individuals with intellectual disability (Lindsay et al., 2014), as well as individuals from the general public (Mouridsen et al., 2008). In one study, a diagnosis of ASD was found to be a protective factor against being involved in the criminal justice system (Raina, Arenovich, Jones & Lunsky, 2013). Overall, these findings are inconsistent with the popular notion that individuals with ASD are necessarily predisposed to criminal offending (Asperger, 1944; Baron-Cohen, 1988) and anecdotal evidence from case studies that suggest that individuals with ASD are more likely to commit specific types of crime (Freckelton, 2013). Indeed, these studies may be less indicative of biased prevalence rates and offense types but more reflective of the subtle differences in pathways to criminal offending in this population and the legal disparities that they receive.

It has been suggested that the discrepancy between rates of offending among individuals with ASD and their prevalence within the criminal justice system may be partially accounted for by the duration of sentencing and detainment in the forensic mental health system. One study found that individuals with ASD are detained in forensic psychiatric facilities for approximately 11 years longer than offenders with other psychiatric disorders (Hare et al., 1999). The difference in length of detainment raises questions about how criminal intent and offending behavior is conceptualized in individuals with ASD. In their review of three cases of offending among adults with ASD, Freckelton and List (2009) compared the difference between legal outcomes when ASD was not originally presented as a mitigating factor with the outcomes of appeals that later account for the influence of an ASD diagnosis on criminal responsibility and culpability. This case series illustrates how insufficient explanations of the unique considerations of criminal responsibility in this population can have significant consequences on the court's appraisal of the offender and sentencing decisions. Moreover, Freckelton and List (2009) highlight the difficulty in making appropriate decisions regarding sentencing when the court does not have sufficient understanding of how an ASD diagnosis might influence factors such as blameworthiness, responsivity to intervention, and how the individual might respond to deterrent approaches and detainment. Misunderstandings about individuals with ASD, and potential mitigating factors to their offending behavior, may have downstream influences on longer detainment in secure facilities due to uncertainty about their rehabilitation needs and risk of recidivism.

## Case Studies of Criminal Offending Among an ASD Population

The majority of the literature on criminal offending among individuals with ASD has placed an emphasis on the principle of theory of mind as a key factor in conceptualizing offending behavior in this population. Specifically, impairments in theory of mind, or the ability to understand the thoughts, emotions, and intentions of other people, make it difficult for an individual with ASD to appraise what other people might think, want, or how they might react. Thus, the individual with ASD may not foresee the negative consequences of their behavior on others or might misunderstand the intentions of others. While theory of mind surely is of critical importance, there are many other factors that are commonly associated with the ASD phenotype that may provide further direction in understanding offending within this population.

One illustrative published cases of criminal offending in ASD is that of a young man charged with multiple counts of theft (Chen et al., 2003). The offender's intense and pervasive interest in collecting various items such as newspapers, cups, boxes, and plastic bags was the predominant factor behind the thefts that resulted in criminal charges. In this case it may be suggested that the obsessional nature of the offender's interest, as well as his inherent impairments in inhibition and limited understanding of social norms, interfered with his ability to comprehend behavioral consequences and the morality of his actions.

Baron-Cohen (1988) reported on a more complex case integrating restricted interests, theory of mind deficits, emotional dysregulation, and poor moral understanding. This case described the situation of a 21-year-old man with Asperger's disorder who was frequently violent towards his elderly girlfriend. This individual demonstrated misconceptions regarding how his violent actions might influence the victim, which impaired his accurate appraisal of consequences of such a violent act.

Barry-Walsh and Mullen (2004) outlined a series of cases in which a preoccupation with fire or interpersonal contact appear to have played a pivotal role in arson-related, harassment, and sexual offenses. In these cases, preoccupations and rigid thinking related to ASD interfered with the offenders' ability to consider consequences of their behavior. Furthermore, their limited ability to interpret other people's behavior and reactions resulted in misappraisals of appropriate behavior in each given situation. Other reports of arson and sexual assault also highlight how language impairments and communication deficits could further contribute to an individual with ASD misunderstanding the nature and context of a situation (Haskins & Silva, 2006).

Murrie, Warren, Kristiansson, & Dietz (2002) presented five cases of men with Asperger's disorder who committed offenses involving arson, sexual assault, and physical assault. While the descriptions of these cases focused on elements of poor social understanding, they also noted difficulties with executive control and comorbid mental health problems that may have contributed to the offending behavior. For example, one case involving the attempted murder of a psychologist by a 44-year-old male to obtain a more favorable outcome in a custody hearing, revealed significant impairments in insight, cognitive flexibility, and abstract reasoning which impaired the individual's ability to consider the consequences of his behavior.

Evident throughout these case studies is the notion that multiple characteristics associated with an ASD diagnosis can play a mitigating role when considering culpability among offenders with ASD. Such factors include those that might *distort* the offender with ASD's understanding of the nature of the situation (including theory of mind, moral reasoning, and language), as well as factors that might *interfere* with the offender with ASD's ability to consider elements of the immediate situation and long-term consequences of their behavior (including executive functioning, emotional or behavioral regulation, and circumscribed interests or repetitive behavior). In addressing these factors, each case study argued that, for an offender with ASD, their inherent impairments have altered their ability to understand the nature of the situation, their own actions, and the actions of others. Integrating these factors into a comprehensive model can help to explain mechanisms by which these factors influence criminal intent and may influence criminal culpability or responsibility.

## Cognitive Model of Offending in ASD

Traditional models of criminal offending, on their own, do not address the specific issue of understanding criminal responsibility in persons with ASD. While the basic tenets may be generally applicable to offenders with ASD, they do not specifically consider many factors that are unique contributors to criminal offending in this population. Nonetheless, traditional models of criminal offending can provide a strong foundation for examining theories about criminal offending among individuals with ASD.

Cognitive theories of offending are established upon the basic cognitive model, which asserts that behavior is largely influenced by the cognitive appraisals an individual makes about a given situation. Such theories lend themselves well to conceptualizing criminal intent as they emphasize the role of individual situational appraisals in decisions to carry out an offence (Clarke & Cornish, 2000).

It should be noted that in Canada, section 16 of the Canadian Criminal Code (1985) indicates that to be held criminally responsible the accused must have been able to appreciate the nature of their actions and must have been aware that their actions were wrong at the time of the offense. In other words, criminal intent (or *mens rea*) must accompany the guilty act (or *actus reus*). As such, an individual may be found not criminally responsible by reason of mental disorder if their mental health diagnosis can be shown to have prevented *mens rea* or *actus reus*. Alternately, an individual might have a disability or mental disorder, but still be held criminally responsible if they could appreciate the nature and quality of the act. In Canada, the threshold to be found not fit and/or not criminally responsible is high (R. v. Taylor, 1992).

In the case of offenders with ASD (particularly those who are higher functioning and are found fit to stand trial), it is likely that they are also found criminally responsible for their offense. However, characteristics and traits that influence criminal intent often also present important mitigating effects that influence criminal culpability and thus hold significance for decisions about sentencing and disposition that may be especially pertinent for offenders with ASD. Cognitive theories of offending, which highlight the role of intent and appraisal, can be especially helpful for understanding how to conceptualize intent and criminal culpability among individuals with ASD.

Specifically, the rational choice theory (Cornish & Clarke, 1986), which is one cognitive theory of offending derived from the field of economics, asserts that the decision to commit a criminal offense is a purposeful decision that results from an evaluative process of weighing the costs and benefits. Rational choice theory is rooted in the classical theory of criminology and was aligned with beliefs that aimed to better balance crime with its accompanying punishment. In this orientation to criminal behavior, it is understood that crime is purposeful and brings some benefit to the offender, and thus comparable consequences are required to deter an individual from committing a crime (Siegel & McCormick, 2015). Classical criminology and rational choice theory have been critiqued as not fully explaining the complexity of criminal behavior (Ritchie, 2011), and the use of harsher sentences has been shown to be ineffective in dissuading individuals in committing crime (Doob & Webster, 2003). Nevertheless, the principle of deterrence is a sentencing objective under the Criminal Code of Canada (section 718(b)). Rational choice theory has practical implications for considering the role of intent among criminal offenders with ASD as well as fair evaluations regarding sentencing and disposition.

In Canadian law, the assessment of intent presumes rational choice at least to some extent (i.e. *R. v. Oommen, 1994*). Within such a model, the extent of criminal intent may be questioned when there are reasonable grounds to believe that this cognitive evaluation process is absent or flawed due to the presence of a psychological disorder, such as ASD. Thus, offenders with ASD by nature of their disorder are typically assumed to have some awareness of the nature of their actions, and therefore the Not Criminally Responsible on Account of Mental Disorder is often not applicable; however, characteristics related to their diagnosis of ASD have implications regarding intent and culpability that should be considered when determining appropriate consequences.

In addition, rational choice theory lends itself well to integration with other models of criminal offending. Tibetts (2014) discussed the evidence in support of this theory, as well as how it is well suited to integration with other theories about criminal behavior. For example, social bonding theory has been combined with rational choice theory to emphasize the role of individual beliefs about the morality of an action in appraising the costs and benefits of a criminal act (Bachman, Patermoster, & Ward, 1992; Paternoster & Simpson, 1996).

Figure 1 proposes a model by which specific impairments related to an ASD diagnosis may be integrated with the rational choice theory to establish a framework or mechanism by which the diagnosis of ASD may warrant consideration of diminished criminal intent and responsibility. Specifically, certain traits related to ASD may *distort* one's ability to make accurate appraisals about the potential costs and benefits of one's behavior. Furthermore, certain characteristics might *interfere* with the process of evaluating costs and benefits, such that balanced decisions cannot be accurately made. In this instance, the inability to fully consider all (or any) potential consequences of a behavior due to neurological differences can result in committing a criminal offense without understanding and being aware of the full implications of the act.

## Mitigating Factors for Diminished Responsibility in ASD

Mitigating factors, as seen in Figure 1, involve both distorting and interfering factors. Distorting factors include theory of mind, moral reasoning, and language. Each is elaborated below.

### *Theory of Mind (Cognitive Empathy)*

The ability to understand the thoughts and emotions of other people has been called theory of mind. Generally, this set of skills is equated with cognitive empathy (Baron-Cohen & Wheelwright, 2004). This component of empathy is differentiated from emotional empathy, which is the ability to show appropriate emotional responses to another person's emotional state. Differences between cognitive and emotional empathy have been thoroughly studied in ASD populations. There is consistent evidence indicating that individuals with ASD have deficits in the area of cognitive empathy, but there their emotional empathy abilities remain intact (Dziobek et al., 2008; Gillespie, McCleery, & Oberman, 2014).

Theory of mind deficits in ASD have been commonly connected to criminal offending (Baron-Cohen, 1988; Baron-Cohen, 2011; Lerner, Haque, Northrup, Lawer, & Burzstajn, 2012; Post, Haymes, Storey, Loughrey, & Campbell, 2014). In fact, exemptions from criminal responsibility due to theory of mind deficits, referred to as the *Mind Blindness Exemption*, are frequently allowed in English courts (Wauhop, 2009). Theory of mind deficits not only make it hard to interpret social situations, but they also lead to increased social naïveté and limited understanding of how to engage in social relationships, and unrealistic views of reasonable reciprocation in relationships. Woodbury-Smith (2014) discussed how these social-communicative deficits result in behaviors that unintentionally make others feel uncomfortable and motivate them to take legal action. Barry-Walsh and Mullen (2004) outlined a number of cases in which offenders with ASD thought their actions were reasonable situational responses, had extremely limited understanding of the effects of their behaviors on others, and could not understand why they were on trial. Such evidence raises questions about criminal intent and suggests that the offender with ASD may be fundamentally unable to recognize what they are doing as wrong, either morally or legally. Accordingly, they may be able to acknowledge their actions (nature of the act) but not recognize the seriousness or implications of their actions (quality of the act), therefore, impacting the evaluation of criminal intent and responsibility.

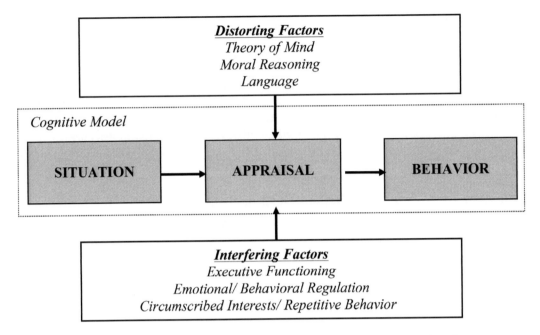

*Figure 1.* A comprehensive integrated model for conceptualizing mitigating factors among offenders with ASD. Specific factors related to an ASD diagnosis are integrated into the basic cognitive model of offending to demonstrate the mechanism by which such factors exert their influence on criminal culpability. This mechanism is by way of distorting or interfering with individual appraisals of a situation, indicating diminished or absent criminal intent.

Support for the role of cognitive empathy in criminal responsibility comes from comparisons between individuals with psychopathy and individuals with ASD (Baron-Cohen, 2011). Specifically, individuals with psychopathy are believed to lack emotional empathy but not cognitive empathy. As such, they are able to understand the consequences of their behavior on others; but place little priority on connecting to the emotional experiences of their victims. Hence, individuals with psychopathy may understand but don't care about their emotional impact on others however individuals with ASD care about their influence on others but may not adequately understand their emotional impact on them.

Misunderstanding of the nature of empathy deficits in individuals with ASD has often resulted in the media equating offenders with ASD to psychopaths (Howlin, 2004). For example, media reports following the Sandy Hook Elementary School shooting were quick to inaccurately link the shooter's diagnosis of ASD to a lack of empathy for the emotional experience of his child victims and their families. Such comparisons are problematic in that those identified as psychopaths within the criminal justice system are generally held criminally responsible for their actions and are believed to be beyond the possibility of treatment or rehabilitation (Samenow, 2004). As discussed above, there is growing evidence that many, if not all, offenders with ASD differ from those with psychopathy with regards to empathy in ways that are relevant to establishing criminal intent and identifying rehabilitation needs.

## Moral Reasoning

There are many reports that basic moral reasoning may be largely intact for individuals with ASD (Leslie, Malloon, & DiCorcia, 2006) and that many individuals with ASD behave with more moral adherence than individuals without ASD due to rigidity in rule following of societal norms (Takeda, Kasai, & Kato, 2007). However, there is also strong evidence that as the rules for moral decision-making become more complex and abstract, moral understanding breaks down for individuals with ASD (Shulman, et al., 2012). Furthermore, there is evidence to suggest that moral decision-making becomes especially difficult for individuals with ASD when they are faced with decisions about the paradoxical concept of accidental harm. Specifically, while individuals who do not have ASD may withhold blame in accidental situations, individuals with ASD still attribute and assign blame (Moran et al., 2011). These findings support the notion that it can be especially difficult for individuals with ASD to make moral decisions in situations that require them to infer the mental and emotional states of other people and to allow for emotional ambiguity.

For individuals with ASD, difficulty with applying moral reasoning raises questions regarding whether they are aware that their actions are fundamentally wrong. This is a persistent issue seen throughout many case studies on offenders with ASD. In the series of cases presented by Barry-Walsh and Mullen (2004), every offender expressed that they felt their behaviors were appropriate responses in the given situations, and they were confused as to why they were on trial. These examples highlight the way in which deficits in moral reasoning may interfere with the ability of an offender with ASD to inherently recognize that an equitable action would even be considered morally wrong (e.g., the 'eye for an eye' analogy). As such, offenders with ASD may be unable to fully appreciate the consequences that are intended to deter them from performing the behavior. Decisions about culpability and sentencing are likely to be substantially influenced by whether an individual is unable to understand that their behavior is immoral, or whether an individual is aware their behavior is immoral but does not care.

## Language

There are relatively consistent findings of impaired pragmatic language and discourse management in individuals with an ASD diagnosis (Eigsti et al., 2011; Marchena & Eigsti, 2015). These abilities refer to the use of language as a tool for social communication. The limited understanding of the pragmatic or social use of language raises concerns about misunderstanding conversations and inappropriate social interaction that may influence criminal offending. Odd phrasing, inappropriate responding, and rigid use of language (Rutter, Mawhood, & Howlin, 1992) may make it difficult for individuals with ASD to clearly express themselves, as well as to interpret and respond to others appropriately. Further, chronic repetitive or perseverative language can also lead to avoidant, or even aversive, response by others. Such challenges increase the likelihood of engaging in social interactions that are not reciprocated nor desired by the conversation partner. Similar to deficits with theory of mind and moral reasoning, difficulties with the interpretation and use of social language are likely to distort one's appraisal of a situation including conversational intent.

Not only do difficulties with pragmatic language interfere with appropriate decision making in situations that result in a criminal offense, but the literal and linear use of language in individuals with ASD may cause such offenders to give the impression of being callous and unemotional once they come into contact with the law. Differences in their use of nonverbal communication such as poorly matched eye-contact and limited integration of body language and facial expression may further present difficulties in impression management which raises concerns about first impressions and biased judgments of criminal intent and responsibility (Freckelton, 2013).

Interfering factors involve executive functioning, emotional/behavioral regulation, and circumscribed interests/repetitive behavior, each elaborated below.

## *Executive Functioning*

Executive functioning involves higher order cognitive skills that allow for flexible thinking, planning, problem solving, and moderating behaviors. It is clear that at least some individuals with ASD experience deficits in various areas of executive functioning including inhibition/impulsivity, working memory, planning, and cognitive flexibility (Geurts et al., 2014). In individuals with ASD, executive functioning abilities develop through adolescence and into young adulthood but may not reach the same optimal level as they do in individuals who do not have ASD (Crone, 2009; Luna, Doll, Hegedus, Minshew, & Sweeney, 2007; Ozonoff & McEvoy, 1994; Robinson, Goddard, Dritschel, Wisley, & Howlin, 2009; Rosenthal et al., 2013).

With regards to criminal responsibility, planning and inhibition serve a critical role in being able to consider the consequences of one's actions and resist impulsive urges. Furthermore, difficulties with cognitive flexibility can interfere with the ability to consider all factors that are relevant to decisions about future behavior and possible consequences. Underdeveloped executive functioning abilities in adolescent offenders who do not have ASD have often been conceptualized as a key contributor to criminal offending (Morais, Joyal, Alexander, Fix, & Burkhart, 2015; Morgan & Lilienfeld, 2000). Likewise, difficulties with executive functioning (especially inhibition) have been highlighted as important contributing factors to criminal offending among individuals with attention-deficit/hyperactivity disorder and fetal alcohol spectrum disorder (Mela & Luther, 2013). With regards to criminal responsibility, Penny (2012) argues in support of the irresistible impulse defense, which applies in situations that an offender has significant impairment in inhibition and impulse control. It is reasonable to expect that such mitigating factors may be very applicable to an ASD population given the executive functioning deficits experienced by individuals with ASD.

## *Emotional and Behavioral Regulation*

As with other psychiatric disorders, difficulties with emotional and behavioral regulation are also commonly reported in individuals with ASD (Laurent & Rubin, 2004; Lerner et al., 2012). Laurent and Rubin (2004) discussed how emotional and behavioral regulation is critical to being able to respond in adaptive and positives ways in social interaction. They argued that poor social understanding puts a strain on one's ability to self-regulate, such that limitations in communicating and interpreting emotional states and intentions often leads to increased confusion, stress, and anxiety. Impulsivity, inflexibility, sensory-motor hypersensitivity, and social confusion can all act as barriers to effective self-regulation in individuals with ASD. Based on an integrated cognitive model of offending, emotional and behavioral difficulties can play a significant role in evaluating criminal intent and culpability. In situations that bring rise to offending behavior, difficulties with emotional and behavioral regulation will likely make it very difficult for individuals with ASD to accurately evaluate the situation, an appropriate response, and the foreseeable consequences of their behavior. The role of emotional and behavioral dysregulation in committing criminal offenses suggests that without such emotional dysregulation and arousal the individual may have been able to reasonably reflect and appraise against carrying out the criminal offense (i.e., rational choice), which presents a challenge to criminal culpability.

### *Circumscribed Interests and Rigid Behaviors*

A core diagnostic feature of ASD is the presence of restricted and repetitive patterns of behavior, interests, or activities (American Psychiatric Association, 2013). Such traits include rigid behaviors or circumscribed interests (Bishop et al., 2013; Lam, Bodfish, & Piven, 2008; Lewis & Kim, 2009) which have been theorized to be linked to criminal offending and specifically criminal responsibility (Freckelton & List, 2009). Rigid behaviors include rituals, habits, strict adherence to routines, and rigid thinking (Bishop et al., 2013). The presence of such traits can result in perservative thinking and behavior, which can interfere with the ability to respond to situations flexibly and in reasonable and appropriate ways. Furthermore, disruption of these behaviors can result in an unmatched response including extreme distress, emotional outbursts, and general over-reactions to the disturbance. Additionally, restricted interests involve preoccupations with particular objects or topics that can be overly specific or extreme in intensity (Spiker, Lin, Dyke, & Wood, 2012). The presence of such traits can result in perseveration and obsession that interferes with an awareness of what level of engagement in the interest is socially appropriate.

Specifically, many individuals with ASD may be so intensely preoccupied with an interest, routine, or belief that it interferes with their ability to consider the broader implications of their actions. Balanced appraisals may be especially difficult in the face of pursuing an obsessional interest that brings pleasure or reduces discomfort caused by rigidity or obsession, thus, perpetuating the intense interest. An example of this is seen in the previously discussed case of the young man charged with multiple counts of theft due to his intense preoccupations with collecting things (Chen et al., 2003). Such an example supports the notion that the presence of circumscribed interests and rigid behaviors may diminish an individual's criminal culpability by way of interfering with their ability to appraise consequences of a situation and adequately provide a measured response.

### Additional Considerations for Offenders with ASD

There are other additional considerations when working with offenders with ASD, including diagnostic comorbidities and the severity of the disability, which are described more fully described below.

## Diagnostic Comorbidities

In the above sections, there are a number of inherent factors that were explored as being delayed or impaired among individuals with ASD and were therefore important to consider when evaluating criminal culpability among offenders with ASD. In addition to these mitigating factors, it is also important to consider how psychiatric comorbidity and severity of ASD symptomatology can exacerbate or otherwise influence these factors.

Research investigating psychiatric comorbidity among individuals with ASD consistently report higher rates of mental health problems in this population as compared to individuals without ASD, especially for depression and anxiety (Howlin, 2004; Sverd, 2003) as well as attention-deficit/hyperactivity disorder and psychotic disorders (Hofvander et al., 2009). It is also well recognized that among criminal offenders with ASD, the rates of comorbid mental illness continue to increase.

In their review of published case studies, Newman and Ghaziuddin (2008) provided evidence that psychiatric comorbidity likely plays a significant role in offending behavior among individuals with ASD. They found that 29.7% of violent criminal offenders with ASD had a confirmed co-morbid psychiatric diagnosis, while another 54% had a probable comorbidity, including mood disorders, ADHD, psychosis, and conduct disorder. Palermo (2004) theorized that many cases of delinquency in ASD occur through interaction between this disorder and mental health comorbidities. For example, sexual offenses involving minors committed by individuals with ASD may be, in part, the result of factors related to this disorder (such as intense preoccupations with sexual contact and poor inhibition) but may also be largely influenced by the existence of sexual deviance and pedophilia (Murrie et al., 2002).

It is important to note that, just as the underlying impairments related to ASD discussed above may distort individual appraisals of situations, symptoms related to other co-existing psychological disorders can have significant influences on the perception of costs and benefits that drive behavioral decisions and influence criminal culpability. For example, the presence of mood disorders has been repeatedly linked to cognitive distortions that may contribute to criminal behavior (Bloom & Schneider, 2006; Murrie et al., 2002). As another example, impairments in executive functioning among individuals with schizophrenia can interfere with an individual's rational decision-making about committing a criminal offense (Tsimploulis, Niveau, Eytan, Giannakopoulos, Sentissi, 2018). When making evaluations about the criminal responsibility of an individual with ASD, it is pertinent to consider how the presence of comorbid conditions at the time of the offense may exacerbate already existing difficulties that are relevant to culpability.

## Severity of Autism

In addition to psychiatric comorbidity, it is also important to consider the heterogeneity and level of severity of the ASD diagnosis. The majority of case reports to date generally illustrate offending behavior in a sub-set of individuals with ASD who are less severely impaired or are considered high functioning (e.g., Asperger's syndrome); however, there are some reports that suggest differences in criminal offending are influenced by level of severity of the ASD diagnosis[1]. In a national study of hospitalized individuals in Sweden, it was found that individuals with Asperger syndrome were more likely to have a conviction of a violent offense as compared to individuals with autistic disorder (Långström, Grann, Ruchkin, Sjöstedt, & Fazel, 2009). Additionally, a Danish study of former child psychiatric inpatients found that by the age of 25-59, individuals with Asperger's disorder were just as likely as matched controls to be convicted of a criminal offense, while individuals with atypical autism and autistic disorder had lower rates of conviction than controls (Mouridsen et al., 2008). With regards to the types of criminal offenses, it had also been suggested that individuals with Asperger's disorder may be more likely to commit crimes involving assault, violence, and threatening behaviour, while those with autistic disorder may show higher rates of aggression and arson (Hare et al., 1999). Taken together these findings suggest that individuals with diagnoses that infer a higher level of functioning (i.e. Asperger's disorder) are more frequently charged and convicted of criminal offenses and may commit different types of crimes than those with diagnoses that infer a lower level of functioning (i.e., autistic disorder) who may be dealt with outside the justice system. These findings implicate considerations for factors such as intellectual capacity, the degree of social and communication skill, and the level of community support or supervision in criminal offending among people with ASD.

## Conclusions, Limitations, and Future Directions

Research on prevalence of ASD within the criminal justice system and rates of offending among these individuals raises concerns about understanding the nature and context of criminal offending among adults with ASD. Specifically, this chapter suggests that misunderstandings regarding criminal intent and responsibility within this population may have downstream influences on the sentencing, rehabilitation plans, and evaluation of criminal risk by the courts and professionals who decide legal dispositions such that a lack of awareness of these mitigating issues may result in inappropriate sentencing decisions. For example, lengthy detainment in both prisons and secure psychiatric facilities present significant vulnerabilities to individuals with ASD by exposure to possible exploitation, confrontation, isolation, and bullying (Dein & Woodbory-Smith, 2010; The National Autistic Society, 2005).

The case studies highlighted in this chapter point to a number of factors related to the ASD diagnosis that can impact the evaluation of criminal intent and responsibility. The proposed cognitive model aims to clarify some of these issues by presenting a framework by which difficulties related to the ASD phenotype may serve as mitigating factors when considering criminal offenses. This model, which is based upon the rational choice theory of offending, emphasizes the pivotal role of cognitive appraisal as a driving force behind criminal offending, and the evaluation of intent is consistent with establishing *mens rea* within the law to be proven by the courts. Specifically, the law conceptualizes offending behavior as being determined by an assumed intact evaluative process of maximizing benefits and minimizing costs of a situation before decision making.

---

[1]Of note, previous literature discussing the relationship between severity of autism and criminal offending has referenced diagnostic categories from previous versions of the psychiatric diagnostic and statistical manual (DSM) to denote higher functioning individuals (e.g., Asperger's syndrome) and lower functioning individuals (e.g., autistic disorder, or atypical autism).

For offenders with ASD, the outlined deficits in theory of mind, moral reasoning, and pragmatic language may distort an individual's recognition and appraisal of potential impact and gravity to their behavior. Likewise, impaired executive functioning, emotional dysregulation, and rigid behavior or circumscribed interests have the potential to interfere with awareness of costs of offending. It is argued that due to these specific impairments, individuals with ASD make decisions to act or behave without understanding the true nature and subsequent consequences of their actions. Moreover, the presence of psychiatric comorbidities and the severity of the ASD symptoms will inevitably impact the evaluative process that an individual utilizes in making behavioral decisions.

Notwithstanding the above, having a diagnosis of ASD or experiencing any one or combination of deficits discussed in this review does not provide a blanket defense to excuse criminal responsibility (Xuan & Weiss, 2014). There is a high degree of heterogeneity in ASD along with a range of severity levels. As such, it is not conclusive that every offender with ASD will experience significant deficits in all the areas mentioned, nor will they all experience impairments to the same extent and in the same way. Furthermore, there is no assurance that the presence of these impairments necessarily indicates or lends to reduced criminal intent or responsibility. Each instance of offending among individuals with ASD must be considered on an individual basis. Hence, a strength of the presented model is that it allows for flexibility of application on a case-by-case basis by considering the various mitigating factors and their potential impact on situation specific offending behavior.

A limitation of this model is that it still relies on a degree of subjective clinical opinion and moral interpretation. Although this model provides structure for evaluating criminal intent and responsibility among offenders with ASD, it does not provide objective predictive values of risk or probability of future offending. Alongside other disorders, research needs to continue to evaluate mainstream risk assessment measures for predictive accuracy with offenders with ASD. Nonetheless, there may be a benefit in establishing such a framework that could be used in conjunction with structured clinical judgment and specialized risk assessment to assist understanding the likelihood of future recidivism in this population.

Although individuals with ASD may only represent a small but growing proportion of offenders in forensic institutions, they can present a substantial burden on the criminal justice system due to their unique needs and pressure on resources tailored to their rehabilitation needs. The complex nature of their profiles and criminal cases have shown to result in their detainment in the forensic system for longer periods both during and following criminal proceedings (Bloom & Schneider, 2006; Hare et al., 1999). The establishment of reliable and valid models to improve understanding and conceptualization of these cases has value in establishing fair and equitable justice for offenders with ASD. More so, from a policy perspective, such models present a benefit in increasing the awareness of the courts and thus efficacy of criminal proceedings and decisions about sentencing and disposition.

Furthermore, while this model has been specifically designed to evaluate criminal intent and responsibility in offenders with ASD, it indicates a method by which criminal culpability and potential diminished responsibility may be conceptualized and applied to many other disorders including other developmental and intellectual disabilities. As such, this chapter may be a beneficial resource for lawyers, judges, clinicians, and policy developers working with some of the most complex yet vulnerable offenders within the criminal justice system.

## References

Allen, D., Evans, C., Hider, A., Hawkins, S., Peckett, H., & Morgan, H. (2008). Offending behaviour in adults with Asperger syndrome. *Journal of Autism and Developmental Disorders, 38,* 748-758. doi:10.1007/s10803-007-0442-9

American Psychiatric Association. (2013). *Diagnostic and statistical manual of mental disorders (5th ed.).* Washington, DC: American Psychiatric Association.

Asperger, H. (1994). Die "autistischen psychopahen" im kindesalter. *Archiv fur Psychiatrie und Nervenkrankheiten, 117,* 76-136.

Bachman, R., Paternoster, R., & Ward, S. (1992). The rationality of sexual offending: Testing a deterrence/rational choice conception of sexual assault. *Law Society Review, 26,* 343-372. doi:10.2307/3053901

Baron-Cohen, S. (1988). An assessment of violence in a young man with Asperger's syndrome. *Journal of Child Psychology and Psychiatry, 29*(3), 351-360. doi:10.1111/j.1469-7610.1988.tb00723.x

Baron-Cohen, S. (2011). *The Science of Evil.* New York, NY: Basic Books.

Baron-Cohen, S., & Wheelwright, S. (2004). The empathy quotient: An investigation of adults with Asperger Syndrome or high functioning autism, and normal sex differences. *Journal of Autism and Developmental Disorders, 34,* 163-175. doi:10.1023/B:JADD.0000022607.19833.00

Barry-Walsh, J. B., & Mullen, P. E. (2004). Forensic aspects of Asperger's syndrome. *Journal of Forensic Psychiatry & Psychology, 15*(1), 96-107. doi:10.1080/14788940310001638628

Bishop, S. L., Hus, V., Duncan, A., Huerta, M., Gotham, K., Pickles, A., & Lord, C. (2013). Subcategories of restricted and repetitive behaviors in children with autism spectrum disorders. *Journal of Autism and Developmental Disorders, 43,* 1287-1297. doi:10.1007/s10803-012-1671-0

Bloom, H., & Schneider, R. D. (2006). *Mental disorders and the law: A primer for legal and mental health professionals.* Toronto, ON: Irwin Law.

Brookman-Frazee, L., Baker-Ericzan, M., Stahmer, A., Mandell, D., Haine, R. A., & Hough, R. L. (2009). Involvement of youths with autism spectrum disorder or intellectual disabilities in multiple public service systems. *Journal of Mental Health Research in Intellectual Disabilities, 2,* 201-219. doi:10.1080/19315860902741542

Cashin, A., & Newman, C. (2009). Autism in the criminal justice detention system: A review of the literature. *Journal of Forensic Nursing, 5,* 70-75. doi:10.1111/j.1939-3938.2009.01037.x.

Chen, P. S., Chen, S. J., Yang, Y. K., Yeh, T. L., Chen, C. C., & Lo, H. Y. (2003). Asperger's disorder: A case report of repeated stealing and the collecting behaviours of an adolescent patient. *Acta Psychiatrica Scandinavica, 107,* 73-76. doi:10.1034/j.1600-0447.2003.01354.x

Clarke, R. V., & Cornish, D. B. (2000). Rational choice. In R. Paternoster & R. Bachman (Eds.), *Explaining criminals and crime: Essays in contemporary criminological theory* (pp. 23-42). Los Angeles, CA: Roxbury.

Cohen, J. A., Dickerson, T. A., & Forbes, J. M. (2014). Legal review of autism, a syndrome rapidly gaining wide attention within our society. *Albany Law Review, 77*, 389-423. Retrieved from: http://www.albanylawreview.org/Articles/Vol77_2/77.2.0389%20 Cohen%20Dickerson.pdf

Cornish, D., & Clarke, R. (1986). *The reasoning criminal: Rational choice perspectives on offending.* New York, NY: Springer.

*Criminal Code of Canada*, R.S.C. 1985, c. C-46.

Crone, E. A. (2009). Executive functions in adolescence: Inferences from brain and behavior. *Developmental Science, 12*, 825–830. doi:10.1111/j.1467-7687.2009.00918.x

Dein, K., & Woodbury-Smith, M. (2010). Asperger syndrome and criminal behaviour. *Advances in Psychiatric Treatment, 16*, 37-43. doi:10.1192/apt.bp.107.005082

Doob, A. N., & Webster, C. M. (2003). Sentence severity and crime: Accepting the null hypothesis. *Crime and Justice, 30*: 143–195. doi: 10.1086/652230

Dziobek, I., Rogers, K., Fleck, S., Bahnemann, M., Heekeren, H. R., Wolf, O. T., & Convit, A. (2008). Dissociation of cognitive and emotional empathy in adults with Asperger Syndrome using the multifaceted empathy test (MET). *Journal of Autism and Developmental Disorders, 38*, 464-473. doi:10.1007/s10803-007-0486-x

Eigsti, I. M., de Marchena, A. B., Schuh, J. M., & Kelley, E. (2011). Language acquisition in autism spectrum disorders: A developmental review. *Research in Autism Spectrum Disorders, 5*, 681-691. doi:10.1016/j.rasd.2010.09.001

Enayati, J., Grann, M., Lubbe, S., & Fazel, S. (2008). Psychiatric morbidity in arsonists referred for forensic psychiatric assessment in Sweden. *Journal of Forensic Psychiatry and Psychology, 19*, 139-147. doi:10.1080/14789940701789500

Freckelton, I. S. C. (2013). Autism spectrum disorder: Forensic issues and challenges for mental health professionals and courts. *Journal of Applied Research in Intellectual Disabilities, 26*, 420-434. doi:10.1111/jar.12036

Freckelton, I. S. C., & List, D. (2009). Asperger's disorder, criminal responsibility, and criminal culpability. *Psychiatry, Psychology and Law, 12*, 16-40. doi:10.1080/13218710902887483

Geurts, H. M., de Vries, M., & van den Bergh, S. F. (2014). Executive functioning theory and autism. In S. Goldstein, & J. A. Naglieri (Eds.), *Handbook of executive functioning* (pp. 121-141). New York, NY: Springer.

Ghaziuddin, M., Tsai, L., & Ghaziuddin, N. (1991). Brief report: Violence in Asperger Syndrome, a critique. *Journal of Autism and Developmental Disorders, 21*, 439-354. doi: 10.1007/BF02207331

Gillespie, S. M., McCleery, J. P., & Oberman, L. M. (2014). Spontaneous versus deliberate vicarious representations: Different routes to empathy in psychopathy and autism. *Brain, 137*, e272-e272. doi:10.1093/brain/awt364

Gordon, V., Donnelly, P. D., & Williams, D. J. (2014). Relationship between ADHD symptoms and anti-social behaviour in a sample of older youths in adult Scottish prisons. *Personality and Individual Differences, 58*, 116-121. doi:10.1016/j.paid.2013.10.022

Hare, D. J., Gould, J., Mills, R., & Wing, L. (1999). A preliminary study of individuals with autistic spectrum disorders in three special hospitals in England. Retrieved December 29, 2007, from: https://pdfs.semanticscholar.org/2d26/017411f22bc-c1517abf92a816153a7a5032b.pdf

Haskins, B. G., & Silva, J. A. (2006). Asperger's disorder and criminal behavior: Forensic-psychiatric considerations. *Journal of the American Academy of Psychiatry and the Law Online, 34*, 374-384. Retrieved from http://jaapl.org/content/34/3/374.long

Hofvander, B., Delorme, R., Chaste, P., Nyden, A., Wentz, E., Stahlberg, O.,... Leboyer, M. (2009). Psychiatric and psychosocial problems in adults with normal-intelligence autism spectrum disorders. *BioMed Central Psychiatry, 9*, 35. doi: 10.1186/1471-244X-9-35

Holden, M., & Shirbon, E. (2018, February 5). Autistic UK man accused of hacking FBI wins appeal against extradition to U.S.. *Reuters*. Retrieved from https://www.reuters.com

Howlin, P. (2004). *Autism: Preparing for adulthood (2nd ed.)*. London: Routledge. Johnson, S. A., Filliter, J. H., & Murphy, R. R. (2009). Discrepancies between self-and parent-perceptions of autistic traits and empathy in high functioning children and adolescents on the autism spectrum. *Journal of Autism and Developmental Disorders, 39*(12), 1706-1714. doi:10.1007/s10803-009-0809-1

Katz, N., & Zemishlany, Z. (2006). Criminal responsibility in Asperger's syndrome. *Israel Journal of Psychiatry Related Science, 43*, 166-173.

King, C., & Murphy, G. H. (2014). A systematic review of people with autism spectrum disorder and the criminal justice system. *Journal of Autism and Developmental Disorders*, 1-17. doi:10.1007/s10803-014-2046-5

Kumagami, T., & Matsuura, N. (2009). Prevalence of pervasive developmental disorder in juvenile court cases in Japan. *The Journal of Forensic Psychiatry & Psychology, 20*, 974-987. doi:10.1080/14789940903174170

Lai, M., Lombardo, M. V., & Baron-Cohen, S. (2014). Autism. *Lancet, 383*, 896-910. doi: 10.1016/S0140-6736(13)61539-1

Lam, K. S., Bodfish, J. W., & Piven, J. (2008). Evidence for three subtypes of repetitive behavior in autism that differ in familiality and association with other symptoms. *Journal of Child Psychology and Psychiatry, 49*, 1193-1200. doi:10.1111/j.1469-7610.2008.01944.x

Långström, N., Grann, M., Ruchkin, V., Sjöstedt, G., & Fazel, S. (2009). Risk factors for violent offending in autism spectrum disorder: a national study of hospitalized individuals. *Journal of Interpersonal Violence, 24*, 1358-1370. doi:10.1177/0886260508322195

Laurent, A. C., & Rubin, E. (2004). Challenges in emotional regulation in Asperger syndrome and high-functioning autism. *Topics in Language Disorders, 24*, 286-297. doi:10.1097/00011363-200410000-00006

Lerner, M. D., Haque, O. S., Northrup, E. C., Lawer, L., & Bursztajn, H. J. (2012). Emerging perspectives on adolescents and young adults with high-functioning autism spectrum disorders, violence, and criminal law. *Journal of the American Academy of Psychiatry and the Law Online, 40*, 177-190. Retrieved from http://jaapl.org/content/40/2/177.long

Leslie, A. M., Mallon, R., & DiCorcia, J. A. (2006). Transgressors, victims, and cry-babies: Is basic moral judgment spared in autism? *Social Neuroscience, 1*, 270-283. doi:10.1080/17470910600992197

Lewis, M., & Kim, S. J. (2009). The pathophysiology of restricted repetitive behavior. *Journal of Neurodevelopmental Disorders, 1*, 114-132. doi:10.1007/s11689-009-9019-6

Lindsay, W. R., Carson, D., O'Brien, G., Holland, A. J., Taylor, J. L., Wheeler, J. R., & Steptoe, L. (2014). A comparison of referrals with and without autism spectrum disorder to forensic intellectual disability services. *Psychiatry, Psychology and Law, 21*, 947-954. doi:10.1080/13218719.2014.918081

Luna, B., Doll, S. K., Hegedus, S. J., Minshew, N. J., & Sweeney, J. A. (2007). Maturation of executive function in autism. *Biological Psychiatry, 61*, 474-481. doi:10.1016/j.biopsych.2006.02.030

Lundström, S., Forsman, M., Larsson, H., Kerekes, N., Serlachius, E., Långström, N., & Lichtenstein, P. (2014). Childhood neurodevelopmental disorders and violent criminality: A sibling control study. *Journal of Autism and Developmental Disorders, 44*, 2707-2716. doi:10.1007/s10803-013-1873-0

Marchena, A., & Eigsti, I. (2015). The art of common ground: Emergence of a complex pragmatic language skill in adolescents with autism spectrum disorders. *Journal of Child Language, 43*, 43-80. doi:10.1017/S0305000915000070

Mayes, T. A. (2003). Persons with autism and criminal justice: Core concepts and leading cases. *Journal of Positive Behavior Interventions, 5*, 92-100. doi:10.1177/10983007030050020401

Mela, M., & Luther, G. (2013). Fetal alcohol spectrum disorder: Can diminished responsibility diminish criminal behaviour? *International journal of law and psychiatry, 36*, 46-54. doi:10.1016/j.ijlp.2012.11.007

Morais, H. B., Joyal, C. C., Alexander, A. A., Fix, R. L., & Burkhart, B. R. (2015). The neuropsychology of adolescent sexual offending: Testing an executive dysfunction hypothesis. *Sexual Abuse: A Journal of Research and Treatment, 28*, 741-754. doi:10.1177/1079063215569545

Moran, J. M., Young, L. L., Saxe, R., Lee, S. M., O'Young, D., Mavros, P. L., & Gabrieli, J. D. (2011). Impaired theory of mind for moral judgment in high-functioning autism. *Proceedings of the National Academy of Sciences, 108*, 2688-2692. doi:10.1073/pnas.1011734108

Morgan, A. B., & Lilienfeld, S. O. (2000). A meta-analytic review of the relation between antisocial behavior and neuropsychological measures of executive function. *Clinical Psychology Review, 20*, 113–136. doi:10.1016/S0272-7358(98)00096-8

Mouridsen, S. E. (2012). Current status of research on autism spectrum disorders and offending. *Research in Autism Spectrum Disorders, 6*, 79-86. doi:10.1016/j.rasd.2011.09.003

Mouridsen, S. E., Rich, B., Isager, T., & Nedergaard, N. J. (2008). Pervasive developmental disorder and criminal behaviour: A case control study. *International Journal of Offender Therapy and Comparative Criminology, 52*, 196 – 205. doi:10.1177/0306624X07302056

Murrie, D. C., Warren, J. I., Kristiansson, M., & Dietz, P. E. (2002). Asperger's syndrome in forensic settings. *International Journal of Forensic Mental Health, 1*, 59–70. doi:10.1080/14999013.2002.10471161

The National Autistic Society. (2005). *Autism: A guide for criminal justice professionals.* The National Autistic Society; London, UK.

Newman, S. S., & Ghaziuddin, M. (2008). Violent crime in Asperger syndrome: The role of psychiatric comorbidity. *Journal of Autism and Developmental Disorders, 38*, 1848-1852. doi:10.1007/s10803-008-0580-8

Ozonoff, S., & McEvoy, R. E. (1994). A longitudinal study of executive function and theory of mind development in autism. *Development and Psychopathology, 6*, 415-431. doi:10.1017/S0954579400006027

Palermo, M. T. (2004). Pervasive developmental disorders, psychiatric comorbidities, and the law. *International Journal of Offender Therapy and Comparative Criminology, 48*, 40-48. doi:10.1177/0306624X03257713

Paternoster, R., & Simpson, S. (1996). Sanction threats and appeals to morality: Testing a rational choice model of corporate crime. *Law & Society Review, 30*, 378–399. doi:10.2307/3054128

Penney, S. (2012). Impulse control and criminal responsibility: Lessons from neuroscience. *International Journal of Law and Psychiatry, 35*, 99-103. doi:10.1016/j.ijlp.2011.12.004

Post, M., Haymes, L., Storey, K., Loughrey, T., & Campbell, C. (2014). Understanding stalking behaviors by individuals with autism spectrum disorders and recommended prevention strategies for school settings. *Journal of Autism and Developmental Disorders, 44*, 2698-2706. doi:10.1007/s10803-012-1712-8

Raina, P., Arenovich, T., Jones, J. & Lunsky, Y. (2013). Pathways into the criminal justice system for individuals with intellectual disabilities. *Journal of Applied Research in Intellectual Disabilities, 26*, 404-409. doi:10.1111/jar.12039

Ritchie, D. (2011). *Does imprisonment deter?: A review of the evidence*. Retrieved from https://www.sentencingcouncil.vic.gov.au

Robinson, S., Goddard, L., Dritschel, B., Wisley, M., & Howlin, P. (2009). Executive functions in children with autism spectrum disorders. *Brain and Cognition, 71*, 362–368. doi:10.1016/j.bandc.2009.06.007

Robinson, L., Spencer, M. D., Thomson, L. D., Stanfield, A. C., Owens, D. G., Hall, J., & Johnstone, E. C. (2012). Evaluation of a screening instrument for autism spectrum disorders in prisoners. *PLoS One, 7(5)*, e36078. doi:10.1371/journal.pone.0036078

Rosenthal, M., Wallace, G. L., Lawson, R., Wills, M. C., Dixon, E., Yerys, B. E., & Kenworthy, L. (2013). Impairments in real-world executive function disease from childhood to adolescence in autism spectrum disorders. *Neuropsychology, 27*, 13–18. doi:10.1037/a0031299

Rutter, M., Mawhood, L., & Howlin, P. (1992). Language delay and social development. In P. Fletcher & D. Hall (Eds.), *Specific speech and language disorders in children* (pp. 63-78). San Diego, CA: Singular Press.

R. v. Oommen (1994) 2 S.C.R. 507

R. v. Taylor (1992) SCC 50, [2014] 2 S.C.R. 495

Samenow, S. E. (2004). *Inside the criminal mind*. New York, NY: Crown Publishers.

Shulman, C., Guberman, A., Shiling, N., & Bauminger, N. (2012). Moral and social reasoning in autism spectrum disorders. *Journal of Autism and Developmental Disorders, 42*, 1364-1376. doi:10.1007/s10803-011-1369-8

Siegel, L. J., & McCormick, C. R. (2015). *Criminology in Canada: Theories, Patterns, and Typologies*. Toronto, ON: Nelson Thomson Learning.

Siponmaa, L., Kristiansson, M., Jonson, C., Nyden, A., & Gillberg, C. (2001). Juvenile and young adult mentally disordered offenders: The role of child neuropsychiatric disorders. *Journal of American Academy of Psychiatry and the Law, 29*, 420-426.

Soderstrom, H., Sjodin, A. K., Carlstedt, A., & Forsman, A. (2004). Adult psychopathic personality with childhood-onset hyperactivity and conduct disorder: A central problem constellation in forensic psychiatry. *Psychiatry Research, 121*, 271-280. doi:10.1016/S0165-1781(03)00270-1

Spiker, M. A., Lin, C. E., Van Dyke, M., & Wood, J. J. (2012). Restricted interests and anxiety in children with autism. *Autism,* 16, 306-320. doi: 10.1177/1362361311401763

Sverd, J. (2003). Psychiatric disorders in individuals with pervasive developmental disorder. *Journal of Psychiatric Practice, 9*, 111-127. doi: 10.1097/00131746-200303000-00003

Takeda, T., Kasai, K., & Kato, N. (2007). Moral judgment in high functioning pervasive developmental disorders. *Psychiatry and Clinical Neurosciences,61*(4), 407-414. doi: 10.1111/j.14401819.2007.01678.x

Tibbetts, S. G. (2014). Integrating rational choice and other theories. In G. Bruinsma, & D. Weisburd (Eds.), *Encyclopedia of criminology and criminal justice* (pp. 2564-2573). New York, NY: Springer.

Tsimploulis, G., Niveau, G., Eytan, A., Giannakopoulos, P., & Sentissi, O. (2018). Schizophrenia and criminal responsibility: A systematic review. *The Journal of nervous and mental disease, 206*(5), 370-377. doi: 10.1097/NMD.0000000000000805

Wauhop, B. (2009). Mindblindness: Three nations approach the special case of the criminally accused individuals with Asperger's Syndrome. *Penn State International Law Review,* 27, 1-31.

Weiss, J. K. (2011). Autism spectrum disorder and criminal justice: square peg in a round hole? *American Journal of Forensic Psychiatry, 32*, 3-19.

Woodbury-Smith, M. (2014). Unlawful behaviors in adolescents and adults with autism spectrum disorders. In F. Volkmar, B. Reichow, & J. McPartland (Eds.), *Adolescents and adults with autism spectrum disorders* (pp. 269-281). New York, NY: Springer.

Xuan, Y., & Weiss, K. J. (2014). Diminished capacity: Mitigating or aggravating factor in sentencing? *Journal of the American Academy of Psychiatry and the Law Online, 42*, 242-243. Retrieved from http://jaapl.org/content/42/2/242.

*Chapter 9*

# Justice-Involved Individuals with Fetal Alcohol Spectrum Disorder: Risks, Interventions, and Protective Factors

*Shelley Watson, Lisa Whittingham, Kelly Coons-Harding, & Elisa Richer*

Fetal alcohol spectrum disorder (FASD) describes the constellation of effects associated with prenatal alcohol exposure (Cook et al., 2016). It is a lifelong and often invisible disability that impacts an individual's cognitive, behaviural, physical, social-emotional, and adaptive functioning. Internationally, it is considered the leading known cause of developmental disability and is a major public health concern. Furthermore, FASD does not represent a homogenous group of individuals; it represents a spectrum of individuals. For example, *fetal alcohol syndrome* (FAS) or *FASD with sentinel facial features* accounts for 10% of persons diagnosed with FASD and is used to describe individuals that exhibit the traditional facial features associated with prenatal exposure (i.e., smooth philtrum), that have neuropsychological impacts, and where there is confirmation that the mother drank during pregnancy (Chudley et al., 2005; Cook et al., 2016; Streissguth, 1997).

The estimates of FASD vary according to country and it has been identified as being more prevalent in some special populations. For example, North American estimates indicate that approximately 1 in 100 live births will have FASD; however, newer estimates indicate a higher prevalence rate of approximately 1-4% of the general population (May et al., 2018; Thanh, Jonsson, Salmon, & Sebastianski, 2014). Around the world, estimates have been shown to vary widely. For example, in South Africa, the prevalence of FASD is estimated to be significantly higher, with rates closer to 10 in 100 (Lange et al., 2017; Roozen et al., 2016). Furthermore, and as most relevant to this chapter, research has indicated that there is higher prevalence of FASD in vulnerable populations, including those involved in the child welfare and justice systems (Tough & Jack, 2010).

Streissguth (1997) suggested that the effects of FASD could be divided into primary and secondary impacts. Primary impacts result from organic brain damage and "they reflect the Central Nervous System (CNS) dysfunction inherent in the diagnosis" (Streissguth, 1997, p. 96). These effects include attentional deficits, poor judgement, memory impairments, and poor impulse control (Streissguth, 1997). Secondary adverse outcomes are the impairments that result from an on-going mismatch between the individual and their environment (Streissguth, Barr, Bookstein, Sampson, & Olsen, 1999; Streissguth, Barr, Kogan, & Bookstein, 1996). These deficits include multiple foster home placements, criminal justice system involvement, poor educational outcomes, poor mental health, and addictions. More recently, some scholars and advocates of FASD have started to divide the impacts of FASD into primary, secondary, and tertiary characteristics (i.e., Malbin, 2002). Primary characteristics are the neurodevelopmental characteristics associated with FASD (i.e., memory impairments); secondary characteristics are the patterns of behavior that develop as result of the inconsistency between the individual and the environment (i.e., anxiety); and tertiary characteristics are the result of the on-going discrepancy between the individual and the environment (e.g., criminal justice system involvement) (Malbin, 2002).

When individuals with FASD are properly supported, they can lead fulfilling and productive lives. That is, many of the secondary and tertiary characteristics are avoidable or can be addressed with proper supports (Malbin, 2002). Unfortunately, because of inadequate supports, many individuals with FASD experience adverse outcomes, such as disrupted school experience, dependent living, incarceration, unemployment, and homelessness (Fast, Conry, & Loock, 1999; Malbin, 2002; Streissguth, 1997; Streissguth et al., 1996; Streissguth et al., 1999; Streissguth et al., 2004). Of all the detrimental outcomes that an individual with FASD can face, involvement in the criminal justice system can be most arduous and severe.

## Fetal Alcohol Spectrum Disorder and the Criminal Justice System

Individuals with FASD are likely to come into contact with the criminal justice system as both offenders and victims. To date, most of the research conducted has focused on individuals with FASD as offenders due to the high incidents of incarceration. The focus of this chapter will be on offenders with FASD, although it is important to note that individuals with FASD are also likely to come into contact with the criminal justice system as victims. Given that less attention has been given to victims with FASD in the literature, future research should focus on this vulnerable group of individuals.

### Persons with FASD as Offenders

General trends indicate that individuals with FASD are overrepresented in the criminal justice system as offenders (e.g., Burd, Selfridge, Klug, & Juelson, 2003; Corrado, Freedman, & Blatier, 2011; Hughes, Clasby, Chitsabesan, & Williams, 2016; McLachlan et al., 2019; Popova, Lange, Burd, & Rehm, 2015; Rojas & Gretton 2007). Systematic literature reviews have found that there is no clear consensus regarding the prevalence of FASD in the criminal justice system; however, the prevalence rate was clearly higher than what is found in the general population, with individuals with FASD being 19 times more likely to be incarcerated compared to those without FASD (Flannigan, Pei, Stewart, & Johnson, 2018; Popova, Lange, Bekmuradov, Mihic, & Rehm, 2011). According to Streissguth and colleagues (2004), 14% of children and 60% of adolescents and adults diagnosed with FASD in their study reported having trouble with the law.

Persons with FASD present with a wide range of complex challenges to a system that is often not equipped to support them. This is not surprising given the intersection between primary and secondary characteristics (Cunningham, Mishibinijima, Mohammed, Mountford, & Santiago, 2010; Rogers, McLachlan, & Roesch, 2013). While the involvement of persons with FASD in the criminal justice system has increasingly emerged as a negative outcome, drawing public, policy, and academic attention, there remains limited available data to inform and direct activities (Flannigan et al., 2018). Adverse outcomes, such as criminal justice system involvement, increase the complexity of care required for individuals with FASD and result in significant social, economic, and personal costs to individuals, families, and society as a whole.

One of the challenges associated with identifying how many individuals with FASD are in the criminal justice system is the barriers to effective assessment and identification. In an earlier study conducted in British Columbia, a cohort of 287 incarcerated adolescents between the ages of 12 and 18 participated in a forensic psychiatric or psychological assessment. Fast and colleagues (1999) found that 23.3% of the individuals screened for FASD met the criteria for a diagnosis; however, only 1% had been diagnosed prior to the assessment. The findings from this study suggest that many individuals with FASD are undiagnosed prior to their involvement with the criminal justice system and are therefore precluded from accessing the supports and interventions that could help reduce the likelihood of criminal behavior. This trend in limited assessments and preventions has been observed internationally. A more recent study conducted in Western Australia with youth sentenced to detention revealed similar findings; of the 88 young people in their study who completed a full assessment, 89% had at least one brain domain of severe impairment, and 36 were diagnosed with FASD, with a prevalence of 36% (Bower et al., 2018).

Finally, the types of crimes committed by individuals with FASD typically reflect their neurocognitive profile (i.e., impulsivity, poor memory) and the primary characteristics of FASD. Although there is little research examining the types of crimes that persons with FASD commit, it appears the most common offenses include property crimes (e.g., shoplifting, theft, burglary) and crimes against another person (e.g., domestic violence, assault) (Streissguth et al., 2004; Wyper & Pei, 2016). Furthermore, research has also suggested that the secondary characteristics, such as addictions, may also contribute to the types of crimes committed by an individual with FASD, such as impaired driving (Wyper & Pei, 2016).

In this chapter, the risk factors for criminality in FASD will be discussed using primary research findings. Interventions that focus on improving supports and services are provided. First, a description of the risk factors that increase the likelihood of persons with FASD coming into contact with the criminal justice system are described. A summary of interventions for persons with FASD who are justice-involved follows, and the chapter concludes with strategies to prevent persons with FASD from coming into contact with the criminal justice system.

## Understanding Risk Factors

Griffiths and Gardner (2002) proposed that challenging behavior, such as criminal offending or the trauma associated with being a victim of an offense, should be understood using a multimodal model rather than from unidisciplinary methods. That is, risk factors should be understood from a comprehensive point-of-view that considers the biological, psychological, and the social variables that may be contributing to the behavior being observed. As Whittingham (2014) illustrated in Table 1, one of the benefits of understanding the risk factors in this way is that it aligns nicely with the primary, secondary, and tertiary characteristics suggested by Streissguth (1997) and Malbin (2002). For example, an individual with FASD may have attentional deficits (primary characteristics; biological impacts) that make it difficult for them to pay attention in class (secondary characteristics; psychological impacts). These impacts often lead to dropping out of high school and being unemployed (tertiary characteristics; social impacts), which in turn may result in repeated criminal justice system involvement.

**Table 1: A comparison between the characteristics of FASD as identified by Streissguth (1997) and Malbin (2002) and the multimodal model (Griffiths & Gardner, 2002)**

| Characteristics of FASD | Multimodal (Bio-psycho-social) Model |
|---|---|
| Primary Characteristics: The direct result of the damage done to the brain by alcohol. | Biological Impacts: Prenatal alcohol exposure causes brain damage and birth defects that alter the ways the individual interacts with the environment. |
| Secondary Characteristics: Develop within the individual over time as a result of poor alignment between the individual and the environment. | Psychological Impacts: The lack of problem-solving abilities, emotional regulation, etc. that increase the likelihood of challenging behavior in an environment that is inconsistent with their abilities. |
| Tertiary Characteristics: The social results of the ongoing mismatch between the individual and the person's needs | Social Impacts: FASD impacts the way a person interacts with the world and the expectations of the persons around them. |

Both conceptualizations recognize that the individual is not the problem, that modification of the environment will lead to an improvement in both the behavior and quality of life and appreciate the complex and multiple influences that create the conditions for criminal offending. However, the biopsychosocial perspective is not new to the medical or psychological professions (i.e., Engel, 1977; Griffiths & Gardner, 2002; Sadler & Hulgus, 1992; Watson, Richards, Miodrag, & Fedoroff, 2012). Therefore, professionals are well-versed in the completion of biopsychosocial assessments and may be better able to assess and develop interventions for individuals with FASD in the criminal justice system. Consequently, the rest of this chapter will focus on the biopsychosocial risk factors for individuals with FASD to become involved in the criminal justice system and to suggest preventative strategies that will reduce the risk of initial contact and the risk of recidivism.

## *Understanding the Risk Factors Associated with FASD for Criminal Behavior*

As stated previously, it is important to understand the complex interaction between the biological, psychological, and social variables that are contributing to the risk of criminal justice system involvement for individuals with FASD. In this section of the chapter, each of these biopsychosocial influences is discussed.

***Biological Impacts or Primary Characteristics.*** Persons with FASD are more likely to become involved in the criminal justice system due to the many challenges associated with the brain damage caused by prenatal alcohol exposure, including difficulty with abstract thinking, communication skill deficits, a diminished ability to express and exhibit empathy, and impulsivity (Wartnik & Brown, 2016). A wealth of literature has emphasized that these impairments can place individuals with FASD at increased risk for delinquent or criminal behavior and for contact with the criminal justice system (e.g., Burd, Martsolf, & Juelson 2004; Conry & Fast, 2000; Conry, Fast, & Loock, 1997; Conry & Lane, 2009; Fast & Conry, 2009; Fast et al., 1999; Sayal, 2007). Often the primary characteristics of FASD lead to higher rates of problematic behavior, such as lying, cheating, disobedience, and stealing (Nash et al., 2013), which are often interpreted as willful, premeditated, and manipulative (Conry & Fast, 2000). There is, however, a strong consensus among researchers, clinicians, and policy-makers that the challenging behaviors exhibited by individuals with FASD that violate social norms are not willful but rather a consequence of neuropsychological deficits (Malbin, Boulding, & Brooks, 2010; Novick-Brown, Connor, & Adler, 2012; Richer & Watson, 2018). Furthermore, it appears that the majority of criminal acts perpetrated by individuals with FASD are reactive and opportunistic rather than premeditated, providing further evidence for the fact that these individuals are not acting willfully (Novick Brown et al., 2012).

In addition, behaviors associated with the deficits in brain functioning can also increase the possibility of situations in which the individuals with FASD will be charged or arrested. Psychological factors, such as poor language comprehension, impaired memory, lack of attention, and inability to reason, may place them at further risk for being evaluated negatively by professionals in these legal environments (Flannigan et al., 2018). For example, the individuals with FASD may be extremely talkative with police officers and lawyers; however, an impairment in receptive language (i.e., ability to understand what is being said to them) may lead the officer to overestimate their competence and level of understanding. As a result of the perceived competence, the officer may believe that the individual was able to understand their Miranda or Charter rights at the time of the arrest and was therefore able to disclose information related to the charges. Unfortunately, the individual may not be aware of the future implications of these actions. Furthermore, individuals with FASD may also *confabulate,* which refers to "the production or creation of false or erroneous memories without the intent to deceive" (Brown, Huntley, Morgan, Dodson, & Cich, 2017, p. 1). Confabulation may look like "lying" or "distorting the truth", which may complicate an investigation, as individuals may not be able to convey events accurately, such as the time, place, or other persons present; in addition, it may also be interpreted as willful lying and can increase the risk of being charged with perjury or cause frustration on the part of the legal professional. Finally, this tendency to distort the truth may also impair an individual with FASD's ability to testify on their own behalf in a meaningful way (Douds, Stevens, & Sumner, 2013).

***Psychological Impacts or Secondary Characteristics.*** Many individuals with FASD exhibit deficits in executive functioning and self-regulation. Zelazo and Mueller (2002) defined executive functioning as the ability to maintain conscious control over thoughts and actions in a way that promotes adaptive responses to novel situations;

whereas, self-regulation is the ability to respond appropriately in situations (and may overlap with executive functioning) (Wyper & Pei, 2016). In one study, many families attributed their adult children's involvement with the law to underlying difficulties with self-regulation and inhibitory control. Moreover, many families report a lifelong pattern of poor frustration tolerance and emotional dysregulation, including violent outbursts that involved death threats, physical assaults, the use of weapons, and destruction of property regardless of their child's age (Richer & Watson, 2018). In many of these cases, the intensity of the aggressive episodes warranted police involvement to keep the individual and family members safe from harm. For example, one parent in Richer and Watson's (2018) study explained "He would threaten to kill our daughter. That was when he first became involved with the police. Threatened to kill us…we had to call the police sometimes because he wouldn't calm down" (p. 94).

Furthermore, poor inhibition or impulse control has also been linked to offending behavior in persons with FASD. Wyper and Pei (2016) defined inhibition as "voluntary control over cognition or behavior, and in particular as the ability to resist a prepotent or impulse response" (p. 106). As noted above, the majority of criminal acts perpetrated by individuals with FASD are reactive and opportunistic rather than premeditated (Novick Brown et al., 2012). In Richer and Watson's (2018) study, parents also described how poor inhibitory control, coupled with difficulty understanding the consequences of their actions, led to impulsive criminal acts. The individuals also identified that each reported offense was opportunistic, reactive, and not planned beforehand. For example, one young person with FASD explained how impulsivity and difficulty understanding abstract concepts, such as ownership, contributed to his criminal behavior:

> When I was younger I didn't realise the consequence of ownership type of thing so I tended to sometimes go into people's houses and be like 'oh that's shiny, that's nice' and I would take it and I wouldn't really feel… bad about it and then I would go in the grocery store or something and say 'I want that but I don't have any money, yoink!' (Richer & Watson, 2018, p. 94)

Finally, alcohol and drug use has also been described as a contributing variable for offending behavior in persons with FASD. Many individuals with FASD are at risk of addictions (Popova, Lange, Burd, Urbanoski, & Rehm, 2013; Streissguth et al., 2004). For many individuals with FASD, involvement with the law often occurs as a result of intoxication related to alcohol, drugs, or some combination of the two. For example, in *R. v. Manitowabi* (2014), an adolescent defendant with FASD was found guilty of first-degree murder for stabbing an acquaintance. During the testimony, the defendant had admitted to smoking a considerable amount of marijuana and consuming alcohol before the stabbing had happened. In addition, addictions and use of illicit substances may serve as a gateway to other risky behavior, such as exotic dancing, prostitution, and stealing (Richer & Watson, 2018). For example, one parent in the Richer and Watson (2018) study stated that substance use interfered with her daughter's ability to maintain steady employment and avoid trouble with the law. Most parents identified that substance use often begins at an early age (i.e., between the ages of 9 and 14 years-old) (Richer & Watson, 2018). Early substance use has been correlated with criminal behavior (i.e., Vaughn, Salas-Wright, & Reingle-Gonzalez, 2016), and it is clear that individuals with FASD are no exception.

***Social Impacts or Tertiary Characteristics.*** Individuals with FASD are also often exposed to adverse life circumstances that contribute to their increased risk of criminal behavior. Adverse childhood experiences (ACES) was coined to describe ten childhood experiences that are identified as risks for a wide array of poor adult outcomes in physical, mental, and behavioral health (Anda, Butchart, Felitti, & Brown, 2010; Baglivio et al., 2014; Flannigan et al., 2018). As Anda and colleagues (2010) identified, these adverse childhood experiences have a strong evidence base for exerting a powerful effect on human development and include factors such as childhood abuse, parent psychopathology, and having an incarcerated parent. Price, Cook, Norgate, and Mukherjee (2017) identified that there may be a greater risk for individuals with both FASD and adverse childhood experiences; however, more research is needed to determine the effects of both factors combined and individually. Independent of FASD, many of these adverse childhood experiences have been associated with deviance and offending in both adolescence and adulthood (Baglivio et al., 2014; Schilling, Aseltine, & Gore, 2007). For example, substance use, life stress, and family factors such as low caregiver supervision and warmth, and verbally aggressive family conflict have been shown to correlate with youth crime (Flannigan et al., 2018). Additionally, Stinson and Robbins (2014) demonstrated the correlation between an earlier onset of problems with a multitude of factors including childhood abuse, maltreatment, multiple complex trauma, and parental substance abuse.

With regards to FASD, Streissguth and colleagues (2004) reported that the family environment, particularly the caregiving provided, had a substantial impact on the outcome of individuals with FASD. Nevertheless, relatively little is known about the specific challenges and stressors that may detrimentally affect the home environment (Watson, Coons, & Hayes, 2013). Most research conducted to date has examined the impact of raising a child with FASD through the lens of parenting stress. For example, a study examining parenting stress in 42 biological mothers of children with FASD found that their children had higher levels of externalizing behaviors (e.g., aggressive, oppositional, or defiant behavior) and lower levels of parental support, which in turn predicted greater maternal stress (Paley, O'Connor, Kogan, & Findlay, 2005). A subsequent study conducted with both biological and adoptive parents of children with FASD found that increased levels of parenting stress were associated with higher ratings of child internalizing (e.g., anxious or depressed behavior) and externalizing behaviors and greater impairments in executive functioning and adaptive behaviors (Paley, O'Connor, Frankel, & Marquardt, 2006). Results in qualitative studies identified that parents reported stressors, including difficulty managing challenging behaviors and providing safety for their child (Caley, Winkelman, & Mariano, 2009), fear for the child's future (Watson, Hayes, Coons, & Radford-Paz, 2013; Watson, Hayes, Radford-Paz, & Coons 2013), and insufficient formal and informal supports (Brown & Bednar, 2004). Collectively, these studies indicate a dyadic relationship between parenting stress and child behavior and suggest that caregiving stress is associated with lack of support and resources for families (Jirikowic, Olson, & Astley, 2012).

Furthermore, a significant social influence on criminal behavior is the peer group surrounding the individual with FASD. Research has hypothesized that impairments in social skills may interfere with the ability to establish and maintain positive relationships (Kully-Martens, Denys, Treit, Tamana, & Rasmussen, 2012). In particular, individual factors such as impulsivity, disregard for boundaries, hyperactivity, and disruptive behavior may lead to rejection by neurotypical peers. For example, some families of individuals with FASD reported that their children often experienced rejection by their peers and that these social difficulties contributed to the development of criminal behavior (Richer & Watson, 2018). One adoptive mother of a 22-year-old son with FASD stated:

> [H]e seems to have friends for a while, and all of a sudden they disappear and we don't know why. He said to me the other day 'I decided all my friends are not really my friend except for two.' One was a girl that we've met once. And the other was a guy that we haven't seen for maybe two years now (Richer & Watson, 2018, p. 94).

Without a positive peer group to turn to, individuals with FASD may be vulnerable to negative peer influences and victimization. Parents often identify that the peers who typically befriend individuals with FASD do not value appropriate social behavior; instead, they tend to encourage them to engage in behavior such as substance use, truancy, and criminality. Moreover, these parents also identified that incarceration may have a detrimental effect on individuals with FASD because it puts them in direct contact with individuals who may take advantage of the vulnerabilities associated with their primary impairments (Kully-Martens et al., 2012). For example, David Boulding (2001) identified:

> I failed to note that my F[etal] A[lcohol] S[yndrome] clients were usually the number two or number three person involved in the offence, but that it was always my FAS[D] clients that were caught. I did not recognize that there must be a reason that other people initiated the offences and were rarely arrested while my clients were always caught. (p. 5).

In addition, many parents have noted that their children's criminal behavior occurred in the presence of peers, and they expressed concern that their children's criminal behavior was influenced by their group of friends. For example, one parent worried that involvement in the criminal justice system exposed her son to a group of peers with a history of involvement in the justice system, thereby compounding the effect of the negative peer group (Richer & Watson, 2018).

Finally, multiple transitions across the lifespan have been connected to the criminal behavior of youth and adults with FASD. Research has demonstrated that children with FASD constitute approximately 16.9% of children in the child welfare system (Lange, Shield, Rehm, & Popova, 2013). Challenges in behavior often lead to frequent foster home placements and poor prospects for adoptions, rendering it difficult to have a stable and consistent home environment. For some individuals with FASD, changes in the family home environment may include a combination of living with biological, foster, and/or adoptive families. Furthermore, living milieus may also include homelessness, residential treatment centers, juvenile detention centers, and jail (Badry, Walsh, Bell, Ramage, & Gibbon, 2015; Pei, Leung, Jampolsky, & Alsbury, 2016). In addition, many individuals with FASD are transient throughout adolescence and adulthood and will *couch surf* with friends for extended periods of times without a fixed address. For example, one parent in Richer and Watson's (2018) study stated, "I don't think I'm exaggerating if I say she lived in 20 different places between the ages 13 and 20" (p. 95). The lack of structure resulting from the multiple transitions often led to unsupervised time, which families identified as a contributing factor to criminal behavior for individuals with FASD. Other parents reported being unaware of the full extent of their children's legal problems because of the multiple home placements. As one parent reported, "We ended up kicking him out of the house... He couch-surfed for a while. And he had all sorts of times when he was involved with the police that we don't know about" (Richer & Watson, 2018, p. 95).

## Interventions for Individuals with FASD in the Criminal Justice System

Because persons with FASD are entering the criminal justice system at alarming rates, it is important to ensure that they are properly supported to reduce the risk of victimization within the system and to ensure that they are getting the support they need to reduce recidivism. While many countries have ensured that there is access to accommodations for persons with disabilities in the criminal justice system, as outlined in the Convention on the Rights of Persons with Disabilities (United Nations General Assembly, 2007), research has shown that many legal professionals have a difficult time identifying individuals with FASD to be able to provide effective accommodations. For example, Douglas, Hammill, Russell, and Hill (2012) assessed justice professionals' ability to detect FASD in defendants. They found that 42% of professionals interviewed had never considered whether the defendant might have FASD. Furthermore, when FASD was suspected by legal professionals, they did not know how to best support the individual. Stromski (2015) interviewed justice professionals and community support workers to determine what accommodations were needed to effectively support persons with FASD in the criminal justice system. She found that both justice professionals and community support workers felt that more interventions were needed for persons with FASD within the criminal justice system, including screening and identification, training and education regarding FASD, and effective case management and supports.

### *Screening and Identification*

The first challenge to supporting persons with FASD in the criminal justice system is identification. Fast and Conry (2009) identified that a comprehensive report from a diagnostic clinic can help legal professionals understand individuals with FASD; however, as Burd and colleagues (2003) demonstrated, very few persons with FASD have been officially diagnosed before entering the criminal justice system and will be able to provide this report. As identified at the beginning of this chapter, persons with FASD are a heterogeneous group, meaning they may lack consistent behavioral or physical features that readily identify them as being a person with a disability (Hamelin, Marinos, Robinson, & Griffiths, 2012). As a result of this lack of identification, persons with FASD are often misunderstood as being willful, manipulative, and antisocial, rather than as an individual with organic brain damage. As David Boulding (2001) wrote:

> I failed to see that if my clients were old, with Alzheimer's Disease instead of 20 years old, male and with a long Criminal Record, they wouldn't be getting my services. Instead, they are labeled as "anti-social" and sent to jail (p. 8).

Screening for persons with FASD has been proposed as a possible solution to ensure that appropriate accommodations are provided (i.e., Burd et al., 2004). Many authors have proposed that screening individuals entering the criminal justice system will potentially decrease future contacts with the criminal justice system by ensuring proper resources (i.e., case management and community-based services) and accommodations are provided to the individual with FASD (Bisgard, Fisher, Adubato, & Louis, 2010; Burd et al., 2003). However, to date, a valid, reliable FASD screening tool has not yet been developed (Allely & Gebbia, 2016). Brown, Wartnik, Connor, and Adler (2010) suggested that any screening tool developed for the criminal justice system should assess the following areas:

- Offense conduct (e.g., evidence of impulsivity, lack of self-preservation)
- Arrest conduct (e.g., talkativeness, suggestibility)
- Interview conduct (e.g., immaturity, poor memory of events)
- Prior legal history (e.g., victimization, being charged for the same offense repeatedly)
- Life history (e.g., multiple foster home placements, school suspensions)

While many authors have advocated for the use of screening in the criminal justice system for persons with FASD, Autti-Rämöo (2016) and Douds and colleagues (2013) have cautioned that screening should not be done blindly as it may have unintended negative effects for the individual. That is, although FASD can be argued as a mitigating factor, it can also have a negative impact on bail or sentencing, including longer sentences. Autti-Ramo (2016) identified that if the criminal justice system is going to screen for FASD, there needs to be clear procedures for the next steps since screening cannot be used as a substitute for a diagnostic assessment. In addition, she advised that the individual with FASD should be included in the conversation about whether to disclose the diagnosis of FASD, and the benefits and risks associated with disclosure should be discussed with them (Autti-Rämö, 2016). At this time, several researchers have identified the growing need for effective diagnostic facilities internationally. For example, Burd and colleagues (2003) found that 27.3% of Canadian correctional services had access to diagnostic services, whereas only 7.4% of correctional facilities surveyed in the United States had access to diagnostic services (Burd et al., 2003). These figures indicate that there needs to be a significant increase in the number of diagnostic services for FASD internationally before screening procedures are introduced.

## *Training and Education for Legal Professionals*

FASD scholars have also identified the need for increased training and education for legal professionals, including police officers. Despite the on-going recognition that persons with FASD are overrepresented in the criminal justice system, the knowledge of legal professionals remains limited. For example, Mutch, Jones, Bower, and Watkins (2016) surveyed a variety of Canadian legal professionals including judges, lawyers, police officers, and correctional officers. While most of the respondents had heard of FAS (85%), many were not aware that this diagnosis was part of a spectrum of disorders (i.e., FASD; 60%). They also found that many of the respondents had received their information about FASD from the media, colleagues, and from reports.

Similar findings regarding training and education have been found internationally. For example, Mutch, Watkins, Jones, and Bower (2013) conducted a survey of legal professionals' knowledge of FASD in Western Australia. They found comparable findings to the Canadian study: most of the respondents (90%) were aware of FAS; however, awareness of the spectrum of disorders associated with prenatal alcohol exposure was lower (64.1%). Interestingly, the most common ways that participants had received information about FASD was also the media, colleagues, and from reports, mirroring the results in Canada.

In both studies (Mutch et al., 2016; Mutch et al., 2013), most legal professionals indicated that they were interested in learning more about FASD, with the exception of police officers, whose agreement was considerably lower than other legal professionals (i.e., 57% agreeing in Canada and 67% agreeing in Western Australia that they wanted more information). One officer in Stromski's (2015) study may have identified the barrier that police officers face with training and education:

> Well... there's so many different ailments out there that we can't, we can't train for every single one ... you know policing ... is quite demanding as far as our training we have to complete every year, so it has to be somewhat generalized in our training. We can't specifically say for these type of people we need more training than this. I don't know the number of people that are affected by this disorder so you know the main ones that we run into are schizophrenia, you know people with just bad depression, anxiety and you know the whole gamete so you know we have to do things that are more generalized. We can't specifically train for one disease (pp. 49-50).

What this police officer may be highlighting is that limits on time and resources may influence limits on training and education. It is important that anyone providing FASD training to legal professionals realizes these limits and ensures that the training and education being provided is relevant to their audience and is solution-focused (Stromski, 2015).

The concerns surrounding the prevalence, or overrepresentation, of those with FASD having contact with the justice system has resulted in a number of important interventions. In 2012, the American Bar Association passed a resolution that all legal professionals need to acknowledge and address the impact of FASD in the criminal justice system, through proper training. The resolution further drew attention to the need for collaboration with health experts and the need for policy reform to address the needs of individuals with FASD. The Canadian Bar Association (CBA) also addressed the issue of FASD in the justice system in 2010, highlighting the ineffectiveness of incarceration for those with FASD, as incapacitation lacks rehabilitative and/or deterrent effects in this population. The resolution also drew attention to the right to substantive justice, and not simply formal justice, before the law. As such, the Canadian Bar Association called on the government to provide resources for alternatives to prison for those with FASD and to develop policies to support and enhance the lives of individuals with FASD (Roach & Bailey, 2010). These resolutions directly informed the first round of calls to reform the *Criminal Code of Canada*, which included Bill C-235, an Act to amend the *Criminal Code* and the *Corrections and Conditional*

*Release Act*, and Bill C-583, an Act to amend the *Criminal Code*. Prior to Bill C-235, previous attempts were made to amend the *Criminal Code*, which included Bill C-656. Although these Bills were ultimately unsuccessful, they have been instrumental in opening up critical conversations in Canada about FASD and the justice system and informing subsequent legislation.

Parents of youth with FASD have also reported the importance of finding a lawyer who is either familiar with the lifelong effects of FASD or is amenable to learning about FASD. Additionally, parents of youth with FASD noted that it was essential to have a probation officer who was willing to take their child's vulnerabilities into account. One parent in Richer and Watson's (2018) study stressed the need to be tenacious: "And you can't take no for an answer. Like for someone to say, 'sorry we can't afford that' is absolutely an abrogation of every human being's rights" (p. 97). Through their unwavering dedication, many parents hope to protect their children from secondary and tertiary characteristics by increasing the awareness of FASD and thereby changing the expectations placed upon individuals with FASD by the judicial system.

## Case Management and Supports

The final intervention needed for individuals with FASD is effective case management and supports involved in the criminal justice system and upon release to reduce the risk of recidivism (Tait, Mela, Boothman, & Stoops, 2017). Researchers have established that without the proper supports in place, persons with FASD are at risk within the criminal justice system due to concerns such as their inability to understand abstract concepts (e.g., justice, guilty), inability to remember facts, and suggestibility (Conry & Lane, 2009; McLachlin et al., 2019; Moore & Green, 2004). While many of the accommodations and supports highlighted by Marinos, Cole, and Stromski (chapter 3) and Pathak, Clarke, and Ioannou (chapter 5) will be effective for persons with FASD, it is important to recognize that these services may not always be available to persons with FASD. Streissguth (1997) established that while all persons with FASD exhibited the symptoms of impaired neurocognitive functioning (i.e., memory impairment) and impairments in adaptive functioning skills (i.e., social skills, money management), only 10% of persons with FASD had an IQ below 70. This finding means that in some regions, persons with FASD may not meet criteria for appropriate services. For example, in the province of Ontario, Canada, the eligibility criteria for developmental services (i.e., case management, behavior therapy) is psychometric confirmation that there are impairments in both cognitive and adaptive functioning and evidence that these impairments appeared before the age of 18 and have a lifelong impact (*Services and Supports to Promote the Social Inclusion of Persons with Developmental Disabilities Act*, 2008). As identified previously, based on these criteria, approximately only 10% of persons with FASD will be diagnosed as having a developmental disability and qualify for developmental services in Ontario. Comparatively, the Americans with Disabilities Act (ADA) is an American federal law that prohibits discrimination on the basis of a disability, including physical or mental impairments that significantly impacts an individual's functioning (SAMHSA, 2014). SAMHSA

(2014) identified that under the Americans with Disabilities Act, persons with FASD should not be discriminated against and should be able to receive supports and treatment that is aligned with their needs and neurocognitive profiles.

One program that has exhibited success is the Alexis FASD Justice program in Alberta, Canada. Adult offenders who are suspected of having FASD are referred for a neurocognitive assessment and "FASD-informed" recommendations are made to court professionals (Flannigan et al., 2018, p. 7). The program goal for the Alexis FASD Justice program is "to increase access to FASD clinical services, improve justice outcomes for adults in the community, decrease costs associated with ineffective justice services, and increase community capacity to meet the needs of these individuals" (Flannigan et al., 2018, p. 7). Research has indicated that legal professionals, Alexis FASD Justice program staff, and clinicians felt that this program was building capacity to be better able to support persons with FASD in the criminal justice system. Furthermore, they found that legal professionals were better able to respond to individual needs based on the information being provided by the FASD-informed recommendations. For example, one professional identified that one of the benefits of this program was the ability to shape expectations and identified that one outcome may be that the offender "com[es] back more often, but that's not a negative thing, that shows that they're making the connection with services . . . we bring them back for reviews to see how they're doing . . . they're positive appearances" (Flannigan et al., 2018, p. 12). While the participants in this study identified the positive benefits of the Alexis FASD Justice program, future research is needed to assess the long-term benefits of this program, such as the impact on recidivism and connection to community services to prevent future offending.

## Preventing Criminal Justice System Involvement for Individuals with FASD

While it is important to consider the risk factors for criminality and interventions for persons with FASD, it is also important to consider the multitude of complex factors in their lives, such as early adversity, adverse outcome, individual strengths and vulnerabilities, service and/or support gaps, and social inclusion. To date, most research regarding preventative measures for reducing the likelihood of secondary and tertiary risk characteristics of FASD has focused on the stressors faced by caregivers of children with FASD, rather than the factors that contribute to resiliency and positive life outcomes. That being said, anecdotal reports and limited research regarding intervention have indicated that using a strengths-based approach, structure and supervision, access to appropriate supports and services, and positive influences can play a critical role in reducing the likelihood that an individual with FASD will enter the criminal justice system.

### *Using a Strengths-Based Approach*

A great deal of literature has focused on identifying and addressing the deficits associated with FASD and little attention has been given to their strengths or what characteristics contribute to positive outcomes. Dubovsky (2015a) identified that some of the positive traits of persons with FASD include: helpful, empathetic, tenacious, and committed. Burles, Holtslander, Bocking, and Brenna (2018) used photovoice[1] to explore the experiences of an individual with FASD. The participant in this study identified strengths such as being resilient, working with his hands, as well as strong visual learning and communication. Furthermore, Dubovsky (2015b) identified that persons with FASD do well when they are given tasks they like to do. Burles and colleagues (2018) concluded that "attention to positive attributes can help individuals with FASD and others to recognize their unique abilities, alongside areas in which they struggle, and facilitate development of a self-identity that transcends stigmatizing stereotypes" (p. 15).

A handful of studies have been conducted that identify individual strengths and explore factors that contribute to positive outcomes among adults with FASD who are involved in the criminal justice system. For example, Pei and colleagues (2016) interviewed adults with FASD and their service providers about their experiences in the justice system. Although there were a number of factors that contributed to adults with FASD entering the justice system, which also hindered them once involved, the participants in this study were able to identify strengths that helped move individuals with FASD through the system, including hope, willingness to change, and resilience. In another study, Currie, Hoy, Legge, Temple, and Tahir (2016) explored the experiences of justice-involved young adults with FASD. Individuals with FASD in this study were able to describe personal qualities, such as being helpful, kind-hearted, artistic, and successful with hands-on, visual, and physical activities. Consequently, there is an urgent need for more research to identify positive qualities among individuals with FASD in order to change the deficit-based narrative that exists among persons with FASD and their involvement in the criminal justice system.

While primary characteristics can make them vulnerable to peer pressure and negative influences, positive peer influences can have an equally important impact on individuals with FASD. David Boulding (2014) also identified that it is important for persons with FASD to have a social network (i.e., friends) that will help implement good decisions and provide support for success. The parents in Richer and Watson's (2018) study discussed their child's lifelong challenge of finding a positive peer group but also identified that opportunities like summer camps for individuals with disabilities were beneficial because these camps provided a safe and structured environment where individuals with FASD could meet individuals who were at similar developmental levels. One parent emphasized the importance of promoting the message that individuals with FASD can overcome challenges and adversity related to prenatal alcohol exposure and can experience positive life outcomes.

Furthermore, many FASD scholars and advocates emphasize the role that a good social network can play throughout the individual's life (Boulding, 2014; Pepper, Coons-Harding, Bibr, & Watson, 2018; Richer & Watson, 2018). Parents often act as a consistent positive influence in their child's life through their role as advocates. Although families face a multitude of barriers, caregivers represented the positive characteristics they hoped to cultivate in their children by remaining optimistic and positive in the face of adversity (Richer & Watson, 2018).

---

[1] Photovoice is a research method that provides participants the opportunity to tell their story through photography and individual or group interviews that discuss the contents of the photographs taken by the participants (Burles et al., 2018).

## Early Identification and Diagnosis

Like many other disorders, individuals who receive early identification and diagnosis fare better (Benz, Rasmussen, & Andrew, 2009). Early identification ensures that individuals with FASD receive the necessary supports and interventions to prevent secondary and tertiary characteristics (Benz et al., 2009; Streissguth, 1997; Streissguth et al., 2004). For example, Streissguth and colleagues (1996) found that receiving a diagnosis before the age of six reduces the risk of many adverse outcomes, including poor educational outcomes and multiple foster home placements. Moreover, Streissguth (1997) found that individuals with FASD who had an early diagnosis were more independent and had fewer problems with employment as adults, plus families report that delays in receiving diagnostic information is a significant stressor (e.g., Pepper et al., 2018; Watson, Coons, et al., 2013).

Researchers have identified that one of the reasons for the challenges in diagnosis is the lack of available diagnostic services. Peadon, Freemantale, Bower, and Elliott (2008) conducted an international survey of FASD diagnostic clinics. They found that overall there were few diagnostic clinics, with most clinics centralized in Canada and the United States. In addition, they found that early diagnosis was complicated by the fact that there are multiple diagnostic criteria (Peadon et al., 2008). The Substance Abuse and Mental Health Admission (SAMHSA) in the United States identified that there are four potential diagnostic criteria that can be used by diagnostic teams, including the Washington 4-digit code, the Center for Disease Control (CDC) and Prevention guidelines, the Canadian guidelines (recently updated in 2015), and the Institute of Medicine (IOM) guidelines (US Department of Health and Human Services, 2014). To add to the complication, some of these diagnostic criteria have been revised and therefore diagnostic clinics may be using different diagnostic criteria or different versions of diagnostic criteria, making it difficult to effectively compare clinics or establish a valid and reliable set of diagnostic guidelines. For example, the CDC guidelines only address fetal alcohol syndrome (FAS); however, as identified earlier, most individuals with FASD do not exhibit the sentinel facial features and therefore are unlikely to be diagnosed as having FASD by clinics using these diagnostic guidelines (U.S. Department of Health and Human Services, 2014).

## Access to Appropriate Supports and Services

One of the benefits of an early diagnosis of FASD is the ability to introduce appropriate supports and services that will reduce the risk of secondary and tertiary characteristics. These supports and services can build on strengths, provide respite and relief to parents, and ensure that there is appropriate supervision and advocacy in a variety of settings including school, work, and healthcare (Benz et al., 2009).

Many individuals with FASD struggle and have challenges coping and meeting the demands in educational and vocational settings, as well as interpersonal relationships (Streissguth et al., 1997). However, many families also emphasized the positive impact that education and employment had on the well-being and self-esteem of their children. For example, one parent in Richer and Watson's (2018) interview study identified that her son "was always looking for work because the biggest, biggest thing that we would notice is that filling his spare time is essential, that he cannot have spare time..." (p. 96).

One of the benefits of appropriate supports and services is the provision of structure and supervision that reduce the risk of tertiary characteristics. For example, research has identified that failure to secure appropriate supports and services earlier in life can result in unstructured time in adolescence and adulthood, which in turn puts the individual at risk of criminal activity, homelessness, or poverty (Coons, 2013; Streissguth, 1997; Streissguth et al., 2004; Watson, Hayes, et al., 2013). Many caregivers have identified their fear about their child with FASD ending up in the criminal justice system as a result of the lack of appropriate structure and support (Boulding, 2014; Fast & Conry, 2009; Richer & Watson, 2018; Streissguth, 1997; Watson, Coons, et al., 2013). Furthermore, these caregivers have suggested that the benefit of adequate supports and services is that it allows for supervision and the opportunity for sharing and supporting the responsibility for decision-making in areas that cause problems (e.g., time and money management). For example, one parent in Richer and Watson's (2018) study identified:

> It was always this fine line of saying what his needs are and people saying you're not letting him take enough risk…you're enabling him and not empowering him… we're sitting here today saying all the risks I didn't let him take. The fact that he hasn't had a criminal record is because we contained his environment (p. 96).

Another conceptualization of the supervision of persons with FASD is the focus on *interdependence* instead of *independence*, which entails greater emotional, social, and financial support for daily living (Clark, Minnes, Lutke, & Ouellette-Kuntz, 2008). Dubovsky (2015b) identified that interdependence is a safety net of individuals that the person with FASD can go to at any time for assistance when needed, similar to the social network of individuals anyone relies on to live in a community as an adult. One of the key differences between persons with FASD and the rest of society is the types of tasks they require assistance with and the intensity of support needed. For example, one parent in Richer and Watson's (2018) study explained:

> He's always had a worker to help him with either daily living skills or community involvement. He still has the special services home worker. She helps him with their dishes and laundry and cleaning the apartment. So Gavin's grown up learning to be interdependent. He never had somebody say to him 'oh you're 16, you should be able to do this.' He never had those kinds of comments (p. 97).

By striving for interdependence rather than independence, parents are able to balance their child's need for autonomy and their need for safety. Despite the identification of the importance of interdependence and community success for persons with FASD, several studies involving caregivers have discussed the challenges of providing effective supervision and support based on interdependence once their adult children move to a different city for post-secondary studies or employment (Clark et al., 2008; Richer & Watson, 2018). Given the lack of FASD-specific or FASD-informed supports available in many communities, most parents are faced with the challenge of finding services suitable to their child's unique vulnerabilities, including individual counselling, residential programs, child and youth workers, and summer camps (Richer & Watson, 2018). This lack of FASD-informed service provision means that many parents have to look beyond government-funded supports to find adequate services for their children and are often left paying out of pocket.

Furthermore, supports and services aimed at improving social skills can help individuals with FASD integrate more easily into peer groups. Caregiver concerns regarding the impact of peer influences on their child's behavior are reflected in existing research, which suggests that the majority of criminal acts perpetrated by individuals with FASD occur with a group of peers and are rarely conducted independently (Novick Brown et al., 2012). As identified earlier in the chapter, without a positive group of friends to turn to, persons with FASD tend to seek social connections with negative peer groups. Thus, by placing them in a setting with other offenders, it is likely that individuals with FASD will seek a sense of belonging among other incarcerated individuals.

Finally, in addition to effective supports and services for individuals with FASD, appropriate supports for family members are also essential. Researchers have found that formal supports such as parent support groups can help to decrease the sense of isolation and hopelessness (Brown &] Bednar, 2004; Coons, Watson, Schinke, & Yantzi, 2016; Pepper et al., 2018; Sanders & Buck, 2010). The perceived benefits of formal supports for families are twofold: first, the supports provide an avenue where caregivers can learn strategies or techniques that help them respond to their child's behavior more effectively; and, secondly, supports can also help caregivers to share their experiences with other families who truly understand what it is like to raise a child with FASD. Parent support groups can help parents to overcome the pressures associated with the social belief that they are accountable for the behavior of their children and the subsequent shame by focusing on the role of central nervous system dysfunction and allowing parents to have more realistic expectations for their children (Coons et al., 2016; Pepper et al., 2018; Richer & Watson, 2018). As one adoptive parent in Richer and Watson's (2018) study, stated:

> [O]ne night [at the parent support group meeting] I shared something that Serena had done and one of the mothers whose daughter is living the exact same life that Serena did said to me jokingly, 'when are you going to get it? That's what these kids do!' And we laughed. And I thought if I'd been home alone, I'd be bawling my eyes out for days. But because she really understood we laughed about it, like I couldn't believe we laughed about this terrible situation, but it broke the pressure (p. 96).

## Conclusions

Persons with FASD are overrepresented in the criminal justice system, in part because of barriers to identification and diagnosis, lack of available appropriate interventions, and a lack of support that considers their unique neurocognitive profiles. While a great deal of work has been done for persons with FASD in the criminal justice system, more work still needs to be done to ensure that the number of persons with FASD in the criminal justice system is reduced. This includes ensuring that persons with FASD are properly supported before they come into contact with the criminal justice system and ensuring that they are properly supported once they have entered the criminal justice system to reduce the detrimental outcomes and the possibility of further involvement. Finally, by increasing the congruence between the individual's neurobehavioural profile and the environmental demands, as demonstrated in our discussion of biopsychosocial approaches (i.e., Griffiths & Gardner, 2002), a preventative strategy based on skill building and enhancing protective factors can be employed to mitigate the impact of secondary impacts such as trouble with the law.

## References

Allely, C. S., & Gebbia, P. (2016). Studies investigating fetal alcohol spectrum disorders in the criminal justice system: a systematic PRISMA review. *SOJ Psychology, 2*(1), 1-11.

American Bar Association. (2012). Resolution 112B. Retrieved from: https://www.americanbar.org/content/dam/aba/administrative/mental_physical_disability/Resolution_112B.authcheckdam.pdf

Anda, R. F., Butchart, A., Felitti, V. J., & Brown, D. W. (2010). Building a framework for global surveillance of the public health implications of adverse childhood experiences. *American Journal of Preventive Medicine, 39*(1), 93-98.

Autti-Rämö, I. (2016). Ethical challenges when screening for and diagnosing FASD in adults. In M. Nelson & M. Trussler (Eds.) *Fetal alcohol spectrum disorders in adults: Ethical and legal perspectives* (pp. 85-97). Switzerland: Springer International Publishing.

Badry, D., Walsh, C., Bell, M., Ramage, K., & Gibbon, J. (2015). The Fetal Alcohol Spectrum Disorder and Homelessness Project: Making connections for promising practice. *Journal of Substance Abuse & Alcoholism, 3(1), 1-4.*

Baglivio, M. T., Epps, N., Swartz, K., Huq, M. S., Sheer, A., & Hardt, N. S. (2014). The prevalence of adverse childhood experiences (ACE) in the lives of juvenile offenders. *Journal of Juvenile Justice, 3*(2), 1-17.

Benz, J., Rasmussen, C., & Andrew, G. (2009). Diagnosing fetal alcohol spectrum disorder: History, challenges and future directions. *Paediatrics & Child Health, 14*(4), 231-237.

Bisgard, E. B., Fisher, S., Adubato, S., & Louis, M. (2010). Screening, diagnosis, and intervention with juvenile offenders. *The Journal of Psychiatry & Law, 38*(4), 475-506

Boulding, D. (2001). *Mistakes I have made with FAS clients*. Retrieved from: http://www.davidboulding.com/uploads/2/4/1/4/24146766/mistakes_i_have_made_with_fas_clients.pdf

Boulding, D. [David Boulding]. (1 July 2014). *Fetal alcohol and the law – Part 2* [Video file]. Retrieved from https://youtu.be/5Z5qVE2lDHE.

Bower, C., Watkins, R. E., Mutch, R. C., Marriott, R., Freeman, J., Kippin, N. R., ... Tarratt, L. (2018). Fetal alcohol spectrum disorder and youth justice: a prevalence study among young people sentenced to detention in Western Australia. *BMJ Open, 8*(2), e019605.

Brown, J. D., & Bednar, L. M. (2004). Challenges of parenting children with a fetal alcohol spectrum disorder: A concept map. *Journal of Family Social Work, 8*(3), 1–18. doi:10.1300/J039v08n03_01

Brown, J., Huntley, D., Morgan, S., Dodson, K. D., & Cich, J. (2017). Confabulation: A guide for mental health professionals. *International Journal of Neurology and Neurotherapy, 4*, 1-9.

Brown, N. N., Wartnik, A. P., Connor, P. D., & Adler, R. S. (2010). A proposed model standard for forensic assessment of fetal alcohol spectrum disorders. *Journal of Psychiatry & Law, 38*, 383-418.

Burd, L., Martsolf, J. T., & Juelson, T. (2004). Fetal alcohol spectrum disorder in the corrections system: Potential screening strategies. *International Journal of FAS, 2*, 1-10.

Burd, L., Selfridge, R., Klug, M., & Bakko, S. (2004). Fetal alcohol syndrome in the United States corrections system. *Addiction biology, 9*(2), 169-176.

Burd, L., Selfridge, R. H., Klug, M. G., & Juelson, T. (2003). Fetal alcohol syndrome in the Canadian corrections system. *Journal of FAS International, 1*(14), 1-10.

Burles, M., Holtslander, L., Bocking, S., & Brenna, B. (2018). Strengths and Challenges: A Young Adult Pictures FASD Through Photovoice. *Review of Disability Studies: An International Journal, 14*(1), 1 – 14.

Caley, L. M., Winkelman, T., & Mariano, K. (2009). Problems expressed by caregivers of children with fetal alcohol spectrum disorder. *International Journal of Nursing Terminologies and Classifications, 20*(4), 181-188.

Canadian Bar Association. (2010). Fetal alcohol spectrum disorder in the criminal justice system. Retrieved from: https://www.cba.org/getattachment/OurWork/Resolutions/Resolutions/2010/Fetal-Alcohol-Spectrum-Disorder-in-the-Criminal-Ju/10-02-A.pdf

Chudley, A. E., Conry, J., Cook, J. L., Loock, C., Rosales, T., & LeBlanc, N. (2005). Fetal alcohol spectrum disorder: Canadian guidelines for diagnosis. *Canadian Medical Association Journal, 172*(5 suppl), S1-S21.

Clark, E., Minnes, P., Lutke, J., & Ouellette-Kuntz, H. (2008). Caregiver perceptions of the community integration of adults with foetal alcohol spectrum disorder in British Columbia. *Journal of Applied Research in Intellectual Disabilities, 21*(5), 446-456.

Conry, J., & Fast, D.K. (2000). *Fetal alcohol syndrome and the criminal justice system*. British Columbia: British Columbia Fetal Alcohol Syndrome Resource Society.

Conry, J. L., Fast, D. K., & Loock, C. A. (1997). *Youth in the criminal justice system: Identifying FAS and other developmental disabilities*. Vancouver BC: Final Report to the Ministry of the Attorney General.

Conry, J. L., & Lane, K. A. (2009). *Characteristics of youth with FASD on adjudicated probation orders*. Vancouver, B.C.: Final report to the Department of Justice Canada and British Columbia Ministry of Children and Family Development.

Cook, J. L., Green, C. R., Lilley, C. M., Anderson, S. M., & Baldwin, M. E., Chudley, A. E., ... & the Canada FASD Research Network. (2016). Fetal alcohol spectrum disorder: A guideline for diagnosis across the lifespan. *Canadian Medical Association Journal, 188*(3), 191-197. doi: https://doi.org/10.1503/cmaj.141593

Coons, K. (2013). Determinants of drinking during pregnancy and lifespan outcomes for individuals with fetal alcohol spectrum disorder. *Journal on Developmental Disabilities, 19*(3), 15-28.

Coons, K. D., Watson, S. L., Schinke, R. J., & Yantzi, N. M. (2016). Adaptation in families raising children with fetal alcohol spectrum disorder. Part I: What has helped. *Journal of Intellectual and Developmental Disability, 41*(2), 150-165. doi: 10.3109/13668250.2016.1156659

Corrado, R., Freedman, L., & Blatier, C. (2011). The over-representation of children in care in the youth criminal justice system in British Columbia: Theory and policy issues. *International Journal of Child, Youth and Family Studies, 2*(1/2), 99-118.

Cunningham, M., Mishibinijima, L., Mohammed, S., Mountford, A., & Santiago, S. (2010). FASD justice committee of FASDONE. Retrieved from http://fasdjustice.on.ca/

Currie, B. A., Hoy, J., Legge, L., Temple, V. K., & Tahir, M. (2016). Adults with fetal alcohol spectrum disorder: Factors associated with positive outcomes and contact with the criminal justice system. *Journal of Population Therapeutics and Clinical Pharmacology, 23*(1), E37-E52.

Douds, A. S., Stevens, H. R., & Sumner, W. E. (2013). Sword or shield? A systematic review of the roles FASD evidence plays in judicial proceedings. *Criminal Justice Policy Review, 24*(4), 492-509.

Douglas, H., Hammill, J., Russell, E.A., & Hall, W. (2012). The importance of foetal alcohol spectrum disorder for criminal law in practice: Views of Queensland lawyers. *Queensland Lawyer, 32*,153-164.

Dubovsky, D. [POPFASD]. (20 October 2015a). *Common strengths of students with FASD* [Video file]. Retrieved from https://youtu.be/67aHbIAXvYY

Dubovsky, D. [POPFASD]. (20 October 2015b). *Fostering Interdependence* [Video file]. Retrieved from https://youtu.be/VQLTIsgz_J0

Engel, G. L. (1977). The need for a new medical model. *Science, 196*, 129-136.

Fast, D. K. & Conry, J. (2009). Fetal alcohol spectrum disorders and the criminal justice system. *Developmental Disabilities Research Reviews, 15*, 250-257.

Fast, D. K., Conry, J., & Loock, C. A. (1999). Identifying fetal alcohol syndrome among youth in the criminal justice system. *Journal of Developmental and Behavioral Pediatrics, 20*(5), 370-372.

Flannigan, K., Pei, J., Stewart, M., & Johnson, A. (2018). Fetal alcohol spectrum disorder and the criminal justice system: A systematic literature review. *International Journal of Law and Psychiatry, 57*, 42-52.

Griffiths, D. M. & Gardner, W. I. (2002). The integrated biopsychosocial approach to challenging behaviours. In D. M. Griffiths, C. Stavrakaki, & J. Summers (Eds.), *Dual diagnosis: An introduction to the mental health needs of persons with developmental disabilities*. Sudbury, ON Habilitative Mental Health Resource Network.

Hamelin, J., Marinos, V., Robinson, J., & Griffiths, D. (2012). Human rights and the justice system. In D. Griffiths, F. Owen, & S. L. Watson (Eds.), *The human rights agenda for persons with intellectual disabilities* (pp. 169 – 194). Kingston, NY: NADD Press.

Hughes, N., Clasby, B., Chitsabesan, P., & Williams, H. (2016). A systematic review of the prevalence of foetal alcohol syndrome disorders among young people in the criminal justice system. *Cogent Psychology, 3*(1), 1 – 8.

Jirikowic, T., Olson, H. C., & Astley, S. (2012). Parenting stress and sensory processing: Children with fetal alcohol spectrum disorders. *OTJR: Occupation, Participation and Health, 32*(4), 160-168.

Kully-Martens, K., Denys, K., Treit, S., Tamana, S., & Rasmussen, C. (2012). A review of social skills deficits in individuals with fetal alcohol spectrum disorder and prenatal alcohol exposure: Profiles, mechanisms, and interventions. *Alcoholism: Clinical and Experimental Research, 36*, 568-576.

Lange, S., Probst, C., Gmel, G., Rehm, J., Burd, L., & Popova, S. (2017). Global prevalence of fetal alcohol spectrum disorder among children and youth: A systematic review and meta-analysis. *JAMA Pediatrics, 171*(10), 948-956.

Lange, S., Shield, K., Rehm, J., & Popova, S. (2013). Prevalence of fetal alcohol spectrum disorders in child care settings: a meta-analysis. *Pediatrics, 132*(4), e980-e995.

Malbin, D. (2002). *Findings from the FASCETS Oregon Fetal Alcohol Project: Efficacy of a neurobehavioural construct; interventions for children and adolescents with fetal alcohol syndrome/alcohol-related neurodevelopmental disabilities (FASD)*. Unpublished manuscript.

Malbin, D., Boulding, D., & Brooks, S. (2010). Trying differently: Rethinking juvenile justice using a neuro-behavioral model. *ABA Criminal Justice Section: Juvenile Justice Committee Newsletter, 5*, 1-14.

May, P. A., Chambers, C. D., Kalberg, W. O., Zellner, J., Feldman, H., Buckley, D., . . . Hoyme, H. E. (2018). Prevalence of Fetal Alcohol Spectrum Disorders in 4 US Communities. *JAMA, 319*(5), 474-482. doi:10.1001/jama.2017.21896

McLachlan, K., McNeil, A., Pei, J., Brain, U., Andrew, G., & Oberlander, T. F. (2019). Prevalence and characteristics of adults with fetal alcohol spectrum disorder in corrections: A Canadian case ascertainment study. *BMC Public Health, 19*(43). https://doi.org/10.1186/s12889-018-6292-x

Moore, T., & Green, M. (2004). Fetal alcohol spectrum disorder (FASD): A need for a closer examination by the criminal justice system. Criminal Reports, 19(1), 99-108.

Mutch, R. C., Jones, H. M., Bower, C., & Watkins, R. E. (2016). Fetal alcohol spectrum disorders: using knowledge, attitudes and practice of justice professionals to support their educational needs. *Journal of Population Therapeutics and Clinical Pharmacology, 23*(1).

Mutch, R., Watkins, R., Jones, H., & Bower, C. (2013). Fetal Alcohol Spectrum Disorder: Knowledge, attitudes and practice within the Western Australian justice system: Final Report. *Foundation for Alcohol Research and Education and Telethon Institute for Child Health Research, The University of Western Australia*.

Nash, K., Stevens, S., Rovet, J., Fantus, E., Nulman, I., Sorbara, D., & Koren, G. (2013). Towards identifying a characteristic neuropsychological profile for fetal alcohol spectrum disorders 1. Analysis of the Motherisk FASD clinic. *Journal of Population Therapeutics and Clinical Pharmacology, 20*(1), e44 – e52.

Novick Brown, N., Connor, P. D., & Adler, R. S. (2012). Conduct-disordered adolescents with fetal alcohol spectrum disorder: Intervention in secure treatment settings. *Criminal Justice and Behavior, 39*(6), 770-793.

Paley, B., O'Connor, M. J., Frankel, F., & Marquardt, R. (2006). Predictors of stress in parents of children with fetal alcohol spectrum disorders. *Journal of Developmental & Behavioral Pediatrics, 27*(5), 396-404.

Paley, B., O'Connor, M. J., Kogan, N., & Findlay, R. (2005). Prenatal alcohol exposure, child externalizing behavior, and maternal stress. *Parenting: Science and Practice, 5*, 29– 56. doi:10.1207/s15327922par0501_2

Peadon, E., Fremantle, E., Bower, C., & Elliott, E. J. (2008). International survey of diagnostic services for children with fetal alcohol spectrum disorders. *BMC Pediatrics, 8*(1), 1- 12. doi:10.1186/1471-2431-8-12

Pei, J., Leung, W. S. W., Jampolsky, F., & Alsbury, B. (2016). Experiences in the Canadian Criminal Justice System for individuals with fetal alcohol spectrum disorders: Double jeopardy? *Canadian Journal of Criminology and Criminal Justice, 58*(1), 56-86. doi:10.3138/cjccj.2014.E25

Pepper, J. M., Coons-Harding, K. D., Bibr, C., & Watson, S.L. (2018). Waving a magic wand: Supports for families raising school-aged children with autism spectrum disorder and fetal alcohol spectrum disorder in Ontario. *Journal of Fetal Alcohol Spectrum Disorder Risk and Prevention, 1*(1), e1-e15.

Popova, S., Lange, S., Bekmuradov, D., Mihic, A., & Rehm, J. (2011). Fetal alcohol spectrum disorder prevalence estimates in correctional systems: A systematic review. *Canadian Journal of Public Health, 102*(5), 336-340.

Popova, S., Lange, S., Burd, L., & Rehm, J. (2015). Cost attributable to Fetal Alcohol Spectrum Disorder in the Canadian correctional system. *International Journal of Law and Psychiatry, 41*, 76–81.

Popova, S., Lange, S., Burd, L., Urbanoski, K., & Rehm, J. (2013). Cost of specialized addiction treatment of clients with fetal alcohol spectrum disorder in Canada. *BMC Public Health, 13*(1), 570.

Price, A., Cook, P. A., Norgate, S., & Mukherjee, R. (2017). Prenatal alcohol exposure and traumatic childhood experiences: A systematic review. *Neuroscience & Biobehavioral Reviews, 80*, 89-98.

R. v. Manitowabi, 2014 ONCA 301.

Richer, E., & Watson, S. L. (2018). "He's on the streets, and stealing, and perpetuating the cycle... and I'm helpless": Families' perspectives on criminality in adults prenatally exposed to alcohol. *Journal on Developmental Disabilities, 23*(3), 90-104.

Roach, K., & Bailey, A. (2010). The relevance of fetal alcohol spectrum disorder and criminal law from investigation to sentencing. *University of British Columbia Law Review, 42*, 1–68

Rogers, B. J., McLachlan, K., & Roesch, R. (2013). Resilience and enculturation: Strengths among young offenders with fetal alcohol spectrum disorder. *First Peoples Child & Family Review, 8*(1), 62 - 80.

Rojas, E. Y., & Gretton, H. M. (2007). Background, offence characteristics, and criminal outcomes of Aboriginal youth who sexually offend: A closer look at Aboriginal youth intervention needs. *Sexual Abuse, 19*(3), 257-283.

Roozen, S., Peters, G. J. Y., Kok, G., Townend, D., Nijhuis, J., & Curfs, L. (2016). Worldwide prevalence of fetal alcohol spectrum disorders: A systematic literature review including meta-analysis. *Alcoholism: Clinical and Experimental Research, 40*(1), 18-32.

Sadler, J. Z., & Hulgus, Y. F. (1992). Clinical problem solving and the biopsychosocial model. *American Journal of Psychiatry, 149*(10), 1315-1323.

Sanders, J. L., & Buck, G. (2010). A long journey: Biological and non-biological parents' experiences raising children with FASD. *Journal of Population Therapeutics and Clinical Pharmacology, 17*, e308–e322

Sayal, K. (2007). Alcohol consumption in pregnancy as a risk factor for later mental health problems. Evidence Based Mental Health,10, 98 – 100.

Schilling, E. A., Aseltine, R. H., & Gore, S. (2007). Adverse childhood experiences and mental health in young adults: a longitudinal survey. *BMC Public Health, 7*(1), 1-10. doi:10.1186/1471-2458-7-30.

*Services and Supports to Promote the Social Inclusion of Persons with Developmental Disabilities Act*, S.O. 2008, c. 14

Stinson, J. D., & Robbins, S. B. (2014). Characteristics of people with intellectual disabilities in a secure US forensic hospital. *Journal of Mental Health Research in Intellectual Disabilities, 7*(4), 337-358.

Streissguth, A. P. (1997). *Fetal alcohol syndrome: A guide for families and communities.* Baltimore, MD: Brookes Publishing.

Streissguth, A. P., Barr, H. M., Bookstein, F. L., Sampson, P. D., & Olson, H. C. (1999). The long-term neurocognitive consequences of prenatal alcohol exposure: A 14-year study. *Psychological Science, 10*(3), 186-190.

Streissguth, A. P., Barr, H. M., Kogan, J., & Bookstein, F. L. (1996). Understanding the occurrence of secondary disabilities in clients with fetal alcohol syndrome (FAS) and fetal alcohol effects (FAE). *Final report to the Centers for Disease Control and Prevention (CDC)*, 96-06.

Streissguth, A. P., Bookstein, F. L., Barr, H. M., Sampson, P. D., O'malley, K., & Young, J. K. (2004). Risk factors for adverse life outcomes in fetal alcohol syndrome and fetal alcohol effects. *Journal of Developmental & Behavioral Pediatrics, 25*(4), 228-238.

Stromski, S. (2015). Searching for Accommodations within the Ontario Criminal Justice System for Persons with Fetal Alcohol Spectrum Disorder: Views of Social Service Agency and Justice Professionals. (Unpublished master's thesis). Brock University, St. Catharines, ON.

Substance Abuse and Mental Health Services Administration (SAMHSA). (2014). *Tip 58: Addressing fetal alcohol spectrum disorder (FASD).* Retrieved from: https://www.ncbi.nlm.nih.gov/books/NBK344239/

Tait, C. L., Mela, M., Boothman, G., & Stoops, M. A. (2017). The lived experience of paroled offenders with fetal alcohol spectrum disorder and comorbid psychiatric disorder. *Transcultural Psychiatry, 54*(1), 107-124.

Thanh, N. X., Jonsson, E., Salmon, A., & Sebastianski, M. (2014). Incidence and prevalence of Fetal Alcohol Spectrum Disorder by sex and age group in Alberta, Canada. *Journal of Population Therapeutics and Clinical Pharmacology, 21*(3), e395-404.

Tough, S.C., & Jack, M. (2010). Frequency of FASD in Canada, and what this means for prevention efforts. In, E. Riley, S. Clarren, J. Weinberg, E. Jonsson (Eds.), *Fetal alcohol spectrum disorder: Management and policy perspectives of FASD* (pp. 27-43). Weinheim, Germany: Wiley-Blackwell.

United Nations General Assembly. (2007). Convention on the rights of persons with developmental disabilities: Resolution/adopted by the General Assembly, 24 January 2007. Retrieved from: http://www.refworld.org/docid/45f973632.html

U.S. Department of Health and Human Sciences. (2014). *TIP 58: Addressing fetal alcohol spectrum disorders (FASD).* Retrieved from: https://store.samhsa.gov/system/files/sma13-4803.pdf

Vaughn, M. G., Salas-Wright, C. P., & Reingle-Gonzalez, J. M. (2016). Addiction and crime: The importance of asymmetry in offending and the life-course. *Journal of Addictive Diseases, 35*(4), 213-217.

Wartnik, A. P., & Brown, J. (2016). Fetal alcohol spectrum disorders (FASD) and the criminal justice system: Causes, consequences, and suggested communication approaches. *Forensic Scholars Today, 1*(4), 1-5.

Watson, S.l., Coons, K.D., & Hayes, S.A. (2013). Autism spectrum disorder and fetal alcohol spectrum disorder. Part I: A comparison of parenting stress. *Journal of Intellectual and Developmental Disability, 38*(2), 95-104.

Watson, S. L., Hayes, S., Coons, K., & Radford-Paz, E. (2013). Autism spectrum disorder and fetal alcohol spectrum disorder Part II: A qualitative comparison of parenting stress. *Journal of Intellectual and Developmental Disability, 38*(2), 105- 113.

Watson, S. L., Hayes, S., Radford-Paz, E., & Coons, K. (2013). "I'm hoping, I'm hoping...": Thoughts about the future from families of children with autism or fetal alcohol spectrum disorder in Ontario. *Journal on Developmental Disabilities, 19*(3), 76-93.

Watson, S. L. Richards, D. A., Miodrag, N., & Fedoroff, J.P. (2012). Sex and genes, part 1: Sexuality and Down, Prader-Willi, and Williams syndromes. *Intellectual and Developmental Disabilities 50*(2), 155-168.

Whittingham, L. (2014). *Fetal alcohol spectrum disorder: Foundations for Effective Supports* [powerpoint slides].

Wyper, K., & Pei, J. (2016). Neurocognitive difficulties underlying high risk and criminal behaviour in FASD: Clinical implications. In, M. Nelson & M. Trussler (Eds.), *Fetal alcohol spectrum disorder in adults: Ethical and legal perspectives* (pp. 101 – 120). Switzerland: Springer International Publishing.

Zelazo, P.D., & Müller, U. (2002). Executive function in typical and atypical development. In U. Goswami (Ed.), *Blackwell handbook of childhood cognitive development* (pp. 445-469). Oxford, UK

*Chapter 10*

# "*I Met Another Man Who Was Wounded with Hatred*": A Therapeutic Jurisprudence Analysis of How We Ignore the Sexual Needs and the Sexual Actions of Persons with Intellectual Disabilities[1]

*Michael Perlin, Heather Ellis Cucolo & Alison J. Lynch*

## Introduction

Almost 25 years ago, one of the co-authors wrote this:

> Society tends to infantilize the sexual urges, desires, and needs of the mentally disabled. Alternatively, they are regarded as possessing an animalistic hypersexuality, which warrants the imposition of special protections and limitations on their sexual behavior to stop them from acting on these "primitive" urges. By focusing on alleged "differentness," we deny their basic humanity and their shared physical, emotional, and spiritual needs. By asserting that theirs is a primitive morality, we allow ourselves to censor their feelings and their actions. By denying their ability to show love and affection, we justify this disparate treatment. (Perlin, 1993-94, p. 537)

And just six years ago, two of the co-authors wrote this, speaking of *sex offenders*: "No other population is more despised, more vilified, more subject to media misrepresentation, and more likely to be denied basic human rights" (Cucolo & Perlin, 2012, p. 4).

We believe that this observation is still salient, and that it characterizes the views, not only of society in general, but of most lawyers and mental health professionals. The idea that persons with mental disabilities have the same right as all others to sexual autonomy – to a free and individualized sexual life with the same options (to have sex, to not have sex; to have sex monogamously, to have sex polygamously; to masturbate, to not masturbate; to have heterosexual sex, to have homosexual sex) as all others have -- is still "beyond the last frontier" for most of society (Perlin & Lynch, 2016;

---

[1] Portions of this paper were presented at the Academy of Criminal Justice Sciences conference, New Orleans, LA, February 2018.

Perlin, Lynch, & McClain, 2019). Similarly, our revulsion for sex offenders knows no lowest limits: "states and municipalities are in a race to the bottom to see who can most thoroughly ostracize and condemn them" (Geraghty, 2007, p. 514; see generally, Perlin & Cucolo, 2017a).

There is remarkably little scholarship that deals with both of these questions: our attitudes towards the sexual autonomy of persons with mental disabilities *and* our attitudes toward persons perceived as being sexually violent predators (SVPs). We believe, though, that it is valuable to consider them together, as we believe that society's responses to the issues raised flow from similar attitudes – about sexuality and disability – and that "twinning" developments in these areas may give us some insights to the roots of these attitudes and to potential means of remediation (Perlin, Cucolo, & Lynch, 2017). We also believe that a consideration of these issues through the prism of therapeutic jurisprudence will best illuminate the underlying issues (Perlin & Cucolo, 2017a; Perlin & Lynch, 2014).

Importantly, each of us has dealt with these issues in practice; Cucolo (HEC) spent most of her litigation career representing persons in *Sexually Violent Predator Act* (SVPA) proceedings. Lynch (AJL) has advocated on behalf of individuals seeking to exercise their rights to sexual autonomy. Perlin (MLP) has done both (although his actual representation of persons in the Sexually Violent Predator Act process primarily dates back to the earlier generation of these laws, when the only question before the court was whether the defendant was a "compulsive and repetitive" offender" (Perlin, 1998, p. 1250; discussing N.J. Stat. Ann. § 2A:164-3, repealed by L. 1978, N.J. Stat. Ann. § 2C:98-2, 1998; see generally, Denno, 1998). In all of these experiences – spanning five decades – we have each noted how pervasive negative social attitudes are whenever "sex" and "mental disability" are thought about in the same conversation, regardless of the context. Developments in these two areas of the law reflect societal fears and unease about the relationships between disability and sexuality, whether that relationship is 'positive' (sexual autonomy) or 'negative' (sexual offending) (see Cucolo & Perlin, 2013; Perlin, 2008).

And there is special irony here, in that there has been an explosion of interest in mental disability law and a significant expansion of rights for the population of persons with mental disabilities, in both institutions and the community in the past forty years (Perlin & Cucolo, 2018, pp. 1-2). Yet, questions related to the sexuality of persons with intellectual disabilities remains one of the last academic taboos:

> With the growth in the field of mental disability law over the past forty years, very few topics involving persons with mental illness remain taboo or off limits to scholars and judges who face these issues daily. However, discussions of the question of whether persons with mental disabilities have a right to voluntary sexual interaction often touch a raw nerve in conversations about mental disability law – even with those who are practicing in the field. (Perlin & Lynch, 2014, pp. 258-59)

In this chapter, we discuss how we globally ignore the human rights of these populations and how this failure to take these rights seriously – a failure that is steeped in sanism – is an "irrational prejudice of the same quality and character of other irrational prejudices that cause (and are reflected in) prevailing social attitudes of racism, sexism, homophobia, and ethnic bigotry" (Perlin, 2008, p. 481). It is also steeped in a false "ordinary common sense" – a "self-referential and non-reflective" way of constructing the world" (Perlin & Cucolo, 2017b, p. 453) that violates every precept of therapeutic jurisprudence. The latter school of thought looks "at the law as it actually impacts people's lives," focusing on its influence on emotional life and psychological well-being (Cucolo & Perlin, 2017, p. 321). This failure also violates constitutional law. We will discuss how these issues can become even more knotty when we are focusing on individuals with intellectual disabilities (Perlin & Cucolo, 2017b; Perlin et al., 2019).

We will also consider how risk assessment is extremely complex and often confused by professionals—a problem exacerbated by the ways that this population is perceived as possessing an animalistic hypersexuality or, contrarily, as being asexual (on the use of conflicting stereotypes in other areas of mental disability law see Perlin, 2003, p. 5). We will address autonomy and risk, how individuals with intellectual disabilities are treated on questions of sexual offending, and the exercise of sexual autonomy. We will conclude by offering recommendations for best practices in this complex and challenging area of law and social policy.

Our title comes in part from Bob Dylan's brilliant song, *A Hard Rain's A-Gonna Fall*, a song that is "as apocalyptic as any in Dylan's songbook" (Perlin & McClain, 2009, p. 258) but yet "a song of indignation, but also a song of resolve" (Thomas, 2017, p. 301). The line we have used – "I met another man who was wounded with hatred" -- follows immediately this line – "I met one man who was wounded in love" (Dylan, 1963, track 6). Persons with mental disabilities who are revealed to be sexual creatures *are* "wounded with hatred," no matter what form that sexuality takes. We hope that our scholarship contributes to a world in which being "wounded in love" will mean something very different.

## Therapeutic Jurisprudence: What Does It Mean?

(For more information, see generally, Perlin & Lynch, 2014; Weinstein & Perlin, 2018)

One of the most important legal theoretical developments of the past three decades has been the creation and dynamic growth of therapeutic jurisprudence (TJ) (Wexler, 1990; Wexler, 2018; Wexler & Winick, 1996). Therapeutic jurisprudence presents a new model for assessing the impact of case law and legislation, recognizing that as a therapeutic agent, the law that can have therapeutic or anti-therapeutic consequences (Perlin, 2009).

Therapeutic jurisprudence asks whether legal rules, procedures, and lawyer roles can or should be reshaped to enhance their therapeutic potential while not subordinating due process principles (Perlin, 2008). David Wexler (1993) clearly identifies how the inherent tension in this inquiry must be resolved: "the law's use of mental health information to improve therapeutic functioning [cannot] impinge upon justice concerns" (p. 21). As such, an inquiry into therapeutic outcomes does not mean that "therapeutic concerns 'trump' civil rights and civil liberties" (Perlin, 2000, p. 412).

Using therapeutic jurisprudence, we "look at law as it actually impacts people's lives"

(Winick, 2009, p. 535), and assess the law's influence on the individual's emotional life and psychological well-being (Wexler, 2006). One governing therapeutic jurisprudence principle is that the "law should value psychological health, should strive to avoid imposing anti-therapeutic consequences whenever possible, and when consistent with other values served by law should attempt to bring about healing and wellness" (Winick, 2003, p. 26). Essentially, therapeutic jurisprudence supports an ethic of care (Winick & Wexler, 2006).

Professor Amy Ronner (2008, p. 627) describes the "three Vs": voice, validation and voluntariness and argues what "the three Vs" commend is pretty basic: litigants must have a sense of voice or a chance to tell their story to a decision maker. If that litigant feels that the tribunal has genuinely listened to, heard, and taken seriously their story, they feel a sense of validation. When litigants emerge from a legal proceeding with a sense of voice and validation, they are more at peace with the outcome. Voice and validation create a sense of voluntary participation, one in which the litigant experiences the proceeding as less coercive. Specifically, the feeling on the part of litigants that they voluntarily partook in the very process that engendered the end result or the very judicial pronouncement that affects their own lives can initiate healing and bring about improved behavior in the future. In general, human beings prosper when they feel that they are making, or at least participating in, their own decisions (Ronner, 2002, pp. 94-95).

Subsequently, we will discuss whether our policies involving sex offenders and sexual autonomy rights comport with these therapeutic jurisprudence precepts.

## Perceptions of Sexual Offenders with Intellectual Disabilities

Individuals with intellectual and developmental disabilities (IDD) are overrepresented in the legal system, both as sexual offense victims and as sexual perpetrators (Griffiths & Marini, 2000). "When considering statistics about offenders with IDD as a group, it is important to avoid false attribution. There is a vast difference in stating that people with IDD are disproportionately represented in regard to the offender populations from the statement that people with IDD are more likely to offend than other populations." (Griffiths, Hingsburger, Hoath & Ioannou, 2018, p. 106). Persons with an intellectual or developmental disability are often at a grave disadvantage in the criminal justice system beginning at the initial arrest and interrogation. The vulnerability of suspects with intellectual disabilities during police interviews has been documented and studied for decades (Kassin et al., 2010). An attorney who represents a cognitively limited offender must recognize that the most prevalent index behaviors in offenders with intellectual disabilities are aggression and violence, followed by sexual offenses and substance misuse (Birgden, 2016). But this does not follow that all sexual offenders with intellectual disabilities are impulsive or over-sexed.

Certain subgroups, such as those with autism spectrum disorder, are incorrectly considered to have a higher prevalence in both correctional and forensic disability settings despite research that shows a lower prevalence of contact sexual offenses for such individuals (Birgden, 2016). A 2014 study from the United Kingdom concluded that autism spectrum disorder was not a risk factor for re-offending or any particular type of offending (Lindsay, 2014, pp. 947-48). Unfortunately, individuals with autism spectrum disorder may exhibit behaviors that would provoke contact with the criminal justice system and subsequent registration system (Cea, 2014). Such individuals have been shown to have experienced higher "rates of physical abuse, neglect and adverse experiences, and demonstrates social naiveté" (Birgden, 2016, p. 654). These characteristics coupled with the potential for poor emotion regulation, reduced empathy, and the limited ability to see from other perspectives may ultimately increase the likelihood of offending (Birgden, 2016).

### Treatment

Clients with various deficits in cognitive functioning have shown to have even greater "significant barriers to successful participation in the conventional treatment program, most often seen in limited intellectual functioning, but also including clients with cognitive limitations, mental illness, and hearing deficits" (*Karsjens v. Jesson*, 2015, p. 52). The compliance challenge of ongoing conditions and obligations might be especially difficult given the characteristics of an offender with a developmental disability:
1. They may not behave appropriately for their age level, and they may choose to socialize with people who are younger (Oppenheim, 2015).
2. They may act impulsively and fail to understand the consequences of or the seriousness of their actions.
3. Their basic 'skill set' – their executive functioning -- might be limited which could impact their ability to understand the consequences of a conviction or plea (Doyle, 2007; Lyden, 2007).

It is the attorney's unquestioned job to protect their client's rights and appropriately identify, through expert assistance, their client's medical needs. "Rights and needs should be considered allied, not dichotomous" (Birgden, 2016, p. 661; on the obligations on an attorney representing an individual with a mental disability, see Perlin & Weinstein, 2016-17). A person with an intellectual disability may not clearly understand their rights; yet this does not deprive them of their decision-making autonomy. It is the attorney's job to make sure that their client understands all aspects of their specific case, to the best of their ability, to be empowered to exercise their legal rights (Perlin & Weinstein, 2016-17, p. 98).

### Assessing Risk in ID/DD population

Assessing risk for individuals with a developmental or intellectual disability is extremely complex and dependent on a vast number of factors. "Risk Assessment for people with ID is far from an exact science. Pertinent assessment tools with other populations need to be adapted and sometimes risk issues are unclear" (Shively, 2015). In order to get a full and complete understanding of cognitive functioning, an attorney must seek out an expert who has the credentials and experience to evaluate such individuals (Perlin et al., 2019). The attorney must ensure that the expert uses the appropriate tests and tools necessary to assess the degree of functioning and any resulting limitations. A current assessment of the individual's intellectual level and how intelligence could impact the ability to understand right versus wrong and sexually appropriate behavior is fundamental. One suggested assessment tool is the *Wechsler*

*Adult Intelligence Scale, 4$^{th}$ Edition* (Wechsler, 2008) that often shows interesting discrepancies between verbal comprehension, perceptual reasoning, working memory, and processing speed. Valid assessments should account for deficiencies in self-control and suggest appropriate guidelines on how much structure an individual may need in daily routines (Shively, 2015).

A dual diagnosis of developmental disability and mental illness is more common with this population and must be fully assessed in order to represent the client effectively (see generally, Birgden, 2016). Attorneys and their experts must also scrutinize the classification of their client. An individual who is "developmentally delayed or mentally disturbed" may be classified as a child offender, even though his actions are often more reflective of his disability than of an actual sexual focus toward children (Friedman, 2009, p. 16). Persons with a developmental or cognitive disability may gravitate towards individuals who are similar to their developmental age. Thus, what is perceived as an inappropriate attraction to children or pre-teens may, in fact, be the result of decreased social opportunities to engage with peers and the failure to comprehend socially appropriate expressions of sexuality (Davis et al., 2016).

The results of a comprehensive evaluation may assist in protecting a person's rights and liberty. For instance, what if the person failed to properly comply with a required aspect of sex offender registration? Research has found that "less-educated sex offenders were more likely to become delinquent in their registration duties, suggesting that as laws become more cumbersome and complex, compliance will become more challenging, especially for those with limited intellectual, social, and psychological resources" (Duwe & Donnay, 2010; as cited in Levenson, Sandler & Freeman, 2012, p. 562). Compliance with registration requirements may be compromised by specific underlying characteristics that contribute to difficulties conforming to rules and norms, such as general criminality, defiance, carelessness, negligence, confusion, or apathy (compared to Geis, 2014: "an incarcerated youth who is experiencing difficulty conforming to a facility's rules might be able to avoid disciplinary charges and sanctions if such behaviors are determined to be a manifestation of his disability" [p. 874]).

Most statutes require that if a defendant gives false information or fails to comply with certain registration requirements, they must do so knowingly and willfully (i.e., *Bartlett v. Alameida*, 2004, p. 1025 [holding that the state was required to prove that Bartlett knew or probably knew of his lifelong duty to register as a sex offender]; *State v. Garcia*, 1987, pp. 35-37 [reversing conviction for failure to register as sex offender because defendant had no knowledge of registration requirement]). The extent of someone's cognitive limitation may prevent them from being found guilty under the "knowingly and willfully" criteria (i.e., *People v. Peterson*, 2010 [holding that defendant who had cognitive limitations and an IQ of 63 was not held responsible for giving false address information to police]).

Persons with limited cognitive functioning may also be susceptible to coercion or improper treatment by authorities (i.e., *State v. Hunt*, 2016 [finding that incriminating statements to police by a defendant with "less than average" cognitive skills were not voluntary]). Probation and parole officers are often the "first responders" when it comes to communicating with registrants on a consistent basis. Attorneys should make efforts, at the outset of their client's integration into the community under registration, to work with parole or probation to find programs that meet the needs of offenders with intellectual disabilities or mental illness (Payne & DeMichele, 2010). In the case of *State v. Young (2000)*, the intermediate appellate court in North Carolina found that notice to the defendant of a state sex offender registration law was functionally "irrelevant" and constitutionally insufficient, largely due to his cognitive limitations. The court urged the legislature to revisit its registration statute to account for such defendants (*State v. Young, 2000*, p. 388).

In short, there are multiple confounding issues that we face in dealing with this population, and the ways that we typically ignore the underlying issues that exacerbate the pre-existing problems and potentially lead to outcomes that are counter-productive to the defendant and to society (Perlin et al., 2019).

**Sexual Autonomy**

There are multiple issues of social policy embedded in any discussion of sexual autonomy, especially for persons with disabilities, which contribute to the paucity of attention paid to these issues that we now address. These range from the most personal of issues (masturbation, reproductive rights, abortion) to issues that necessarily involve institutional policies that implicate others' interests as well (impact of drugging side effects, sex education, right to sexual surrogacy services) to issues that implicate other areas of the law (torts and administrative law). Failure to take seriously issues of patient sexual autonomy is self-defeating. It ignores the reality that most patients will be reintegrated into a community in which sexuality is an important component, and it stems from our discomfort with even defining 'sex' (see generally Perlin & Lynch, 2016).

Hand in glove with this fear is the concomitant failure to consider that the opportunity to engage in an intimate relationship may be critical to a patient's adjustment to the outside world once released (Perlin, 2008). The opportunity to take part in intimate relationships may be critical to a patient's successful reintegration into the outside world (see Emens, 2009, p. 1315: "the state should reduce barriers to entry to intimate relationships for people with disabilities"). As part of a treatment plan, or as part of a discussion about reintegration into the community after a long-term hospitalization, it is appropriate to bring up issues surrounding sexual expression and autonomy. It will be present in the lives of these individuals, so there is not a strong clinical argument to be made that ignoring it will prevent it from becoming a problem, either during or after treatment (on how these issues are treated radically differently in different nations; Fischel & O'Connell, 2016).

Recent research has begun to paint a more comprehensive picture of these issues. First, scholars are beginning to acknowledge that we need to create more nuanced instruments that seek to determine whether persons with mental disability have the capacity to consent to sexual interactions (Hillman, 2017; Perlin et al., 2019). This problem is confounded by the fact that assessment tools validated for the general population have not been validated for this specific sub-population (Thom, Grudzinskas, & Saleh, 2017; on the need for the assessment process to be individualized, see Lyden, 2007).

And, apart from treatment, we must consider these issues on their own merits. Regardless of a treatment plan, are individuals who are institutionalized or undergoing treatment given the appropriate amount of autonomy to make decisions about their sexuality? In all likelihood, that answer is generally "no" (see generally, Perlin, 1993-94).

The reality is that institutionalized persons with mental disabilities—including forensic patients—do have at least some right to sexual expression and autonomy (Perlin & Lynch, 2016). By rejecting this legal reality, public opinion creates a social disconnect and allows for an irrational universe in which the extent to which a patient's rights may be vindicated may well rest on a triviality, such as which institution within the same geographic region of a state a patient is housed (Perlin, 1993-94, pp. 531-32).

An argument frequently made in opposition of providing autonomy and support for sexual expression is that of capacity: people undergoing treatment will not have the capacity to make these decisions. However, this is again short-sighted and based on perceptions, fears, and bias, rather than facts and data (Perlin & Lynch, 2014, p. 263: "We must start with the assumption that all individuals have the capacity to consent to sexual relations, and that the presence of a mental disorder, in itself, does not mean that the individual lacks this capacity"). Importantly – and we have known this for decades – it is essential that we educate mental health professionals about the multiple issues involved in assessing sexual consent capacity of persons with intellectual disabilities (Kennedy, 1999). There will not be a "one size fits all" approach to determining whether someone has the capacity to understand how to exercise their own sexual autonomy in a safe way.

By way of example, as recently as five years ago, an article published in a peer-reviewed scientific journal began with this startling comment: "The recognition that individuals with disabilities have a *desire* [emphasis added] for sexual relationships with other people is a relatively new concept in the scientific community" (Gilmour, Smith & Schalomon, 2014, p. 569; as cited in Perlin & Lynch, 2014, p. 258). Here, it is also important to acknowledge that there are often radically different views held by clinical staff and ward staff on these issues (Dein et al, 2016; Perlin, 2005; Perlin & Lynch, 2016). On the one hand, anecdotally, when Michael Perlin presents on these topics in Grand Rounds presentations, invariably, a majority of the line staff, nurses and psychiatrists react negatively to the idea of patients being granted sexual autonomy; on the other hand, in general, psychologists, social workers, and patient advocates respond favorably (Perlin & Lynch, 2016). Sheehan notes that hospital staff aides often refused to even fill out incident reports on patient sexual activity because they found the subject matter so unsavory (Sheehan, 1982). Administrators and psychiatrists frequently cite potential liability risks in their opposition (Mossman, Perlin & Dorfman, 1997). Importantly it has been shown that nursing staff disapproval results in the further stigmatization of the behaviors in question (Berer, 2004; Quinn & Happell, 2015).

We have also learned that tailored sexual education – something often entirely missing in both institutional and community settings – can improve capacity to make sexuality-related decisions among individuals in this population (Dukes & McGuire, 2009). This flies in the face of prevailing social attitudes of many parents and treatment providers. Widespread sex education for persons with intellectual disabilities has been largely thwarted by parental objections to sexual education for their children with intellectual disabilities (Perlin & Lynch, 2016). These objections flow from feelings that their children are not capable of understanding the information, or they feel it would be "bad for them" by giving them "wrong ideas" and "overstimulat[ing] them" (Fegan, Rauch & McCarthy, 1993, p. 11). Many parents of this population also have succumbed to what is called the "forever child syndrome," as a result of which children are regarded as "eternally innocent" and asexual (Kempton & Kahn, 1991, pp. 94 – 97; as cited in Reed, 1997, p. 804). As a result, basic information and education is often not given to individuals with significant intellectual disabilities with regards to sexuality (Wade, 2002; as cited in Perlin & Lynch, 2016). This will hamper their development in community settings, where opportunities to engage in safe explorations of sexuality may arise, and this group of individuals may be unprepared because they have been so sheltered in the name of "protection" (compared to Freeman-Longo, 1997, pp. 320-21 [discussing how sex education for adolescent abusers and would-be abusers may deter future child sexual abuse]).

Thus, we know that adults with intellectual disabilities know much less – far less -- about sex (and sexual abuse) than non-disabled teenagers aged 16 (Murphy, 2003). This lack of knowledge extends to all important areas of sexual information – pregnancy, masturbation, contraception, birth control, STDs, types of relationships, and legal aspects of sexual relationships (Murphy & O'Callaghan, 2004).

## Applying Therapeutic Jurisprudence Principles to These Questions

The question to be posed here is this: does our current system comply with the precepts of therapeutic jurisprudence discussed earlier in this chapter? Think about the range of topics that one must consider when one thinks about patient sexuality: sterilization, the special circumstances of forensic facilities, medication side effects, sex education, sexual interaction when one or both participants have irreversible neurological deficits, institutional placements, institutional conditions, and reproductive technologies and rights (see generally, Perlin & Lynch, 2016). In each instance, an evaluation of our findings in the context of Ronner's (2002, 2008) therapeutic jurisprudence prescriptions would show that our policies fail miserably (a finding that should not surprise us terribly, given the legal system's long-standing and well-documented woeful track record of comporting with therapeutic jurisprudence in many of these areas).

It is also important to note that any analysis of therapeutic jurisprudence in this context must also take into account the implications of international human rights law. The late Professor Bruce Winick (2002) taught us over fifteen years ago that "therapeutic jurisprudence principles can point the way to law reform" in all matters of international human rights law (p. 544). Writing more recently, one of the co-authors (Michael Perlin) stressed that "it is essential that scholars begin to take seriously the relationship between [Michael Perlin] and I[nternational] H[uman] R[ights]" (Perlin, 2014, p. 539). Two of the co-authors have written about how, in considering questions of sexuality, "the use of the [therapeutic jurisprudence] filter – in the context of the articulated principles of international human rights law – offers us a means of approaching these questions in a new and, potentially, socially redemptive way, and in a way that, optimally, erases sanist attitudes" (Perlin & Lynch, 2015b, pp. 47-48). It is essential that litigators and other scholars consider this approach.

Based on this, it is imperative to not only educate self-identified therapeutic jurisprudence practitioners about this particular gap in the advocacy for this underserved population, but to also begin working outside the therapeutic jurisprudence world and bring in others who do work with these individuals. Case managers, social workers, and others outside the traditional legal system will be invaluable partners to the therapeutic jurisprudence community as we look to reshape our understanding of this topic and to bring positive change to the way these issues are handled by the courts and by advocates (on the interdisciplinarity of therapeutic jurisprudence, see Hartley & Petrucci, 2004).

## Conclusion

We have regularly ignored the sexual interests and needs of persons with intellectual disabilities, and we have erred – tragically – in the way we treat sexual offenders with intellectual disabilities. This is bad policy, bad law, and bad human rights. In a recent article that co-authors Michael Perlin and Heather Ellis Cucolo wrote about the global inadequacy of counsel in the representation of those alleged to be sex offenders, we concluded:

> We believe that it is only through the use of TJ that we can best diminish the shaming and humiliating aspects of these processes. We know that nothing so clearly violates "the dignity of persons as treatment that demeans or humiliates them" as shaming. To be consistent with TJ principles we must, rather, focus on reintegrating sex offenders into society and promoting sex offenders' self-respect and dignity while fostering family and community relationships (Cucolo & Perlin, 2017, pp. 322-23).

In a recent article that co-authors Michael Perlin and Alison Lynch wrote about why law schools must teach students about sexual autonomy issues, we concluded:

> Learning through the use of therapeutic jurisprudence can help students recognize the inherent power imbalances in the law [as it treats persons with mental disabilities on the question of sexual autonomy] and combine their training to "think like lawyers" with the empathy and understanding that TJ promotes (Perlin & Lynch, 2015a, p. 224).

It is rare for the topics we have addressed here to be "twinned" in an academic presentation or in scholarship (also see, Perlin et al., 2017; Perlin et al., 2019), but we believe that it is vital we do so. Universally, we have ignored the legal and human rights of these populations, and have trivialized their legal, behavioral and human needs. We hope that by focusing on both of these cohorts together, we may break this cycle. Both populations have been "wounded in hatred," to return to our title; we hope that, to quote another Bob Dylan song, finally, "things have changed" (Dylan, 1963).

## References

*Bartlett v. Alameida*, 366 F.3d 1020, 1025 (9th Cir. 2004).

Berer, M. (2004). Sexuality, rights and social justice. *Reproductive Health Matters, 12*(23), 6-11.

Birgden, A. (2016). Enabling the disabled: A proposed framework to reduce discrimination against forensic disability clients requiring access to programs in prison. *Mitchell Hamline Law Review, 42*, 637-694.

Cea, C. N. (2014). Autism and the criminal defendant. *St. John's Law Review, 88*, 495-529.

Cucolo, H. E. & Perlin, M. L. (2012). Preventing sex-offender recidivism through therapeutic jurisprudence approaches and specialized community integration. *Temple Political and Civil Rights Law Review, 22*, 1-44.

Cucolo, H. E. & Perlin, M. L. (2013). "They're planting stories in the press": The impact of media distortions on sex offender law and policy. *University of Denver Criminal Law Review 3*, 185-246.

Cucolo, H.E. & Perlin, M.L. (2017). Promoting dignity and preventing shame and humiliation by improving the quality and education of attorneys in sexually violent predator (SVP) civil commitment cases. *Florida Journal of Law and Public Policy 28*, 291-328.

Davis, T. N., Machalicek, W., Scalzo, R., Kobylecky, A., Campbell, V., Pinkelman, S. & Sigafoos, J. (2016). A review and treatment selection model for individuals with developmental disabilities who engage in inappropriate sexual behavior. *Behavior Analysis in Practice, 9*(4), 389–402.

Dein, K. E., Williams, P. S., Volkonskaia, I., Kanyeredzi, A., Reavey, P., & Leavey, G. (2016). Examining professionals' perspectives on sexuality for service users of a forensic psychiatry unit. *International Journal of Law and Psychiatry, 44*, 15-23.

Denno, D. W. (1998). Life before the modern sex offender statutes. *Northwestern University Law Review 92*, 1317-1387.

Doyle, S. (2007). The notion of consent to sexual activity for persons with mental disabilities. *Liverpool Law Review, 31*, 117-118.

Dukes, E. & McGuire, B. E. (2009). Enhancing capacity to make sexuality-related decisions in people with an intellectual disability. *Journal of Intellectual Disability Research, 53*, 727-734.

Duwe, G. & Donnay, W. (2010). The effects of failure to register on sex offender recidivism. *Criminal Justice and Behavior, 37*, 520-536.

Dylan, B. (1963). A hard rain's a-gonna fall. On *The Freewheelin' Bob Dylan* [CD]. New York, NY: Sony Music Entertainment.

Emens, E. F. (2009). Intimate discrimination: The state's role in the accidents of sex and love. *Harvard Law Review, 122*, 1307-1402.

Fegan, L., Rauch, A. and McCarthy, W. (1993). *Sexuality and People with Intellectual Disability II*. Sydney, Australia: MacLennan & Petty Pty Ltd.

Fischel, J. J. & O'Connell, H. R. (2016). Disabling consent or reconstructing sexual autonomy. *Columbia Journal of Gender and Law, 30*, 428-571.

Freeman-Longo, R. E. (1997). Reducing sexual abuse in America: Legislating tougher laws or public education and prevention. *New England Journal on Criminal and Civil Confinement, 23*, 303-331.

Friedman, I. (2009). Sexual offenders: How to create a more deliberative sentencing process. *The National Association of Criminal Defense Lawyers Champion, 33,* 12 - 18.

Geis, L. M. (2014). An IEP for the juvenile justice system: Incorporating special education law throughout the delinquency process. *University of Memphis Law Review, 44,* 869-919.

Geraghty, S. (2007). Challenging the banishment of registered sex offenders from the state of Georgia: A practitioner's perspective. *Harvard Law Review 42,* 513-529.

Gilmour, L., Smith, V. & Schalomon, M. (2014). Sexuality and ASD: Current state of the research. In V. Patel, V. Preedy, & C. R. Martin (Eds.). *Comprehensive guide to autism, (pp.* 569 – 584). New York, NY: Springer.

Griffiths, D., Hingsburger, D., Hoath, J., & Ioannou, S. (2018). Ethical considerations in working with people with intellectual disabilities who have offended. In B. Lindsay & J. L. Taylor (Eds.). *The Wiley handbook on offenders with intellectual and developmental disabilities: Research, training and practice* (pp. 105-122). Chichester, UK: Wiley.

Griffiths, D. & Marini, Z. (2000). Interacting with the legal system regarding a sexual offence: Social and cognitive considerations for persons with developmental disabilities. *Journal of Developmental Disabilities, 7,* 77-121.

Hartley, C. C. & Petrucci, C. J. (2004). Practicing culturally competent therapeutic jurisprudence: A collaboration between social work and law. *Washington University Journal of Law and Policy, 14,* 133-181.

Hillman, J. (2017). Sexual consent capacity: Ethical issues and challenges in long-term care. *Clinical Gerontologist, 40,* 43 - 50.

*Karsjens v. Jesson,* 109 F. Supp. 3d 1139, No. 0:11-cv-03659-DWF-JJK (D. Minn. 2015).

Kassin, S. M., Drizin, S. A., Grisso, T., Gudjonsson, G. H., Leo, R. A. & Redlich, A. D. (2010). Police-induced confessions: Risk factors and recommendations. *Law & Human Behavior 34,* 49-52.

Kempton, W. & Kahn, E. (1991). Sexuality and people with intellectual disabilities: A historical perspective. *Sexuality and Disability, 9,* 94-97.

Kennedy, C. H. (1999). Assessing competency to consent to sexual activity in the cognitively impaired population. *Forensic Neuropsychology 1* (3), 17 - 33.

Levenson, J., Sandler, J. C. & Freeman, N. J. (2012). Failure-to-register laws and public safety: An examination of risk factors and sex offense recidivism. *Law and Human Behavior, 36,* 555-565.

Lindsay, W. (2014). A comparison of referrals with and without autism spectrum disorder to forensic intellectual disability services. *Psychiatry, Psychology and the Law, 21,* 947-948.

Lyden, M. (2007). Assessment of sexual consent capacity. *Sexuality and Disability, 25,* 3 - 20.

Mossman, D., Perlin, M. L., & Dorfman, D. A. (1997). Sex on the wards: Conundra for clinicians. *The Journal of the American Academy of Psychiatry and the Law, 25*(4), 441-460.

Murphy, G. (2003). Capacity to consent to sexual relationships in adults with learning disabilities. *Family Planning and Reproductive Health Care, 29,* 148 - 149.

Murphy, G. & O'Callaghan, A. (2004). Capacity of adults with intellectual disabilities to consent to sexual relationships. *Psychological Medicine, 34,* 1347 - 1357.

N.J. Stat. Ann. § 2A:164-3, repealed by L. 1978, N.J. Stat. Ann. § 2C:98-2 (West 1998).

Oppenheim, J. (2015). The negative impact of Megan's law consequences on communities. *The Arc*. Retrieved from https://www.thearc.org/document.doc?id=5253

Payne, B. K. & DeMichele, M. (2010). The role of probation and parole officers in the collaborative response to sex offenders. *Federal Probation, 74*, 23-27.

*People v. Peterson*, 935 N.E.2d 1123 (Ill. App. Ct. 2d Dist. 2010)

Perlin, M. L. (1993-1994). Hospitalized patients and the right to sexual interaction: Beyond the last frontier? *NYU Review of Law and Social Change 20*, 517-547.

Perlin, M. L, (1998). "There's no success like failure/and failure's no success at all": Exposing the pretextuality of *Kansas v. Hendricks*. *Northwestern University Law Review, 92*, 1247-1277

Perlin, M. L. (2000). A law of healing. *Cincinnati Law Review, 68*, 407-433.

Perlin, M. L. (2003). "She breaks just like a little girl": Neonaticide, the insanity defense, and the irrelevance of ordinary common sense. *William & Mary Journal of Women and the Law, 10*, 1-31.

Perlin, M. L. (2005). "Limited in sex, they dare": Attitudes toward issues of patient sexuality. *American Journal of Forensic Psychiatry, 26*, 25-45.

Perlin, M. L., (2008). "Everybody is making love/or else expecting rain": Considering the sexual autonomy rights of persons institutionalized because of mental disability in forensic hospitals and in Asia. *University of Washington Law Review 83*, 481-512.

Perlin, M. L. (2009). "His brain has been mismanaged with great skill": How will jurors respond to neuroimaging testimony in insanity defense cases? *Akron Law Review, 42*, 885-916.

Perlin, M. L. (2014). "The ladder of the law has no top and no bottom": How therapeutic jurisprudence can give life to international human rights. *International Journal of Law and Psychiatry, 37*, 535-542.

Perlin, M. L. & Cucolo, H. E. (2017a). *Shaming the constitution: The detrimental results of sexual violent predator legislation*. Philadelphia, PA: Temple University Press.

Perlin, M. L. & Cucolo, H. E. (2017b). "Tolling for the aching ones whose wounds cannot be nursed": The marginalization of racial minorities and women in institutional mental disability law. *Journal of Gender, Race & Justice 20*, 431-458.

Perlin, M. L. & Cucolo, H. E. (Ed.). (2018). *Mental disability law: Civil and criminal* (3d ed.) New York, NY: Lexis-Nexis Press.

Perlin, M. L., Cucolo, H. E & Lynch, A. J. (2017). Sex, sexuality, sexual offending and the rights of persons with mental disabilities. *Laws, 6*(4), 1 – 10. doi:10.3390/laws6040020

Perlin, M. L. & Lynch, A. J. (2014). "All his sexless patients": Persons with mental disabilities and the competence to have sex. *Washington Law Review, 89*, 257-300.

Perlin, M. L. & Lynch, A. J. (2015a). How teaching about therapeutic jurisprudence can be a tool of social justice, and lead law students to personally and socially rewarding careers: Sexuality and disability as a case example. *Nevada Law Journal 16*, 209-225.

Perlin, M. L., & Lynch, A. J. (2015b). "Love is just a four-letter word:" Sexuality, international human rights, and therapeutic jurisprudence." *Canadian Journal of Comparative & Contemporary Law, 1*, 9-48.

Perlin, M. L. & Lynch, A. J. (2016). *Sexuality, disability and the law: Beyond the last frontier?* New York, NY: Palgrave MacMillan.

Perlin, M. L., Lynch, A. J. & McClain, V. R. (2019). "Some things are too hot to touch": Competency, the right to sexual autonomy, and the roles of lawyers and expert witnesses. *Touro Law Review, 35,* 405-434.

Perlin, M. L. & McClain, V. R. (2009). "Where souls are forgotten": Cultural competencies, forensic evaluations and international human rights, *Psychology, Public Policy & Law, 15,* 257-277.

Perlin, M. L. & Weinstein, N. (2016-2017). "Said I, 'but you have no choice'": Why a lawyer must ethically honor a client's decision about mental health treatment even if it is not what s/he would have chosen. *Cardozo Public Law, Policy and Ethics Journal, 15,* 73-116.

Quinn, C., & Happell, B. (2015). Consumer sexual relationships in a forensic mental health hospital: Perceptions of nurses and consumers. *International journal of mental health nursing, 24*(2), 121-129.

Reed, E. J. (1997). Criminal law and the capacity of mentally retarded persons to consent to sexual activity. *Virginia Law Review, 83,* 799-826.

Ronner, A. D. (2002). Songs of validation, voice, and voluntary participation: Therapeutic jurisprudence, Miranda and juveniles. *Cincinnati Law Review, 71,* 94-95.

Ronner, A. D. (2008). Learned-helpless lawyer: Clinical legal education and therapeutic jurisprudence as antidotes to the Bartleby syndrome. *Touro Law Review, 24,* 627-696.

Sheehan S. (1982) *Is there no place on earth for me?* New York, NY: Random House.

Shively, R. (2015). Risk assessment for individuals with intellectual disabilities (ID). *The Arc* (pp. 11-13). Retrieved from: https://www.thearc.org/document.doc?id=5253

*State v. Garcia,* 752 P.2d 34, 35-37 (Ariz. Ct. App. 1987)

*State v. Hunt,* 2016 ME 172, 151 A.3d 911 (Me. 2016)

*State v. Young,* 535 S.E.2d 380 (N.C. App. 2000).

Thom, R. P., Grudzinskas, A. J. & Saleh, F. W. (2017). Sexual behavior among persons with cognitive impairments. *Current Psychiatry Reports, 19,* 25. https://doi.org/10.1007/s11920-01700777-7

Thomas, R. F. (2017). *Why Bob Dylan matters.* New York, NY: Dey Street Books, Harper Collins.

Wade, H. A. (2002). Discrimination, sexuality and people with significant disabilities: Issues of access and the right to sexual expression in the united states. *Disability Studies Quarterly, 22,* 9-27.

Wechsler, D. (2008). *WAIS-IV administration and scoring manual.* San Antonio, TX: Psychological Corporation.

Weinstein, N. & Perlin, M. L. (2018). "Who's pretending to care for him?" How the endless jail-to-hospital-to-street-repeat cycle deprives persons with mental disabilities the right to continuity of care. *Wake Forest Journal of Law and Policy8,* 455-502.

Wexler, D. B. (1990). *Therapeutic jurisprudence: The law as a therapeutic agent.* Durham, NC: Carolina Academic Press.

Wexler, D. B. (1993). Therapeutic jurisprudence and changing concepts of legal scholarship. *Behavioral Science and the Law,* 11. 17-29.

Wexler, D. B. (2006). Practicing therapeutic jurisprudence: Psychological soft spots and strategies. In D. P. Stolle, D. B. Wexler, & B. J. Winick (Eds.), *Practicing therapeutic jurisprudence: Law as a helping profession (pp.493-498)*. Durham, NC: Carolina Academic Press.

Wexler, D. B. (2018). Mental health law and the seeds of therapeutic jurisprudence. In T. Grisso & S. L. Brodsky (Eds.), *The roots of modern psychology and law: A narrative history (pp.78-93)*. Don Mills, Canada: Oxford University Press.

Wexler, D. B. & Winick, B. J. (1996). *Law in a therapeutic key: Recent developments in therapeutic jurisprudence*. Durham, NC: Carolina Academic Press.

Winick, B. J. (2002). Therapeutic jurisprudence and the treatment of people with mental illness in Eastern Europe: Construing international human rights law. *New York Law School Journal of International & Comparative Law, 21*, 537-571.

Winick, B. (2003). A therapeutic jurisprudence model for civil commitment. In K. Diesfeld & I. Freckelton (Eds.), *Involuntary detention and therapeutic jurisprudence: International perspective on civil commitment (pp. 23-55)*. Farnham, UK: Ashgate Publishing.

Winick, B. J. (2009). Foreword: Therapeutic jurisprudence perspectives on dealing with victims of crime. *Nova Law Review, 33.* 535-54.

Winick, B. J. & Wexler, D. B. (2006). The use of therapeutic jurisprudence in law school clinical education: Transforming the criminal law clinic. *Clinical Law Review, 13,* 605-607.

# Authors

**John Clarke** is the Manager of Autism and Behaviour Services for the Centre for Behavioural Health Sciences. He has worked in the Intellectual and Developmental Disabilities sector for almost 30 years. For the last 5 years, he and his colleagues at CBHS have had a focus on ensuring people who have been diagnosed with an intellectual or developmental disability have an equitable opportunity to participate in the Justice System.

**Mihael Cole** is an Assistant Crown Attorney and has been for over a decade. He regularly appears in both Superior and Provincial Courts. For many years his practice focused predominantly on sexual assault and child abuse. His current title is High Risk Offender Crown for the Toronto Region. Mr. Cole is also the past president and current board member of the Canadian Criminal Justice Association. He is the proud father of two young boys.

**Heather Ellis Cucolo** is an adjunct professor at New York Law School (NYLS), an adjunct professor at Emory University School of Law, and fellowship faculty at Albert Einstein College of Medicine. She co-owns an educational company, Mental Disability Law and Policy Associates, and is on the board of trustees for the International Society of Therapeutic Jurisprudence. She has taught and lectured — both domestically and internationally — and has published numerous articles, casebooks, and other texts in the areas of mental disability law, criminal law and procedure, international law, forensic psychiatry, and sex offender law.

**J. Paul Fedoroff, MD** is the Director of the Sexual Behaviours Clinic (SBC) in The Royal's Integrated Forensic Program. Under his leadership, the SBC was awarded the prestigious American Psychiatric Association Gold Award for best outpatient clinical research program in 2015. Last year the SBC was presented with the "Innovation" award from the City of Ottawa Crime Prevention Committee. Dr. Fedoroff is a Full Professor of Psychiatry in the Faculty of Medicine with cross appointments in the Faculty of Law and the Department of Criminology at the University of Ottawa. He is also a Senior Researcher with The Royal's Institute of Mental Health Research. He has been President of the International Academy of Sex Research and of the Canadian Association of Psychiatry of the Law. His research focusses on the assessment and treatment of problematic sexual behaviors, and he has published over 100 peer reviewed scientific papers and chapters on the topic. Dr. Fedoroff and the SBC research team are experienced in multidisciplinary, international research collaborations and recently guest-edited a special edition of The International Review of Psychiatry (Murphy & Fedoroff, 2019). Dr. Fedoroff also recently published a book about the paraphilias (Fedoroff, 2020).

**Mary Gilmore (Fraser)** graduated from Brock University in 2018 with an Honours BA in Child and Youth Studies as well as a BA of Education. Living in Pelham with her husband, she is currently a supply teacher with the District School Board of Niagara. During her time at Brock, she worked closely with Professors Voula Marinos and Dorothy Griffiths to complete her thesis on persons with IDD and the criminal justice system.

**Dorothy Griffiths, PhD** is Emerita Professor at the Departments of Child and Youth Studies and Applied Disability Studies and former Co-Director of the International Dual Diagnosis Certificate Programme, Brock University, St. Catharines, Ontario, Canada. She has lectured and published extensively regarding persons with intellectual disabilities who have behavioral and mental health challenges and of those who have become involved with the criminal justice system. She has received the Order of Canada, the Order of Ontario, and the Queen's Jubilee Medal for her work.

**Layla Hall** earned her MSc in 2013 and is currently a Clinical Psychology PhD candidate at Queen's University, Ontario. The focus of her research and clinical training has been in the field of Autism Spectrum Disorder, Developmental Disability, and Dual Diagnosis. She is presently working as a Psychometrist at Surrey Place, a provincially funded agency for children and adults with developmental disabilities in Toronto. She has published in the field of autism on topics related to criminal offending, social cognition, mental health, and genetics.

**Dr. Kelly Coons-Harding** received her PhD in Interdisciplinary Rural and Northern Health from Laurentian University (2017) in Sudbury, Ontario, Canada. Dr. Harding is currently a Research Associate for the Canada Fetal Alcohol Spectrum Disorder Research Network (CanFASD), a national, interdisciplinary research network whose mission is to support Canada's leadership in addressing the extraordinary complexities of FASD. Dr. Harding is also an Adjunct Professor in the Psychology Department at Laurentian University. Dr. Harding has been involved in the field of FASD since 2010, predominantly through research and working with families raising children with FASD. Her research interests focus primarily on FASD prevention, women and alcohol, health care professionals' knowledge, self-efficacy, and attitudes regarding FASD, and health services delivery in rural and Northern regions.

**Stephanie Ioannou** is a Board Certified Behavior Analyst who has provided assessment and treatment to persons with dual diagnosis and sexual offending behavior in community settings. Within a bio-psycho-social framework, she has worked with adults with dual diagnosis and challenging behaviors and has provided clinical oversight of the delivery of ABA services to children/youth with Autism and their families.

**Amanda Jones** is a Registered Nurse with an Honors degree in Psychology and Criminal Justice. She obtained her Masters in Child and Youth Studies at Brock University. Her work experiences in the office of the Attorney General, youth probation, and as a child and youth worker contributed to her studies and thesis investigating the relationship between individuals with intellectual disabilities and the criminal justice system. She participated in a panel on "risky" youth at the Annual Canadian Sociological Association Conference in 2014. She continues to enjoy working with youth and vulnerable populations through emergency and surgical nursing.

**Alison J. Lynch** is a staff attorney at the New York State Protection & Advocacy System in Brooklyn, NY. She works in the Protection of Individuals with Mental Illness (PAIMI) program, and is also part of the Representative Payee Review program. Before coming to the New York P&A in 2014, She served as a staff attorney for the PAIMI and Client Assistance Program (CAP) at Disability Rights New Jersey, in Trenton. She received her undergraduate degree from Mount Holyoke College in psychology and neuroscience, and this has inspired her interest in advocating for individuals with mental illness and developmental disabilities. Her legal career has also been devoted to working with this population, particularly with individuals in jails, prisons and psychiatric hospitals around New York State. She received her JD from New York Law School in 2013 and her M.A. in Mental Disability Law Studies in 2015.

**Voula Marinos** is an Associate Professor in the Departments of Child & Youth Studies, and M.A. in Social Justice & Equity Studies at Brock University, Ontario. She received her PhD in Criminology from the Centre of Criminology, University of Toronto. She completed a postdoctoral fellowship at the Faculty of Law, Queen's University. Her publications are focused on topics including diversion, mental health, disabilities and the law, and plea bargaining. Much of her socio-legal research includes interviews with justice professionals and court observations. She lectures widely to lawyers, police, and community-based organizations providing services to youth and adults.

**Michael L. Perlin** is Professor of Law Emeritus at New York Law School (NYLS), where he was Director of NYLS's Online Mental Disability Law Program and Director of NYLS's International Mental Disability Law Reform Project in its Justice Action Center. He is the co-founder of Mental Disability Law and Policy Associates and is currently Adjunct Professor of Law, Emory University School of Law and Instructor, Loyola University New Orleans, Department of Criminology & Justice. He has written 31 books and nearly 300 articles on all aspects of mental disability law, many of which deal with questions of sexual offenses, sexual autonomy, and therapeutic jurisprudence Among his books (co-authored with Alison J. Lynch) is *Sexuality, Disability and the Law: Beyond the Last Frontier?* (Palgrave Macmillan) (2016). He has litigated at every court level from police court to the US Supreme Court, and he has done advocacy work on every continent. He is the honorary life president of the International Society for Therapeutic Jurisprudence and a member of that society's current Board of Trustees.

He is also a member of the Lawrence Township (NJ) Community Concert Band and the board of directors of the Washington Crossing (NJ) Audubon Society.

**Rebekah Ranger** is a forensic research coordinator at the University of Ottawa Institute of Mental Health Research and the Royal Ottawa Mental Health Centre. She has been affiliated with the Institute since 2007, when she began doing research and clinical training as a student. Rebekah has completed sexual behaviors clinic assessments on hundreds of men and has worked with offenders in several capacities including in community re-integration and federal institutions. Her research is published and presented to national and international audiences. She is currently a part-time graduate student in Conflict Studies at Saint Paul University, Ottawa, Ontario.

**Deborah Richards, MA, CHMH, RP** is a psychotherapist and consultant in private practice in Ontario, Canada. Her focus is working with individuals who have intellectual disabilities, genetic and mental health disorders, and problematic sexual behaviors. She has collaborated in research and published in the area of sexuality and disability. Deborah has presented at conferences and seminars both nationally and internationally. She is an adjunct professor at McMaster University in the Department of Psychiatry & Neurosciences and the Department of Family Medicine.

**Elisa Richer** holds an MA in Applied Psychology from Laurentian University. She contributed to research studies on families of individuals with Fetal Alcohol Spectrum Disorder (FASD) and concentrated her research at the graduate level on the risk and protective factors for criminality among adults with prenatal alcohol exposure. Influenced by the experiences shared by the families who courageously participated in the studies on FASD, she has worked with individuals and families both in inpatient and outpatient settings to continue advocating for the specific mental health needs of families in Northern Ontario. She is currently working as a counsellor at Laurentian University.

**Samantha Stromski** has a Master of Arts Degree from Brock University. Her research focuses on individuals with intellectual disability who interact with the Justice System, particularly what accommodations and supports are needed to assist this population in navigating their way through the court process. She now works in the field, putting research into practice by assisting individuals with Dual Diagnosis who are involved in the justice system.

**Shelley Watson** is Associate Vice-President, Learning and Teaching and a Professor in the Psychology Department at Laurentian University in Sudbury, Ontario, Canada. She holds a PhD in Educational Psychology and has created specialized courses on disability issues, teaching within the Psychology and Interdisciplinary Health programs. Her research focuses on intellectual disability and human rights issues, with specific emphasis on sexuality and abuse prevention, as well as Fetal Alcohol Spectrum Disorder (FASD) prevention. She is a point person for assisting agencies with policies and practices to help prevent abuse as well as training for sexual abuse prevention.

**Lisa Whittingham** is a PhD student in the department of Child and Youth Studies at Brock University, Ontario, Canada. Her research interests include the experiences of vulnerable populations in the criminal justice system and interventions for persons with intellectual and developmental disabilities, particularly for individuals described as complex or at risk. Prior to starting her PhD, Lisa worked for many years as a behavior therapist with adults with intellectual and developmental disabilities in the community, many of whom were involved in the criminal justice system.

# Index

## A

Accessibility of Ontarians with Disabilities Act (AODA) 56-57
accommodations vii, 10, 53, 197
Americans with Disabilities Act 56, 186-187
arrest 24, 29-32, 33, 36, 41-42, 45, 141, 147, 179, 202
attention deficit hyperactivity disorder (ADHD) 127, 130
autism spectrum disorder (ASD) xi, xii, 3, 11, 19, 69, 125, 139, 155-169, 171-172, 196, 202-203, 210
autonomy 205

## B

barristers 84
benefits of identification 25
biological factors 55, 129
biopsychosocial xi, 12, 15, 17, 42, 53, 55-56, 64, 75-76, 102-103, 129, 131, 178, 192, 194, 196

## C

Canada Evidence Act 59
Canadian Charter of Rights and Freedoms 70
Canadian Criminal Code 15, 28, 31, 43, 58, 60, 64, 159
Canadian Mental Health Association 83, 104
capacity 210
classification xi, 20, 23, 82, 119, 204
cognitive ability 3, 32
communication 8-9, 14, 26-27, 31, 36, 40-41, 59, 71, 85-86, 99, 101, 113, 125, 133, 155, 159, 163-164, 167, 179, 188, 197

community support x
comorbid 8-9, 24, 27, 29, 38, 69, 157, 159, 166, 197
Competence Assessment for Standing Trial for Defendants with Mental Retardation (CAST-MR) 72
competency to stand trial 48
counterfeit criminality 32
court report 101
criminal justice system i, v, vii, ix-xii, 1, 3- 20, 23-25, 27-33, 35-36, 38-41, 40-47, 53-57, 59-60, 63-69, 71-72, 77-85, 87, 91, 95, 97, 102-105, 111, 115-117, 119-121, 123-129, 135, 137-139, 147-148, 150-151, 155, 157, 162, 167-169, 171, 173, 176-179, 182-188, 190-197, 202-203, 216-217, 219
criminal responsibility 36, 38, 48, 62, 71, 73, 79, 126, 156, 158, 159, 161-162, 164-166, 168, 170, 173-174
culpability 156, 158-160, 162-163, 165-166, 168, 170
custody 13, 24, 30, 33-35, 123-127, 130, 132, 134-135, 137-138, 141-143, 147, 159

## D

developmental disability 3-4, 6, 8, 12-14, 18, 23-24, 26, 58, 61, 68-69, 73, 77, 135, 137, 150, 175, 186, 202-204, 215
diagnosis 5, 9, 12-13, 16-18, 20, 24, 29, 35, 41, 42, 45, 47, 49, 58, 64, 68, 69-70, 79, 104, 116, 124-128, 130, 146, 147, 149-150, 155-163, 166-168, 175, 177, 184, 189, 191-194, 204, 216
Diagnostic and Statistical Manual (DSM-5) 68

dignity vii, 109
dual diagnosis 12-13, 16, 24, 29, 35, 58, 61, 68-69, 116, 126-127, 130, 132-133, 204, 216, 218
Dual Diagnosis Justice Case Manager 61, 126, 127, 130, 132-133

## E

emotional regulation 77, 155, 171-178

## F

fetal alcohol spectrum disorder (FASD) xi-xii, 3-4, 10, 12, 18, 30, 65-66, 69, 125, 127, 134-135, 148-150, 164, 175-198, 216, 218
Fetal alcohol syndrome.
See also Fetal alcohol spectrum disorder
fitness to stand trial.
See competency to stand trial

## G

gaps xi- xii, 13, 60, 68, 134, 187
Good Lives Model (GLM) 141

## H

HCR-20 Violence Risk Assessment 74
human rights 11-12, 19, 34, 53-56, 58, 63-65, 139, 140, 142, 147, 151-152, 194, 199-200, 207-208, 211-213, 218

## I

identification xi, 6, 14, 20, 23, 25, 27-31, 36, 37, 38, 40-43, 54, 60, 85, 124-125, 127, 144, 148, 177, 183, 189-191
intellectual disability ix, 3-5, 7-11, 16-20, 23-36, 3844, 46, 48-49, 53-55, 60-62, 65, 67-68, 73, 78-84, 86-87, 89, 97, 100, 102-104, 110, 118-121, 123, 127, 130, 132, 136, 139, 144, 148-152, 157, 172, 203, 209-210, 218
intelligence quotient (IQ) 4-5, 7-8, 26-28, 36, 69, 71, 73, 111, 116, 125, 186, 204
International Classification of Disorders (ICD-11) 68
interview 72, 82, 184

## J

jail 40-42, 48, 94, 123, 142, 182-183, 212

## L

language ix, 3, 8-10, 14, 26, 31, 37-38, 55, 67, 71, 84, 132, 133, 155-156, 159, 161, 163-164, 168, 172-173, 179
Law Commission of Ontario 11, 19, 38, 46, 63, 65, 134-135, 150
learning disability 84
lifestyle planning 131, 151

## M

memory 10
mens rea 7-8, 15, 31, 159-160, 167
mental age 4, 27-28, 62, 96, 99
mental disability 215, 217
mental disorder 7, 15, 28, 58, 60, 149, 160, 206
mental health 8, 11-20, 25-31, 33, 35, 37-39, 41, 47-49, 58, 59-61, 64, 67-68, 77-80, 83, 104, 111, 116, 126-128, 130, 133-135, 137, 145, 147-151, 155-157, 159-160, 166, 169-170, 176, 193-194, 196, 199, 201, 206, 212, 216-218
mental illness 7, 9, 24, 29, 39, 45, 60-61, 67-69, 71-72, 79, 81, 86, 127, 151, 155, 166, 200, 203, 204, 205, 213, 217
mitigating factors 161
multidimensional xi, 4, 11-12, 15, 53

## O

offending behavior ix, 4, 8, 12, 74-75, 102, 120-121, 141-144, 150, 157-159, 165-168, 180, 216
Ontario Human Rights Code 57, 65
Ontario Review Board 72-73, 81

## P

Perske, R. (1972) 120
personality disorders 78
person-centered xi, 11-12, 53, 115, 129, 130-132, 135, 137, 142, 144, 146-147
phallometric assessment 75
police 6, 8-9, 14-18, 33, 35, 39, 41-44, 57, 84-89, 93, 102-104, 117, 125-126, 130-132,

134, 138, 147, 179-180, 183-185, 202, 204, 210, 217
post-traumatic stress disorder (PTSD) 127
prevalence ix, 4-6, 8-9, 16-20, 23-25, 39, 44, 46, 48-49, 68-69, 73, 77, 80-82, 110-111, 118-120, 124, 148-150, 157, 167, 171, 175-177, 185, 192, 194-197, 202
prevention 47, 76, 78, 112, 116, 150, 173, 197, 209, 216, 218
psychiatric and/or psychological assessments 87
psychological factors 103, 121, 129

## Q

quality of life 13, 110, 129, 131, 148, 151, 178

## R

recidivism 112, 144
risk assessment vii, 19, 74, 80-81, 109-121, 133, 143-144, 168, 201, 203, 212
risk management 152

## S

sanism 200
screening 10, 23, 30-31, 40-43, 74, 80, 125, 150, 157, 173, 183-184, 192-193
sentencing 23, 25-26, 28, 30-31, 33, 36-37, 40-43, 46, 61, 73, 125, 133, 156-158, 160, 163, 167-168, 174, 184, 196, 210

sexual autonomy 199-202, 205, 206, 208-209, 211-212, 217
sexual offender 119, 149
social inclusion 56
stability 135
strengths 27, 36, 55, 60, 85, 187-189, 194
substance abuse 76

## T

therapeutic jurisprudence xii, 15, 64, 200-202, 207-213, 217
training 47, 138, 148, 184
traumatic brain injury 12

## U

United Kingdom 15, 83, 84, 136, 202

## V

Victim/Witness Assistance Program 61
Violent Risk Appraisal Guide (VRAG) 74, 112

## W

Witness iii, 31, 49, 61, 65, 83, 86, 88, 91, 92-93, 95, 104